101 GM Muscle Car
Performance Projects

Colin Date and Mitch Burns

MOTORBOOKS

First published in 2005 by Motorbooks, an imprint of MBI Publishing Company, Galtier Plaza, Suite 200, 380 Jackson Street, St. Paul, MN 55101-3885 USA

Motorbooks titles are also available at discounts in bulk quantity for industrial or sales-promotional use. For details write to Special Sales Manager at MBI Publishing Company, Galtier Plaza, Suite 200, 380 Jackson Street, St. Paul, MN 55101-3885 USA.

ISBN 0-7603-1756-9

Editorial: Peter Bodensteiner and Lindsay Hitch
Layout: Christopher Fayers

Printed in China

            Library of Congress Cataloging-in Publication Data
Date, Colin
   101 GM muscle car performance projects / by Colin Date.
     p. cm. -- (Motorbooks workshop)
   ISBN 0-7603-1756-9 (SB : alk. paper)
    1. General Motors automobiles--Conservation and restoration. 2. Muscle
cars--Performance. 3. Muscle cars--Customizing. 4. Muscle cars--Motors--Modification.
I. Title: One hundred and one General Motors muscle car performance projects. II. Title.
III. Series.

TL215.G4D38 2005
629.28'72--dc22

On the front cover: 1970 Cranberry Red Chevelle SS 454.

On the frontis: The balancer removal tool is an absolute must.

On the title page: 1964 Pontiac GTO.

On the back cover: After removing the air cleaner, disconnect the throttle linkage with a flat-blade screwdriver and Crescent wrench.

Author bios:
Colin Date is the author of *Original Mustang 1964 1/2–1966* and the photographer of *Ultimate Auto Detailing Projects*. He has been a freelance writer for a variety of muscle car magazines and currently publishes *Legendary Ford Magazine*. He lives in Dana Point, California.

Mitch Burns is an automotive enthusiast with over 10 years of experience in classic restorations and performance. He is currently the technical editor of a classic car magazine and works full time in the aerospace industry. He was born and raised on the coast of the Carolinas and now resides in Southern California.

CONTENTS

CONTENTS

ACKNOWLEDGMENTS

When a book this involved comes together, it's due to the efforts of more than just a couple of gearheads. There are a few folks to thank here, but we need to put MBI Publishing editor Peter Bodensteiner at the top of the heap. Without him, the opportunity would have never come to pass. Thanks, Peter.

A close second would have to be Mitch Burns. Without Mitch, his writing skills, and his vast knowledge of all things automotive, this project would have buried me. What can I say? Thanks, my friend.

Jeff Farina for never hesitating to lend a hand with a set of wrenches or floor jacks. Not to mention ice cold brew on those 100-degree days. . . .

My awesome wife, Dianne, for working the same crazy hours I do, and for never once saying, "You're still working on that book?"

Tony Genty of Original Parts Group, Inc., for letting me "borrow" all those GM A-body parts for photography purposes. Without him, my credit cards would have tapped out long ago.

To the good Lord, who always makes things "come together at just the right time."

— Colin Date

I would like to thank the following people for their help, support, and graces with this project:

Peter Bodensteiner and Lindsay Hitch at MBI Publishing for their utmost patience and the special opportunity to write this book.

Colin "Wildfire" Date for his valued friendship and expertise behind the lens.

My mom (P.T.) for her endless support, understanding, and prayers.

My dad for his wisdom and guidance.

My sister Michael and her husband John for helping me more than I can ever repay. Thank you.

My sister Karen and her husband Bob for use of their overcrowded garage and the homemade salsa.

My sister Robin, her husband Steve, and good old *Split Decision* for the great getaways and relaxation.

Brian Engels and the Mansfield family for their constant flexibility and patience.

Jeff "Grumpy" Farina for his sacrifices, time, knowledge, and endless supply of Tecate (Mooch: R.I.P.).

James "Big Ferg" Ferguson for being the technical go-to guru he is. Thanks, BOSS!

My bandmates and comrades Tim Hoferer and Nathan Aurich for picking up all of my slack and running with it.

Alejandra Toscano Barbosa for her quiet inspiration and the caramel coffee.

All the friends I forgot, never called back, or have not seen much of this past year—thanks for not disowning me.

— Mitch Burns

INTRODUCTION

Working on old cars is a labor of love. It takes a lot of time, patience, and hard work to get the job done right. Whether you plan on performing a factory-correct restoration or building a high-performance street machine, the down-and-dirty hands-on training will prove to be an invaluable learning experience. The primary focus of this book is to offer the average backyard mechanic insightful tips and information on performing a wide variety of projects for his/her vehicle. The projects range in skill and difficulty, but they are straightforward and easy to understand.

With so many different components and systems on one car, I decided to break things down a bit and focus on certain areas of the car and the relative projects one at a time. Therefore, you will notice the book is divided into sections (interior, transmission, electrical, etc.). The projects listed and performed inside each section are common examples of what it takes to properly restore and build a car in your own garage or driveway.

You will also notice by flipping through the pages, that each project starts off with an information box, which explains to the reader everything that may be involved in that particular job. Displayed in a chart format, the information box estimates the amount of time the project will take, the tools needed for the job, and the recommended level of skill to adequately perform the project. Keep in mind, the time is approximate. Depending on your mechanical placement and your current working conditions, this may change significantly. It's more important to take your time and do the job right than to cut corners, break parts, and possibly end up having to start the entire project over. In other words, be patient.

The tools of the trade play a very important part in every project. These items are listed with each job as a guide for what is necessary and relative to that project. Many of these tools are widely used throughout the book and should definitely be a part of your personal collection. The exact socket and wrench sizes are omitted since not all makes and models contain identical hardware. The suggested specialty tools may also vary on application, however the basic idea is just to inform you of what is needed for the job.

The recommended talent or skill level inside the information box represents the difficulty of each project. From beginners to veterans, this book is intended for a wide range of enthusiasts and offers something for everyone. However, the goal of the book is to teach something new and increase your mechanical skill and knowledge. These projects will explain the mysteries and take you step-by-step in the process of removing, rebuilding, and replacing all of the necessary components for your vehicle.

In addition to the aforementioned categories, the information box also breaks down the applicable years for the projects, the estimated costs, and the necessary parts and materials to complete the projects. The information is easy to follow and gives you a clear, detailed picture of what the entire project entails.

Although the projects are often heavily technical, they should be used and viewed solely as a source of reference, along with service guides and any other informative books related to the projects. Wiring schematics, torque specifications, and other technical data can typically be found in the original factory manuals and should always be acknowledged as part of the procedure.

To me, nothing is cooler than the unique look, sound, feel, and performance of these old GM cars. They have been favorites of mine since the beginning. I have always held a certain respect and love for the simple, yet timeless design and ingenuity that was poured into them. For years, they have been tested and proven on both the streets and the racetracks, and they are often regarded as some of the best-built cars in American automobile history. Today, as the classic-car market continues to soar, there is no doubt GM muscle cars have stood the test of time and are destined to be legends. I hope you enjoy and value the opportunity and experience of owning, and more importantly, driving your classic GM machine. Have fun!

TOOLS AND SAFETY

Completing a project well is all about having the right tools. The investment in a quality collection of tools will more than pay for itself in the long run. Although there never seems to be an end to the tool list, here is a general guide for getting started.

Adjustable wrenches—Commonly referred to as crescent wrenches, these wrenches come in handy when dealing with an irregular-size bolt or fastener.

Allen wrenches—Allen wrenches are available in both standard and metric sizes and are used with cap screws or hex-keyed bolts.

Breaker bar—This simple, yet highly effective tool increases torque to help loosen and tighten bolts. The head is usually a 3/8-inch or 1/2-inch-drive socket head and pivots 180 degrees for easy use.

Crankshaft socket—This oversized socket fits over the front of the crankshaft at the harmonic balancer and allows you to easily turn the motor by hand with a breaker bar.

Dial calipers—Calipers are used to take precise measurements related to bore, diameter, depth, and length up to 0.001 inch. Owning a quality pair of calipers is crucial to assembling an engine.

Feeler gauge—Setting and adjusting the valves on any engine requires a feeler gauge. The tool contains a wide selection of shims of varying thicknesses for determining the proper gap/tolerance.

Flashlight—Portable, self-standing flashlights always make working under a dark car a little easier. Small, hand-held lights are also very handy in confined spaces.

Floor jack and jack stands—When it comes to hoisting and supporting your vehicle, be sure to use a heavy-duty floor jack and jack stands. They are typically rated by the amount of weight they can safely lift and support.

Hacksaw—They are great for cutting thick hose, hard lines, and bolt threads. These lifesavers are cheap, and blades are easy to replace when dulled.

Hammers—Sledge (suspension), ball peen (sheet metal), dead blow, and rubber mallets (trim and fragile parts) are commonly used in the automotive repair world.

Metric sockets and wrenches—Although just about everything on these cars was assembled with standard hardware, it is a good idea to keep a set of metric sockets and wrenches accessible. Metric sizes are slightly off from standard sizes and may work with a rounded or stripped bolt head or nut.

Multi-meters—They are great for tracing and troubleshooting electrical problems in your car. Most meters measure amps, volts, and resistance.

Pliers—It's best to have an assortment of sizes and styles—from conventional and needle-nose pliers to channel locks and vice grips—in preparation for any job.

Power drill—A reliable drill is a necessity when tackling heavy projects. Purchase quality drill bits that are specific to the job.

Ring compressor—This engine-building tool is used to compress the piston ring and allow the piston assembly to slide into the bore in the engine block.

Ring expander—This is necessary when installing piston rings onto the piston. It safely widens the diameter of the ring to fit into the recessed grooves in the side of the piston.

Screwdrivers—Flat-head (standard) and Phillips-head screwdrivers are a must in the toolbox. They come in a variety of sizes for every application and are fairly inexpensive.

Standard socket set—This should include 1/4-inch, 3/8-inch, and 1/2-inch-drive socket wrenches with both shallow and deep-set sockets. Sockets come in six-point and twelve-point configurations.

Standard wrenches—Combination wrenches (open on one end and closed on the other) and boxed wrenches are staple tools for every mechanic. Sizes typically range from 1/4 inch to 1 inch.

Timing light—An automotive timing light is a must for anyone who enjoys tuning a car. Some lights allow you to set the proper degree and timing by adjusting a small knob on the face of the light.

Torque wrench—Every serious mechanic needs a torque wrench. It is the ultimate assembly tool. Select the appropriate wrench that will work in your desired range.

Safety should always be top on the list for any automotive project. Patience, foresight, and a little common sense can prevent most accidents and injuries. Below is a list of basic automotive safety rules and guidelines that will ultimately make the job easier.

- Always disconnect the negative battery cable when working with any electrical components.
- Always wear protective eye gear or safety goggles when cutting, grinding, drilling, or prying.
- Properly dispose of used oils and fluids by sealing them in a container and taking them to a recycling or waste center.
- Use a quality floor jack and a pair of jack stands to support a vehicle in the air.
- When the vehicle is lifted from the ground, always block the wheels and set the parking brake.
- Place the transmission in neutral and work to the side of the vehicle whenever possible.
- Make sure your work area is adequately ventilated.
- Keep your work area clean and organized.
- Clean up any oil or fluid spills immediately.
- Always work on a flat, level surface.
- Always wear a dust mask or respirator when working with harmful chemicals or agents.
- Keep a fire extinguisher and first aid kit within easy reach.
- Inspect heavy-lifting equipment, such as engine hoists and stands, for proper operation and stability prior to use.
- Wear protective work shoes.
- Always work in a well-lighted area.
- Avoid wearing loose clothing when working around moving parts.
- Never smoke around gasoline, cleaning solvents, or the battery.
- Keep all electrical connections and extension cords away from moisture or water.
- Shield your eyes when working around the battery and sulfuric acid.
- Never use gasoline to clean your hands or skin.

 Heads a project that a novice could complete.

 Lets a novice know that a little help may be needed.

 Indicates a project that requires that you have a fair amount of mechanical expertise and be comfortable with complex assemblies.

 Implies that you are well versed in wrenching. Perhaps you've even had some training. A project at this level could be attempted with the assistance of a more experienced mechanic.

 Marks a job best left to the pros, but those who aspire to professional tuner status could press ahead.

HOW TO READ THIS BOOK

While we'd be gratified if you read this book from cover to cover, we all know that our busy schedules will prevent that. So, the sections cover groupings of projects based on a muscle car's different systems. For the most part, maintenance projects are listed at the beginning of the section. These projects are usually the easier ones and offer novice mechanics an opportunity to get comfortable wrenching. To assist you in your planning for a project, each begins with an easy-to-read listing of information to give you an idea of what challenges you face. The items listed are:

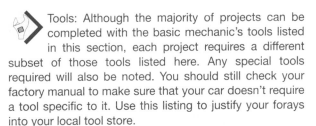 Time: Many projects can be finished in a couple of hours. Others can take days. Wouldn't you like to know in advance? If you're a complete novice, you might want to factor in additional time. Old pros will probably breeze through some projects in significantly less time.

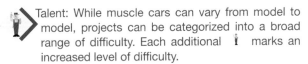 Tools: Although the majority of projects can be completed with the basic mechanic's tools listed in this section, each project requires a different subset of those tools listed here. Any special tools required will also be noted. You should still check your factory manual to make sure that your car doesn't require a tool specific to it. Use this listing to justify your forays into your local tool store.

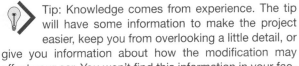 Talent: While muscle cars can vary from model to model, projects can be categorized into a broad range of difficulty. Each additional marks an increased level of difficulty.

 Applicable Years: Select projects apply to only certain model years.

 Cost: The approximate cost for components required for the project.

Parts: The listing of parts required to perform the modification. However, you should still check your factory manual to ascertain that your car doesn't require anything special.

 Tip: Knowledge comes from experience. The tip will have some information to make the project easier, keep you from overlooking a little detail, or give you information about how the modification may affect your car. You won't find this information in your factory manual.

Performance Gain: What to expect from your time, money, and effort.

Complementary Projects: This listing will point to other projects that could help you get even more out of the current project. Again, you won't find this information in your factory manual.

INTERIOR

Refurbishing your car's interior is always a time-consuming affair. It's the fine attention to detail that truly makes the difference in the appearance of your vehicle. There are many tricks and tips to performing quality interior work. This section will shed some new light on the installation and restoration of these items.

Door panels courtesy of P.U.I. Industries

Restoring the Floorpan

 Time: Approximately 8 hours

 Tools: Scrapers (putty knife), drill motor with wire bristle attachment

 Talent:

 Applicable years: All

 Cost: About $70

 Parts: Marine Clean (industrial strength cleaner and degreaser), Metal Ready (rust remover, preprimer), POR-15 (rust-preventative paint), and plenty of elbow grease

 Tip: Let POR-15 dry completely before recoating, and wear as much protective material as possible. POR-15 is almost indelible.

PERFORMANCE GAIN: Solid, life-long rust protection for all types of metal. POR-15 is like liquid metal.

COMPLEMENTARY PROJECTS:

Project 2: Installing New Carpet and Sound Deadener;

Project 8: Installing New Seat Upholstery

Let the scraping begin. It's the sound deadener that has to come up, and that can be an effort. We use putty knives and literally pry off all the old tarlike material.

What's the old saying? If it's worth doing, it's worth doing right? Well, that old adage certainly applies here. If you're going to install new sound deadener and carpeting, it's well worth spending an extra day to add some long-term rust protection while you're at it.

Here we've taken a standard-issue '69 Buick Skylark and stripped out the seats and seat belts. That nagging apprehension while tearing away at the old carpeting and undercarpet sound deadener (vintage 1969) gradually fades when we discover the floorpans are actually in pretty good shape. The only problem spots encountered are in the rear seat area—not a big surprise. GM's A-body cars (Chevelle, GTO, Cutlass, Skylark, etc.) are all prone to floor rust in the recessed areas directly beneath the rear seat, and this Buick is no exception.

With some basic scraping tools, a little determination, and products from POR-15, we are able to give the Buick's floorpans a new lease on life.

When you don't know what's lurking beneath it, removing old carpeting can be a little scary. We are lucky that, for the most part, the floor is solid and the original factory paint still looks pretty good—if you think lime green poly looks good, that is!

Check out the first photo. Once the old carpeting comes out, it's time to bring out the elbow grease. In areas where the sound deadener just doesn't want to come up, we use a drill with a wire bristle attachment to remove all those last little annoying bits. It's imperative to strip the floors clean. In areas where there is clean paint, you'll need to scuff up the surface in preparation for the POR-15 rust preventative.

The rear floorpan proves to be the only difficult area. This area is typically rusty on GM A-bodies. Once again, we are fortunate that none of the rusted-through holes are larger than the diameter of a pen. After inspecting the holes, we pull the rubber drain plugs that were originally installed at the factory.

We remove all the scaly surface rust in the rear seat area with a heavy-duty wire scrub brush. After scrubbing, we notice that the floor itself is getting pretty thin. At this point, you could probably punch a hole through it with a small hammer. Fortunately, this area is directly under the rear seat and is not a load-bearing section. The seat itself mounts to higher locations on the floor. After all the loose rust and old sound deadener/insulation is removed, it's time to clean the floors.

Following the manufacturer's directions, we spray generous portions of Marine Clean to the entire floorpan. Marine Clean is a heavy-duty industrial cleanser made by POR-15.

Next, (left) we apply the Metal Ready, again according to the manufacturer's directions. Metal Ready is a rust remover/primer. Like the Marine Clean, you must coat the entire door. We now apply (right) the POR-15 rust-preventative paint. It's literally painted on with a brush, in small sections. You'll find that the POR-15 goes on like black paint, but slightly thicker. A few words of caution: This stuff is toxic and should only be used in a well-ventilated area. It's also very important to wear gloves when "painting on" POR-15. If you get it on your skin, it'll come off, but only after about two weeks of scrubbing. If you get it on your clothes, enjoy the new design.

Use Marine Clean to eat away at any small bits of sound deadener that refuse to budge. Finish it off with the wire scrub brush. Then rinse the entire floor with clean, room-temperature water. Be sure to remove all the factory drain plugs (rubber and metal).

Next, pat the floorpans dry with a clean towel. It's important to remove all traces of water in preparation for the next step.

It can take a number of applications to clean up the surface rust in the rear pan sections. Spray on the Metal Ready, allow it to sit for a while, and then reapply. The process is explained in depth on the label, and times vary according to the amount of rust that needs to be treated. Again, rinse the entire floor with clean, room-temperature water, following

the manufacturer's directions. Pat everything dry with towels. You have now successfully prepped the floor.

The last photo shows what comes next. Use the POR-15 sparingly. It doesn't need to go on thick, all in one coat, and it's not cheap. After the entire floorpan is coated, allow approximately 5 hours' drying time, and then apply another coat. We treat the rear sections (which were thin and corroded) to several coats over 24 hours. The small rust holes literally disappear after the third coat, and the floor is now solid as a rock. POR-15 is like a liquid metal, protecting and strengthening as it dries.

Replace the drain plugs, and you're ready for new sound deadener and carpet.

Installing New Carpet and Sound Deadener

 Time: 3–5 hours

 Tools: Standard socket set, standard wrenches, Phillips screwdriver, scraper, utility knife, scissors, heat gun (recommended), spray adhesive

 Talent:

 Applicable years: All

 Cost: About $150

 Parts: Carpet, floorpan sound deadener

 Tip: After purchasing a new carpet kit, remove the pieces from the box and lay them out flat. This will help take the folds and creases from packaging out of the rug before it goes into the car. If the weather permits, lay the carpet outside in the direct sun with the plastic backing facing up, allowing the sun's heat to soften the fold and ease the installation.

PERFORMANCE GAIN: A quiet, factory-fresh-looking floor that now accentuates every flaw and well-worn item in the interior . . . Oh, well!

COMPLEMENTARY PROJECTS:

Project 1: Restoring the Floorpan

As we all know, the interior carpet is subject to some of the most brutal and constant abuse your car will ever see. How many times have you launched a full soda or cup of coffee into your floorboard, only to let it sit there as you watch the carpet soak it up? If you're lucky, you have a dark interior that helps hide these types of mishaps. When you mix that with 30-plus years of intense engine heat and floorpan moisture, the results can be startling.

Installing new carpet and sound deadener is always near the top of the list after any muscle car purchase. It will make a drastic difference in your interior, regardless of whether or not you make any other changes. Original-style replacement carpet costs in the neighborhood of $100 to $125 and can be ordered from just about any restoration house or carpet manufacturer in the color of your choice.

The first order of the day will be to completely gut the floor of the interior. Remove the front and rear seats, the seatbelts, the door sill plates, the kick panels, the floor shifter, and the center console if so equipped. For removal and replacement information on these items, refer to the appropriate projects covered in this book. With the floor stripped of all attachments, it's time to give the old rug the heave-ho, and no, there is no reason to save the mess.

Be careful and move slowly when pulling the factory carpet up off the floorpan. Often, the build sheet of the car was attached to the underside of the carpet or even folded and taped to the pan. These sheets are much sought-after and thoroughly explain and validate by code the factory build of that particular vehicle. Oddly enough, I have found multiple build sheets for different cars under the same rug of carpet. Let me tell you, nothing is cooler than buying an old beater, taking it home, ripping apart the interior, and scoring the original build sheet of the car. Not only does it serve as a great point of reference, but it also lets you know the car was not previously dismantled or altered. This can be a huge vote of confidence after forking out your hard-earned cash on some random, redheaded stepchild of an automobile.

On the other hand, removing the factory sound deadener is a little less exciting and a lot more labor intensive. Most factories at the time utilized tarpaper insulation as a cheap way to shut out extreme high and low temperatures and excess noise. Although the material leans a bit on the heavy side, the stuff actually works very well. Pulling it up cleanly and completely, however, is another story. Get out your best scraper and a drum full of elbow grease, and have at it. A power drill or an air compressor with a wire wheel attachment will help clean out the small cracks and crevices in the pans. How far you want to go is entirely up to you. If you plan on refurbishing and rust treating your floorpans while you're at it, make sure everything is totally stripped clean and free of all old residue and grease.

The tarpaper insulation is applied with a high-heat source, such as an adjustable heat gun, and stuck to the floorpans in the precut pattern. If the deadener covers seatbelt holes or the mounting holes of the front seat, now is the time to cut provisions in the material to allow access to the bolts.

15

Start by loosely fitting the rug into position. Use the center hump in the floor as the focal point and work your way down into the pans.

Most carpet kits are cut slightly oversized to ensure the proper fit. Cut the excess sides of the rug with a pair of shears or a sharp utility knife.

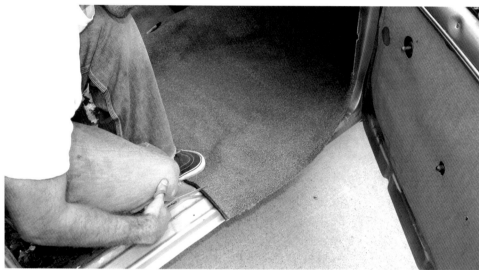

Laying the carpet is a relatively basic procedure, but it requires much attention to detail for the best results. Most aftermarket carpet kits are premolded and designed to fit the shape and contour of the factory floorpan. Since the front piece always overlaps the rear, I have found it easier to install the rear section of the carpet first. Place the rug into the rear floorboard area and glue it down in the corners with spray adhesive. The rear top flap of excess carpet should also be folded over and glued down to sit under the bottom of the rear seat. Each side will most likely require minor trimming to neatly tuck the carpet back underneath the rear panels and the windlace. Take your time and be careful not to cut too much. Your patience will definitely pay off in the long run.

Depending on the car, the front section of the carpet can prove to be a little more involved than the rear and in need of greater modification. Obviously, floor shift/console cars will need to be heavily cut around the shifter area to fit. Start by loosely fitting the rug into a position that will cover the entire area of the pan. Most of the time, there is plenty of excess carpet on all sides to allow for trimming. Use the center hump in the floorpan as the focal point—work down from the hump into the passenger and driver side pan. In tightly bunched areas, apply direct heat to the plastic back side of the rug with a heat gun. This will result in a softer, much more flexible material to work with temporarily.

Spray the back of the carpet with adhesive and stretch it into place. If bunching still persists, you may need to cut a small slit into the rug, forcing it to lie flat without kinking or creasing.

Once the carpet is thoroughly tacked down, grab a sharp utility knife and a pair of shears and trim off all of the overhanging material. Focus on one area at a time, and be sure to leave enough carpet to tuck back under the kick panels and the door sill plates.

Cutting out the shifter hole on a floor shift car is simple. With the carpet fully installed, make a small incision with a utility knife in the center of the hole. Slowly extend the cut to each side of the opening, and remove the excess. The shifter boot or console will completely cover the hole and the surrounding area and will make for a clean finish. Don't forget to cut holes in the carpet and sound deadener for the seatbelts before reinstalling the seats. (Note: You can always locate the holes from the underside of the car and punch through the bottom with a sharp nail if needed.)

PROJECT 3

Removing, Inspecting, and Refinishing the Steering Column

 Time: 2–3 hours (plus overnight drying time)

 Tools: Phillips screwdriver, flat-blade screwdriver, 12-point standard wrenches, standard socket set, steering wheel puller, sandpaper (500- or 1,000-grit), spray paint, non-petroleum-based cleaner

 Talent:

 Applicable years: All

 Cost: $0

 Parts: None

 Tip: Grab another person to help pull the steering column through the firewall. This can be done by one, but an extra set of hands always helps.

 PERFORMANCE GAIN: A fresh coat of paint looks great, but crisp, tight steering will offer immeasurable handling benefits.

COMPLEMENTARY PROJECTS:
Refurbishing or replacing the steering wheel

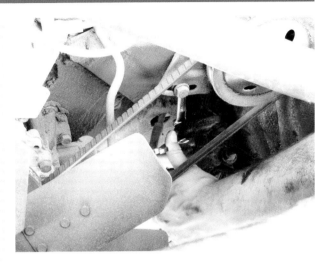
Using 12-point wrenches, disconnect two steering coupler nuts and bolts.

Remove the pin that retains the park "lock-out" arm assembly.

This project will make your steering column look factory fresh and operate like new. We will cover removal of the entire column, checking the bearings, repainting, and reinstalling.

To disconnect the base of the steering column from the gearbox, remove the two steering coupler nuts and bolts. The steering coupler acts as a rubber isolator between the steering shaft and gearbox and it eliminates road vibration through the steering wheel. At this point, remove the pin that retains the park "lock-out" arm assembly. The park lock-out arm prevents the transmission from shifting out of park unless the ignition key is in the "on" position.

Inside the car, using a Phillips screwdriver, remove the horn pad (the design varies from vehicle to vehicle). Disconnect the horn wire assembly. The wire terminals are "push-in" and will easily pull out of the inner horn contact. Then, bracing the steering wheel, remove the 7/8-inch steering wheel nut.

Now, remove the steering wheel itself. The spline of the upper steering shaft is tapered, securing the wheel. Following the manufacturer's instructions, use a steering wheel puller (available at most auto parts stores) to pull the wheel directly off the spline.

Using a Phillips screwdriver, remove lower steering column cover and unplug the turn signal wiring harness. Remove four

We removed the steering column, the antitheft lock cover, the locking steering ring, the hazard hand switch, the ignition cylinder, and the upper steering column bracket.

The end of the shaft. Note the sharp edges on the spline. Rounded edges indicate a need for replacement.

With the cancel cam/horn contacts removed, rotate the shaft by hand.

3/8-inch sheetmetal screws that retain the firewall seal, leaving the seal attached to the steering column. Remove the two 9/16-inch upper column bolts. Lower the column and unplug the ignition switch wiring harness. Rotate the steering column to clear the park lock-out arm through the hole in the firewall and remove the column.

Using a Phillips screwdriver, remove the antitheft lock cover at the top of the column. With a flat-blade screwdriver, pry and remove the C-clip and remove the locking steering ring. Remove turn signal/canceler/inner horn contact. Then, remove the turn signal lever and the ignition cylinder lock.

Using a Phillips screwdriver, remove the three screws that retain the signal switch assembly, and then unscrew (by hand) the hazard switch located on the side of the column and set aside.

To check the bearings, turn the steering shaft by hand (both the upper and lower portions of the shaft). It should rotate smoothly and freely in either direction. If there are signs of excessive "play" (more than 1/8-inch in either direction), grinding, or rubbing, chances are the bearings need replacing. Upper and lower bearing replacement is a fairly complex procedure that could involve disassembling the entire column. If you determine that your bearings require attention, consult a professional.

If everything seems OK with the bearings, you can prepare the entire column for painting. Smooth out any gouges or scratches left by dangling keys with fine-grit (500 or higher) sandpaper. Wipe the unit down with a non-petroleum-based cleaner and dry with a lint-free cloth. In a well-ventilated area, spray the column with primer. Let it dry approximately one hour and then paint. We use two coats of black acrylic lacquer and let it dry overnight. Repaint the upper steering column bracket at the same time (as a separate unit).

Make sure the cylinder lock is reinstalled and then replace: 1. turn signal lever; 2. turn signal/canceler/ inner horn contact; 3. locking steering ring and C-clip; 4. antitheft lock cover; 5. hazard hand switch; 6. ignition switch; 7. the upper steering column bracket; and 8. the tilt-column lever (if applicable).

Our refinished column is now ready to be reinstalled. Slip the column in through the firewall the same way it was removed. Be sure to reconnect the ignition and signal switch wiring harnesses. Make sure the upper column bolts are reattached as well as the four firewall seal screws.

Reattach the steering wheel, and tighten the 7/8-inch steering wheel nut, using the socket wrench. Reattach the horn wire contacts and horn pad.

Installing a Trunk Divider Board and Rear Seat Shelf

 Time: 1 hour

 Tools: Utility knife, 3M Super 77 spray glue

 Talent:

 Applicable years: All

 Cost: $75

 Parts: Trunk divider board and insulation, rear package tray and insulation

 Tip: When removing your trunk divider board and rear seat shelf, don't automatically destroy and discard the cardboard and/or insulation. If you have a hard time locating new ones, the original pieces serve as accurate templates from which to make your own replacements.

 PERFORMANCE GAIN: A well-insulated interior reduces noise, hot and cold temperatures, and exhaust fumes from the trunk area

COMPLEMENTARY PROJECTS:

Rear speaker installation

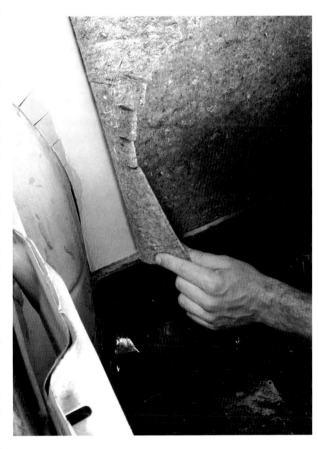

We end up having to slightly cut the cardboard around the curved edges to allow it to sit flat behind the rear seat.

Although minor projects compared to upholstery work or a dash installation, the trunk divider and rear package tray are two fundamental components in the interior that almost always need addressing in any restoration. Over the years, the sun and rain (water leaks) take their toll on these cardboard cutouts and leave many with nothing but a pile of brittle scraps in the back of the trunk. The good news is these are both extremely easy to remove and replace and can be bought for most cars right over the counter or via mail order. The two pieces work hand in hand and are often replaced together for sheer simplicity.

The trunk divider, constructed of a thick cardboard material, separates the trunk cargo area of the car from the inside

passenger compartment. It's located directly behind the rear seat and mounts to the top of the metal package tray. In between the divider board and the back of the rear seat is a precut layer of jute insulation to further support the cause.

To replace or install the divider, you first need to remove both sections of the rear seat. The bottom of the seat is the first to go. It is secured by its own frame inside a notched bracket welded to the floor. It sounds complicated, but trust me, it's not. After you get it apart, it will make perfect sense. Push the bottom of the seat down and toward the rear of the car at the same time. Note: It may take a little force to release the seat from its location. This will pop the lower seat frame out of the bracket

After laying the insulation and the seat shelf in place, simply glue the excess flap of vinyl down to the metal tray below.

and allow the bottom half to be removed. There are two mounting slots or brackets in the floor, one on each side of the car.

The back of the rear seat literally hangs on a series of hooks that are welded to the top of the metal package tray. It's normally fastened to the floor by two bolts hidden behind the bottom of the rear seat. Remove the bolts and nuts and simply lift the seat back up and off of the hooks.

Replacing the trunk divider board (or what's left of it) and its insulation is about as easy as it gets—no tools or sweat required. Both hang on the seat back mounting hooks and quietly do their jobs. If for some reason you are unable to find a new replacement board and insulation, making your own version of the factory piece is not too difficult. Create a basic template of the size and shape needed for your vehicle, and cut it out of a rigid, thick piece of cardboard. Do the same for the insulation. Using a can of 3M spray glue, affix the insulation to the front of the divider board (facing the front of the car).

The rear seat shelf works in a similar fashion. It is located between the top of the back seat and the rear back glass. Nothing more than vinyl-covered cardboard, the shelf simply continues and completes the colored trim of the interior. If your

car was factory optioned to include a rear speaker package, the rear seat shelf was made with built-in protective grilles to cover the speakers below. Again, jute insulation was installed beneath the tray for added sound and noise dampening.

After removing the old package tray and insulation, clean out and inspect the rear window channel for corrosion or holes in the metal. These cars are famous for rusting and leaking in this area. Water tends to pool in the corners of the back glass and, over time, can eat its way right through the metal and into your interior. If your old seat shelf is warped and rippled (wet cardboard) or shows any signs of water damage, the leaking areas will need to be fixed or repaired before going any further (no JB weld or silicone). Otherwise, your new seat shelf and trunk divider will ultimately meet the same fate.

As you most likely figured out, the insulation goes down first with the help of a little glue. The shelf slides into place through a slightly recessed groove on each side. Make sure the tray is fully seated rearward under the lip of the glass channel. On the opposite end of the shelf is a small strip of vinyl and backing foam. This is to be folded down and glued to the front of the trunk divider board. That way, when the back seat is once again installed, there is no gap or major seam between the rear seat and the shelf.

Removing, Refinishing, and Reinstalling the Door Panels

Time: 4 hours

Tools: Door panel clip remover, window crank remover, Phillips screwdriver

Talent:

Applicable years: All

Cost: Under $40 (including the price of the tools); add $40 for new front armrest pads (optional)

Parts: Door panel water shields, vinyl dye, silicone spray

Tip: Use water shields to protect your door panels from moisture.

PERFORMANCE GAIN: A show-winning interior

COMPLEMENTARY PROJECTS:

Armrest pad replacement; Project 6: Replacing the Window Regulator and Door Latch Assembly

Unscrew the lock knob. Use a Phillips screwdriver to remove the three long screws that retain the armrest base.

You've just come back from the paint shop with a drop-dead-gorgeous new paint job. The outside of your car looks great! How about once you open the door? Have you neglected the inner door panels? Years of exposure to the sun and the moisture that gets trapped inside the door shell can have devastating effects on a door panel. Fading, cracking, and general wear and tear don't add up to a show car, and this project will help you fix all that.

This project doesn't take a lot of skill, just some time and a little patience. The key to the project is taking things slowly, one step at a time. If you're restoring a classic muscle car, the last thing you want to do is start damaging your interior. Although there are a lot of interior restoration parts now on the market, many of them are expensive. Why rush things and damage a perfectly good door panel? Granted, you could order a new set from a classic car parts supplier, but you'll probably end up shelling out at least a few hundred bucks. With some fairly inexpensive tools, we'll show you the correct way to remove your door panels. We'll also cover refinishing them with vinyl dye and silicone spray. Just look at the first and last photos in this project—tell us it's not worth it!

Let's get the car in the shade. This is not a job you want to do under an 80-degree sun. Starting with either side, unscrew the door lock knob. Then, take a Phillips screwdriver and remove the three long screws that hold the armrest base to the door panel. After removing the armrest base, take the window crank remover and carefully slide it behind the window crank. You don't want to mark up the vinyl, so go easy. On page 23, you can see what you're trying to remove. That's a C-clip that snaps onto the base of the window crank. It actually secures the crank to the post that operates the window regulator. Slowly turn the tool so that it catches the C-clip and pops it off. You may want to hold your hand or a rag under the crank to catch the flying clip. You can then safely pull the crank off its post. Repeat this procedure with the inner door handle and, if so equipped, the quarter-vent window crank.

Use the specially designed window crank remover to pop the C-clips that retain the cranks. Do not try to pry the cranks off with a screwdriver.

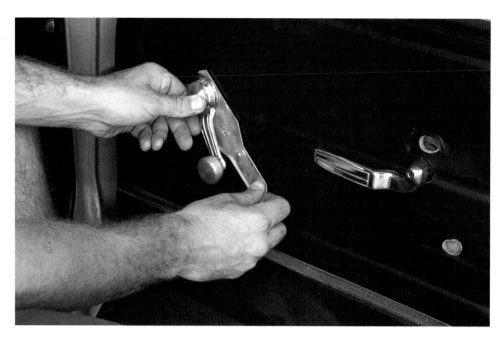

Next, release the clips that attach the door panel to the door shell. You can use a flat-blade screwdriver to do this, but a door panel clip remover will work best. Depending on the year and make of car, there could be four or five clips at each end of the door. They are best removed by gently sliding the tool in between the panel and the steel door. You want to feel for the clip locations. Once you've located them, carefully pry each clip out of its seat in the door. The clip should remain attached to the door panel. Once you've pried loose all the clips, you'll need to free the bottom part of the panel. Again, depending on the year and make, it could be held in with either sheetmetal screws or more clips.

With the cranks and handle removed, it's time to pull the panel itself. Since the panel rail (the rounded upper edge of the panel) actually slots into the top of the door shell, you'll need to lift the panel to break it loose. Just go easy, and work the panel up first, then off.

Now it's time for a little refinishing action. Get some vinyl upholstery cleaner (or soapy warm water) and scrub clean all the vinyl areas of the panel. Be careful not to soak the vinyl. The innards of the panel are just heavy-gauge cardboard. Make sure you remove all grease, dirt, gum, etc. (a lot can accumulate over 30-plus years). Next, dry the panel thoroughly.

We've masked off the decorative chromed Mylar welts on the door in anticipation of spraying it with vinyl dye. Since vinyl dye is permanent, cover up any areas that you don't want colored. Mask off any lower carpet on the door panel as well as other emblems and striping. When you're ready, spray on the vinyl dye. We're using Omni-Pak's Lacquer Blend. The spray nozzle comes with an adjustable fan spray pattern. Following the manufacturer's directions, we're laying on several thin coats—just enough to get a good solid coverage. Be sure to use vinyl dye in a well-ventilated area.

Before reinstalling the panels, we're adding some much needed weatherproofing. Door panel water shields are coated with a thick, waxlike substance that will repel any moisture that gets down inside your door shell. Since the door panels are basically vinyl-covered cardboard, they are extremely sen-

The door panel clip remover is your best bet for popping those clips. The tool can be found at any auto parts supply store for around $10. A flat-blade screwdriver will work, but you risk breaking the edge of the door panel.

sitive to the elements. A complete set of four water shields retails for around 12 bucks anywhere door panels are sold (most specialty classic auto parts companies). You can tack them to the door shell with spray glue or masking tape.

Now, it's time to reinstall the panel, basically putting it all back together in reverse order. Take care to insert the upper rail of the panel first, and slide it into the right position. Push the clips back into their mounting points. In this instance, we elect not to use the four screws that originally retained the bottom portion of the door panel (for cosmetic reasons). You can

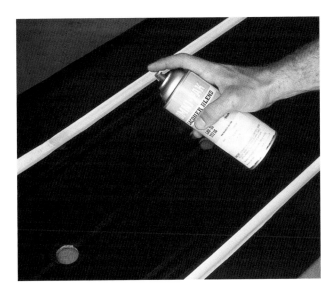

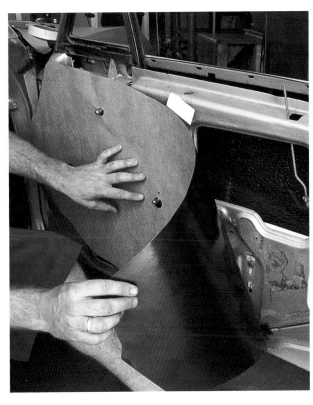

With the chrome strips masked off, we apply the vinyl dye to immediately give the old faded vinyl a new lease on life.

Adding door panel water shields is a must to keep refurbished door panels from warping and cracking.

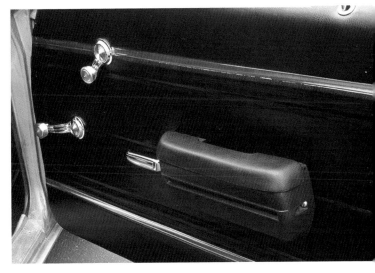

The tiny C-clips snap into position on the back of the window crank handle and the inner door handle. You'll need to push them back in place before reinstalling your cranks.

The finished panel looks great. Granted, we've taken things to the next level by adding new armrest pads (about $20 each) and new window cranks. The clear GM originals tend to yellow over the years, looking pretty dingy. We sprang for a new set and it was totally worth it—approximately $20 each for a genuine GM replacement or $5 each for an overseas reproduction.

actually use strong double-sided tape for a cleaner appearance.

After the panel is secured, reattach the cranks. The photo shows how the C-clips need to be seated on the cranks before attaching them. Then, reattach the armrest bases and pads. Again, we've gone the extra mile and added new armrest pads (about $20 each for the front). After everything's back in place, spray the entire panel down with a light coating of silicone and wipe clean. You have to agree that it was all worth it. Our last photo shows a panel worthy of any show.

PROJECT 6

Replacing the Window Regulator and Door Latch Assembly

Time: 3 hours

Tools: Phillips screwdriver, impact driver (optional), hammer, socket wrenches, open-ended wrenches, window crank removal tool, white lithium grease, flashlight, small inspection mirror

Talent:

Applicable years: All

Cost: Window regulator assemblies $80 each, door latch assemblies $110 each

Parts: Window regulator assemblies (Original Parts Group Part Number CH25879 right and CH25880 left), door latch assemblies (OPG Part Number C980007 right and C980008 left)

Tip: We recommend wearing long sleeves while working inside the door assembly. Sharp edges can easily cut skin. If necessary, use a flashlight and small inspection mirror to make sure that the rollers are firmly set in their tracks.

PERFORMANCE GAIN: Smooth door latch and window operation, but nothing in terms of drag strip performance

COMPLEMENTARY PROJECTS:

Replacing the door glass; Project 5: Removing, Refinishing, and Reinstalling door panels

Are the door locks or latches on your late 1960s or early 1970s GM car jamming or not working altogether? How about the windows? Do they rattle or jam in their tracks? Maybe it's time for a door tune-up.

Before starting, roll your window to its "up" position to allow easy access to the inner door assemblies. Clamp the window in this position, taking care not to scratch the glass (when the window regulator assembly is removed, nothing will be supporting the glass).

To get things started, we remove the window crank with the removal tool. Slip the tool behind the crank until it is pushed against the retaining pin. Gently pry the tool until the crank is removed.

Next, we remove the inner door handle. Use a 5/16-inch open end wrench on the single nut located under the handle. Then, remove the two screws under the molded armrest and the two sheetmetal screws at the bottom of the door panel (in the carpeted area). Pry the four retaining clips with the window crank tool and pull the panel.

Now that everything's exposed, we remove the three door latch retaining screws. A Number 3 Phillips screwdriver can be used, but if the screws are rusted, you can easily strip the heads. We recommend an impact driver for this procedure. At this point, you should also unscrew and remove the door lock knob, then gently pry loose the door lock ferrules (the circular trim rings around the door locks).

Using a socket wrench, remove the three screws that retain the inner door latch mechanism. You should also inspect the control rod and the lock rod. Look for stress cracks or lots of rust. If the rods appear questionable, replace them.

Our control and lock rods are OK, so we attach them to the new door latch assembly. Fortunately, the rods require no screws or nuts and "snap" back into place. We then reinstall the new latch assembly. Take care not to overtighten the screws.

Using a locking plier or other clamp, make sure the window is clamped in the up position. This will prevent the window from falling into the door when the regulator assembly is removed. Using a socket wrench, remove the four retaining bolts that hold the front end of the regulator assembly.

Next, we remove the door guide rail. The door guide rail acts as a fixed point that holds the bottom of the window regulator assembly. Very Important: Mark the location of the bolt closest to the doorjamb. The bolt is adjustable, and its position is set at the factory. It is critical that the bolt is returned to its original location. Using a socket wrench, remove the two bolts and pull the door guide rail.

Then, reach into the door cavity and work the regulator assembly back and forth to remove the rollers from the window roller track. This will be a tight operation, so watch those sharp metal edges.

This is the window regulator.

Install the new window regulator assembly. First, bend the fixed window guide rail flanges open slightly using pliers, and insert the regulator roller into the window channel track. Then crimp it back into its original position. It may be necessary to wind the window crank to line up the four mounting bolt holes in the regulator assembly with the holes in the door. Using a socket wrench, retighten all four bolts. Do not over-tighten them.

Remove the clamp and gently lower the window. Place the door guide rail inside the door, and attach the "scissor" arm of the regulator assembly to the door guide rail channel.

Tighten the bolts, making sure that the rear-most bolt is in its original position. Using white lithium grease, lubricate all moving parts (window regulator, door latch, guide rollers) at their hinge points. This is done after installation to avoid getting grease all over the window, door, your hands, etc.

Now, it's time to reinstall the door panel. You can use your old door panel clips, but we recommend using new ones, as the originals have probably lost some of their shape and tension. Reattach your window cranks and inner door handle, and enjoy the fruits of your efforts.

Shown here is the door latch assembly.

INTERIOR

PROJECT 7

Installing a New Dash Pad

 Time: 2–3 hours

 Tools: Small Phillips screwdriver, small standard screwdriver, utility knife, small standard wrenches

 Talent:

 Applicable years: All

 Cost: $150–$300 (depending on the size of your dash pad)

 Parts: New reproduction or refinished dash pad

 Tip: If at all possible, hire a kid with small limbs to do the job for you. Wedging yourself upside down under the dash is not exactly fun. Seriously, if you get stuck on something, try a factory assembly manual as a point of reference.

! PERFORMANCE GAIN: A clean, factory-fresh dash pad

Constantly straight and center, it's hard to get away from an unsightly dash. When you peek your head inside the window of any older car, the dashboard trim and instrumentation are among the first things you notice. The attention paid to even the smallest of details uniquely distinguishes each car with its own signature look and layout. However, these pieces (especially the dash pad) take quite a beating from years in the scorching hot sun. Most original dashes today are faded, dried out, and cracked in half. You can always buy a dash cover to hide the problem, but nothing looks cooler than a clean, factory-fresh dash.

Removing the dash pad is never a simple affair. In fact, it often requires contorting yourself into a human pretzel and crawling up behind the dash carrier. Every car will be different, depending on make, year, and model, but equally challenging.

When removing the old pad, start with easiest things first. Loosen and remove any external hardware securing the dash pad to the shell. Look at the underside of the pad for hidden clips or retainers. If you are unsure how your dash pad is mounted, pick up a factory assembly manual for your vehicle from any restoration house. It may even offer some insight into removing and replacing the piece.

Most factory dash pads have a series of threaded studs inserted into the bottom of the pad. The studs drop down through slotted holes in the carrier and fasten on the underside with nuts. Most of these are blind holes and cannot be seen from the underside of the dash without disassembly. You literally have to feel them out.

Starting on the passenger side of the dash, remove the glove box liner and door if necessary. With a small flashlight, you should be able to locate the first couple of nuts and remove them. As you work your way into the driver's floorpan, things will get tighter and more difficult to see. You will need to rely on your feelers alone to locate and remove the remaining nuts. Be patient and don't give up—after you find the mounting locations in the removal, you will have a much better idea of how to go about the reinstallation.

If you purchased a new reproduction dash pad from an aftermarket company, you may need to trim off a little excess vinyl at the face and in the corners of the pad. Do so with a sharp utility knife, but be careful not to cut too much. If you want to retain the original dash pad, there are plenty of outfits that restore and recover dashes, as well as other interior trim items. They are not exactly cheap when you factor in all of the shipping costs, but some do great work and offer a quality alternative to either aftermarket repros or junkyard trash.

The dash pad will install in the same manner in which it was removed. Loosely place the pad into position to determine the amount of material (if any) to be trimmed. Install the dash pad into the carrier and tighten the retaining nuts. Reattach the glove box liner and any other items that were removed during the disassembly.

Honestly, this is not one of the more enjoyable projects in this book. In fact, it's a serious pain that you hope to do only once in a lifetime. You might be tempted to farm it out and just cough up the cash. But the sheer satisfaction you get from doing even the dirtiest jobs yourself is really what car crafting is all about.

Above: Using a small flashlight and a boxed wrench, we are able to locate and remove the first couple of nuts.
Below: The stud in the dash pad slides down inside the slotted hole and is tightened on the underside by the nut.

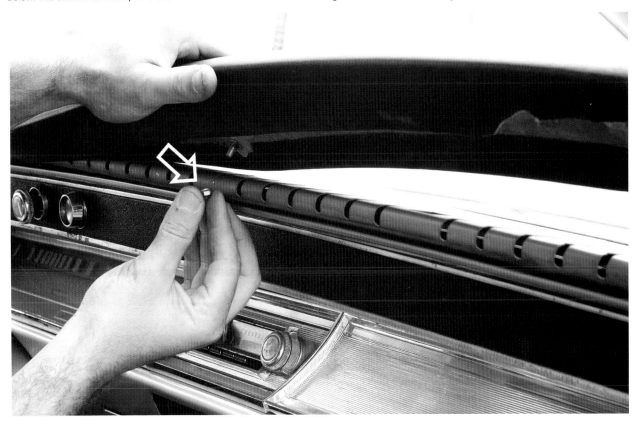

PROJECT 8

Installing New Seat Upholstery

 Time: Varies depending on number of seats and style; at least 2–3 hours

 Tools: Standard wrenches, hog ring pliers, flat-blade screwdriver, needle-nose pliers (optional)

 Talent:

 Applicable years: All

 Cost: $100–$500

 Parts: Upholstery, hog rings

 Tip: Before installing new vinyl seat covers, lay them out in the sun to loosen the material and relieve any folds or creases in the vinyl from packaging.

 PERFORMANCE GAIN: None that are track-proven, but the added comfort and style far make up for it.

COMPLEMENTARY PROJECTS:

Installing new seat foam, seat springs, and headrests

Whether your vehicle came equipped with cloth- or vinyl-covered seats, chances are they need a full cosmetic makeover. Seat upholstery is almost always tattered and torn, regardless of the car. Mexican blankets are cool and work fine while the rest of the car is coming together, but no restoration would be complete without a freshly recovered interior. It's amazing what new skins will do for the look and feel of your car's inner delicates.

There comes a time when everyone is faced with the classic dilemma: D.I.Y. or farm it out to a hired hand? Interior work requires a great deal of patience and can sometimes turn out to be more than we bargained for. Fortunately, many common mistakes and obstacles can be avoided and overcome with a little instruction and guidance.

Naturally, replacing the upholstery requires the seats to be removed from the car. Starting with the front, unbolt the seat from the floorpans. On a split-bench, there will be two bolts at the front of the seat (one on each side) and possibly four at the rear. The rear bolts can be difficult to access, as the clearance is pretty tight under the seat. An open or boxed wrench should do the trick, however. Bucket seats follow the same basic approach. Loosen the bolts and simply lift the front seats out of the passenger compartment.

Removing the two-piece rear seat can be a bit more of a challenge. Typically, the bottom is secured by the frame of the seat to retaining hooks welded onto the floorpan. Force-fully push the seat rearward to its furthermost point. In this position, the seat frame will clear the retaining hooks in the pan and can be lifted up and out of the floor. Do this in one continuous motion.

When the seat bottom is removed, the mounting points of the seat back are accessible. The seat back is bolted to the rear wall of the floorpan at the bottom and hooked to the rear package tray at the top.

The covers are secured to the frame and the springs of the seats by small fasteners called hog rings. The upholstery is stretched over the foam padding and tucked to the underside of the seat assembly. The hog rings loop through the edge of the material and into the holes in the seat frame (see photo 2). Out of the bag, the metal rings have a "U" shape to them, with slight notches cut into both sides. The arms of the hog ring pliers fit snugly into these notches, allowing the rings to be folded over and closed.

To remove the covers, gently pry the hog ring open with a small flat-blade screwdriver. Loosen all of the rings from the seat assembly and remove the skins. During the process, take note of the original mounting locations of the rings to the seat to help in getting the new covers stretched and installed correctly.

While you're at it, this is a good time to replace your existing seat foam as well. The underlying foam is what actually makes the seats comfortable. Over time, the foam deteriorates and ends up as a big pile of dust under the seat. Unless you enjoy being poked in the rear with sharp, metal seat springs, spend the extra coin, and install some new padding. Most seat foam comes premolded to a specific application and is available from just about any restoration house. Upholstery is readily available for practically any older GM vehicle and comes in most, if not all, of the original colors and patterns.

After tearing the seats apart, you'll have a pretty good idea how to install the new covers. It can be tricky in some areas, especially in the corners and at the bottom of the seats. Try to stretch the new material as evenly as possible over the foam.

It may take several tries, working from one side to another, to really nail it. This is a project that takes practice and patience to achieve the desired results. Take your time and be sure to buy plenty of hog rings—the more the better.

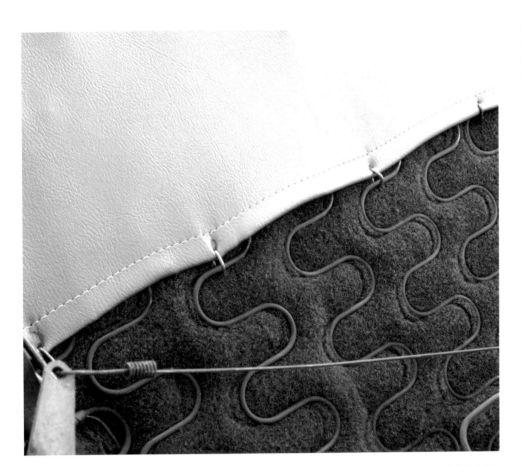

The underside of the seat cover attaches to the bottom seat springs on this split-bench.

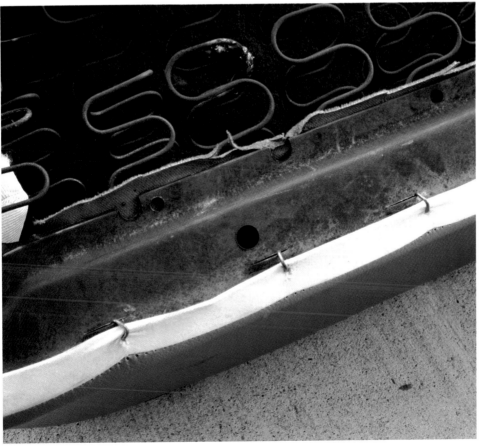

The hog rings secure the upholstery to the frame of the seat.

Above: New upholstery kits often include hog rings and specialty pliers.

Right: Squeeze the ring with the arms of the pliers to close the loop and tether the new cover to the seat assembly.

PROJECT 9

Converting to Bucket Seats

 Time: 1 day

 Tools: Phillips screwdriver, standard socket set, standard wrenches, razor blade, measuring tape, welder, putty knife or scraper, power drill with wire wheel attachment (recommended)

 **Talent:** ▮▮▮

 Applicable years: All

 Cost: $25 (brackets)

 Parts: Bucket seat conversion brackets

 Tip: Be careful not to overheat the metal of the floorpan when welding the brackets in place. Excessive heat can weaken and warp the sheet metal.

 PERFORMANCE GAIN: Your interior will take on the sporty look and feel of a true performance car.

COMPLEMENTARY PROJECTS:
Replacing the center console; Project 2: Installing New Carpet and Sound Deadener

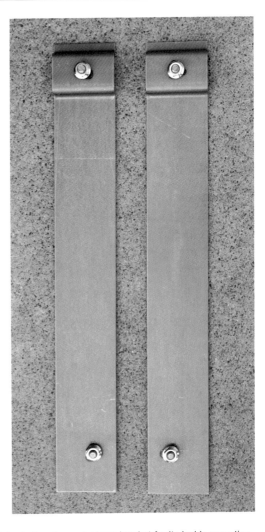

Each bucket seat uses just one bracket for its inside mounting location. The outside will reuse the existing bench seat holes in the floorpan.

Converting a stock bench seat car to have high- or low-back bucket seats is nothing new. For many, the lure of the sleek and sporty bucket interior is too strong to resist. Performance-minded drivers prefer bucket seats for their planted, boxed-in feel. The stock bench is OK for cruising, but around heavy corners it can get a little crazy, especially in four-speed cars. By eliminating the bulky bench seat and installing a pair of buckets, you will not only gain more control behind the wheel, but also open up the cabin for additional upgrades such as a console and floor shifter.

The first thing to do is to remove the old bench seat. There are two bolts in the front (one at each corner) and two bolts at the rear. These can be tough to access if the seat is back

all the way. If the seat is intact and the adjusting mechanism still works, slide the seat up toward the front of the car. With the mounting bolts removed, detach the lap belts from their through-hole in the back of the seat. After many years of service and abuse, the poor bench can finally be retired.

Now we move on to the flooring. Remove the door sill plates with a small Phillips screwdriver and keep track of each side and its mounting hardware. If your sill plates are beat up, this is a good time to replace them. They are fairly inexpensive and make a huge difference in the appearance of the interior. With the old bench now history, you can easily access the seatbelt anchor bolts and remove them. If your car has retractable lap belts, the belt housing/cover on the floor simply pops off

31

with a little prying force. Again, label your parts and hardware for proper reinstallation. To remove the carpet, it may be necessary to loosen both plastic kick panels, located in the corner of the floor underneath the dash. This will also help in getting the carpet back in place when finished. You will likely need to remove the lower steering column protector from the firewall for the same purpose.

Pulling the carpet is basic. The front piece will overlap the rear by 3 to 6 inches. With the ends free and untucked, carefully pull the carpet back from the firewall and remove from the car—guiding it around and underneath the driver's pedals. Most factory sound deadeners were made of heavy tarpaper and glued to the floorpans with heat, much like laying a roof on a house. Needless to say, it's not the easiest stuff to remove and clean. Check out the carpet installation project (Project 2) for some tips and guidelines. A drill or an air compressor with a wire wheel attachment will make the cleanup a lot faster.

In order to make the seat swap, you will need to purchase a pair of bucket seat conversion brackets. Many aftermarket companies carry and stock the brackets for a variety of cars. Each bucket will use one bracket for its inside mounting location. The outside mounting holes already in the floorpans from the bench will be reused, making it easy to square up and take accurate measurements. Using either side to start, install one of the bucket seats in the outer mounting holes in the pan. Place the conversion bracket under the seat's inside mounting points and mark the pan in relation to the bracket when correct. Do the same thing with the other side of the car.

The conversion brackets need to be welded in place. Most people do not own or know how to safely operate a welder, but that's OK. There are tons of body shops, interior shops, and machine shops that can spot weld these brackets into position. This is a small hurdle to overcome.

With the brackets firmly welded in, return the sound insulation and carpet to the car. Chances are, you will need to pick up some new insulation to replace what was removed. The carpet will need slight modification to accommodate the newly installed mounting brackets. This can be done with the carpet in the car. Using a small razor blade, cut around the stud of the bracket just enough to let it poke through and attach to the seat. The seatbelts, sill plates, and kick panels can now be reinstalled.

To install the seat, simply lower the bucket into its inner and outer mounting locations. The brackets should come with a pair of serrated locknuts and washers for each side. Clean any old, dirty threads before reinstalling the new seats. Hand tighten the bolts and nuts at first to allow for adjustment. When everything is finally in place, return and tighten evenly.

After "mocking up" the seat in position, scribe a mark in the floorpan where the bracket is to be welded.

BODY AND EXTERIOR

Body and trim work is often regarded as a mysterious craft in the world of automotive restoration. It's a delicate process that involves plenty of time, space, and specialty tools. The labor is heavy, but the effort can easily last the lifetime of your car.

Removing the Moldings

 Time: 15–30 minutes

  Tools: Molding removal tool (specialty), rubber mallet, standard socket set

  Talent:

Applicable years: All

 Cost: $10–$20 for tools

 Parts: Molding clips or retainers, speed nuts

Tip: When purchasing new moldings or trim for your car, thoroughly inspect them before paying or taking delivery. They are very vulnerable to scratches, kinks, and blemishes.

COMPLEMENTARY PROJECTS:

Project 11: Refinishing the Moldings

Molding removal is essential in the restoration of any vehicle. Although most are simple to take on and off, they require delicate hands to do so without damaging them or the rest of the vehicle in the process. First and foremost, you need the proper tools. A variety of specialty tools are available to aid in removing and installing these moldings.

The windshield moldings on older vehicles are often the most damaged or worn among the bunch. They are constantly baked under the sun and have a nasty habit of catching small rocks and bits of debris from the road. Over time, the once highly polished stainless or chrome can become more of an eyesore than a beauty mark.

To remove the windshield moldings, first purchase the proper removal tool. Don't use a screwdriver! You can very easily break the retainer clips and damage the molding. Most molding removal tools are designed with a thin, "hooked" head to slide between the molding and the glass and release it from the clip. Grab the tool by the handle and insert the hook under the molding. Gently slide it along the windshield until you feel it snag on a clip.

Typically, the clips are spaced about 8 to 10 inches apart. By slightly tugging on the handle of the removal tool, the hook will bend the edge of the clip back just enough to release the tension on the molding. Repeat this procedure for the remainder of the clips.

Next, we tackle the ever-so-delicate roof-drip moldings. These thin, stainless moldings literally "pinch" over the drip channel in the roofline. The best way to remove them is to use a small block of wood and a rubber mallet. In some cases, you can actually remove them by hand. They are extremely fragile

The proper removal tool is essential for replacing your windshield reveal moldings.

Using a small block of wood and a mallet, carefully loosen and remove the roof drip molding.

and easy to kink, so be very careful. Start from whatever end of the molding is easiest. Wedge the end of the wood block underneath the lip and lightly tap it with the mallet. Try to avoid a "square" hit on the lip of the molding. This will only damage the piece and make it more difficult to remove. The key is to position the block just behind the lip between the roof channel and the molding. It should take minimal force to pop and release the trim from the roof.

Although they vary in size, shape, and design, the vast majority of all body moldings and trim pieces use similar hardware and retainers. In the process of stripping a car, you will see what I mean. The back sides of the moldings have channels that the clips or retainers slide into. In this particular case, we are using universal spring retainers. The body of the retainer is designed to enter the channel diagonally, while the spring-loaded arm is bent in the opposite direction (see photo 3). This applies tension into the lip of the molding and holds the retainer in place. The stud on the face of the retainer is then inserted into its designated hole and secured on the back side with a nut.

As we all know, no two cars were built or designed exactly the same. The methods listed here hold true for most GM muscle cars. Although your car may be slightly different, the principles remain true.

Once the retainers are installed, simply slide them into position for mounting.

Refinishing the Moldings

BODY AND EXTERIOR

 Time: 10–20 minutes per molding, depending on size

 Tools: Specialty molding removal tool, power buffing wheel, fine wet sandpaper, stainless or aluminum polish, and clean rags

 Talent:

 Applicable years: All

 Cost: $10 in supplies

 Parts: N/A

 Tip: Be careful not to burn the finish of the metal on the buffing wheel. The wheel turns at a high speed and produces quite a bit of heat from friction.

 PERFORMANCE GAIN: Maybe it's just me, but a nicely detailed car just feels faster when you're sitting behind the wheel. Taking the time to clean and detail your moldings will make a world of difference in the presentation of your car.

COMPLEMENTARY PROJECTS:
Replacing broken or missing retainers and clips

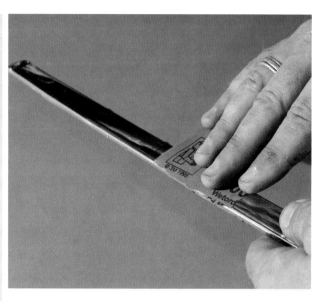

To remove any roughness in the finish, lightly wet-sand the molding until it is smooth and clean.

Considering the amount of chrome, stainless steel, and polished aluminum that was originally bolted on or stuck to these old boxes, cleaning and polishing your body moldings and trim can drastically improve the appearance of your car. Think about it—from grilles and bumpers to window reveals and door moldings, these cars are clad to the hilt with all things bright and shiny. It was the style of the times, and I, for one, love it! Nothing looks better rolling down the high-

way than a nicely restored car with highly detailed trim and appointments. Picture a '65 Marina Blue Impala SS convertible (the luxury flagship of the time for Chevrolet) dancing and sparkling in the afternoon sun like a 2-ton disco ball. Now that's what I call Saturday night fever!

In reality, most of us probably fall a little short of the kingpin styling and prestige of such an Impala. We can always dream, right? The truth is, any car will greatly benefit from time invested in precise detail work. However, this is an area that many car crafters seem to glaze over or forget about altogether. You see it all the time: Somebody will strip a car down, spend $4,000 on bodywork and a new paint job, and proceed to reinstall the same faded-out and pitted-up chrome and trim that came off the car. That makes no sense; not to mention, it heavily detracts from the overall appearance you just spent a grip of cash to improve. Sure, reproduction replacements are not always the best alternative, but they do the job. Chroming is a no-brainer. There should be at least a couple of quality chroming outfits within reasonable range in your area. For stainless and aluminum, you would be surprised how much you can do with a buffer, a little polish, and your own two hands. In fact, we will show you just how easy it is to put a little sparkle back into your cars' cosmetics.

The windshield reveal moldings are constantly under fire from the rays of the sun (or rain and snow depending on the car's origin). Over time, the moldings fade and dull and can even rust, due to the harsh elements of the outdoors. We will pull the original set of moldings off the car and treat them to some long-overdue TLC.

Make sure the buffing wheel is free of all grease and grime before using it on one of your moldings.

With the moldings removed, give them a quick once-over cleaning with a little soap and warm water. Using superfine wet sandpaper, lightly wet-sand each of the moldings lengthwise to remove any burrs or pits in the surface (see photo 1). Go easy, and cover the molding evenly. Wet-sanding is a delicate process and does not require much force. When completed, wipe the molding dry with a clean rag and proceed to the buffing wheel. Again, the trick here is to go easy. If you press the molding too hard into the wheel or stay in the same spot for too long, you run the risk of burning and ruining the finish of the molding. Working in a smooth side-to-side motion, run the molding back and forth under the wheel at a slight angle (see photo 2). It helps to roll the piece in your hand along the wheel to prevent constant direct friction in one specific area. Occasionally, pause and inspect the finish to decide what is adequate. If you plan on restoring a car and currently do not own a bench grinder/buffing wheel, I strongly recommend buying one. It will help tremendously on a variety of projects such as this.

The last and final step is hand polishing. This is where the magic happens. In a small circular pattern, apply a soft polishing compound (Wenol brand recommended) with a clean rag or towel. Light pressure is all that is needed. When the compound begins to dry or disappear, wipe the molding off with a separate clean towel. You may need to repeat the process a couple times to achieve your desired results. You will be amazed at the brilliant finish, and to think it only costs an afternoon and about 10 bucks!

Much like waxing a car, rub the compound in a small circular pattern with light pressure across the surface of the molding.

Removing and Refinishing Painted Moldings

 Time: 1–3 hours

 Tools: Screwdriver, standard socket set, can of spray paint, masking tape, fine sandpaper

 Talent:

 Applicable years: All

 Cost: Approximately $10

 Parts: n/a

 Tip: Always paint in an open, dry area. Too much moisture in the air can cause the paint to bubble up and run. A warm, sunny climate is ideal.

PERFORMANCE GAIN: Unfortunately, this project will not make your car any faster, but at least you will look better at the red light!

COMPLEMENTARY PROJECTS: Replacing the headlights; Project 11: Refinishing the Moldings

Face it—if you drive an old car on a semiregular basis, you are bound to catch a few chips and dings here and there. Along with the paint job, the body moldings are very fragile pieces of the exterior that often take the brunt of time on the open road. Most were made of thin aluminum or pot metal and don't exactly stand up well to tiny rocks and dirt clods being hurled at them at 70-plus miles per hour. In fact, just about every original car I have seen has some sort of trim damage from the road (and the years under the scorching sun). Although minor in comparison to some, it's the attention

With most of the bright work still in good shape, we decided to focus on the rapidly flaking painted sections of the front grille assembly.

Treat the painted surface of the molding with fine sandpaper to etch the metal and allow the paint to fully adhere.

Spray paint has a nasty habit of traveling. Make sure you mask off other areas of the molding that are not intended for paint.

to finishing details like this that can really set a car apart from the rest of the pack.

In the world of aftermarket reproduction trim, there are typically two options—bad and worse. Cheap labor and cheaper materials somehow fail to duplicate that sought-after factory fit and finish. What a surprise, right? Oddly enough, a lot of people are content with that. But to the serious restoration specialist, "repops" are definitely not an option. That leaves us either scrounging through scrap yards hoping to find something in better shape than what we already have (not likely), or embarking on a fanatical and quite expensive journey to locate NOS pieces. Considering the big picture, most of us are probably better off making the best of what we have, and that is not necessarily a bad thing. In extreme cases, some pieces will need to be sent out to a competent pro for reworking. But for everything else, you can knock it out yourself in

the comfort and convenience of your own garage. The fix is easy and costs next to nothing. So with that said, let's get started!

We decided to nominate a pair of painted aluminum headlight bezels for the job. The bezels are decent, but with spotted and flaking paint, they lack the clean show quality look the rest of the car deserves. We start by removing the bezels from the front-end assembly with a small Phillips screwdriver (see photo 1). On this '67 Chevelle SS, there are just two screws on the top and two valance-mounted retainers securing the bezel on the bottom. Once they are off, we use superfine sandpaper to slightly scuff them up for better paint adhesion. It's only necessary to sand the painted areas of the molding.

After sanding and cleaning the parts of all dirt and grease, it's time for the tedious chore of masking. If you have ever painted anything before, you know the importance of properly masking off with clean, straight lines. The tape's edges will ultimately determine the finished product. Make sure the tape is secure and flat on the surface to be painted. This will help prevent bleed-through and runs in the paint. By taking the extra time to carefully prep and mask the parts, you will ensure quality results.

With all the hard stuff out of the way, the actual painting process can be fun. I love watching an old cracked-up, faded paint job transform into a clean, glossy coat of glass. It can be addicting—all of a sudden you'll find yourself wanting to spray paint everything in sight. Anyway, follow the manufacturer's directions on the paint and always lay down at least a couple of coats, especially for high-profile items such as grilles and bezels. If at all possible, paint outdoors in a dry and warm, sunny climate. Garages are often damp and are prone to holding moisture. The sun will not only speed up curing times for the paint, but it will also supply plenty of natural light. After the painting is done, allow ample drying time before reinstalling the pieces on the car.

Restoring Die-Cast Badges and Emblems

Time: Varies; pictured emblem took 1 1/2 hours total, excluding drying time

Tools: Masking tape; X-Acto knife; paint stripper, brake fluid, or carb cleaner; grease remover such as Acryli-Clean or Prep-Sol; old toothbrush; lint-free cloth, paint (quality enamel spray paint such as Plasti-kote)

Talent: 👤

Applicable years: All

Cost: Materials approximately $15–$20

Parts: Your old emblem(s)

Tip: Work in a well-ventilated area, spray in light, and apply multiple coats. Wear gloves.

PERFORMANCE GAIN: Nothing in quarter-mile times, but a lot in terms of that finishing touch!

COMPLEMENTARY PROJECTS:

Project 11: Refinishing the Moldings

With our GS emblem masked and the "red" portion of the letters trimmed out, we apply several light coats of red enamel.

You've spent months (or maybe years) restoring your classic muscle car, and now it's time for a few finishing touches. Maybe your once-colorful, glittering emblems have degraded to worn-out, faded ghosts barely representing the proud marque they're attached to. Some of the more popular nameplates and badges are available as repros, but if your car is even slightly off the beaten path, your replacement choices are limited and can be extremely expensive. A NOS version of a rare emblem can run hundreds of dollars and after dropping (how much?) on your resto to date, it's about time you catch a break. Using a very simple method, a little patience, and some basic supplies, you can restore tired emblems and nameplates to their former glory.

Most of the older cars (up until the early 1970s) are adorned with die-cast metal emblems or nameplates and are painted or screened using various enamels. They were affixed to body panels and grilles using self-tapping or "speed" nuts. A few makes, however, located their emblems on the sail panel or on a fender using barrel clips. All can be easily removed with patience and simple tools.

Use your own judgment as to the condition of your original badges. Even an emblem with pitted chrome can be made to look just about factory fresh using this method. This project does not cover how to repair severely pitted or cracked metal, which would require the skills of a specialist and several hundreds of dollars.

The first step is to access the emblem mounting area and remove the nuts with a wrench or pliers. Take care that the emblem doesn't fall off and damage the car or the badge. In cases where the emblem is located on a sail panel or other area where there is no obvious access to the nuts, chances are the badge is fastened using barrel clips. In this instance, gently pry the emblem away from the surface area, taking care not to scratch the paint. The emblem should "pop" out of the barrel clip. When the badge restoration is complete, simply push it

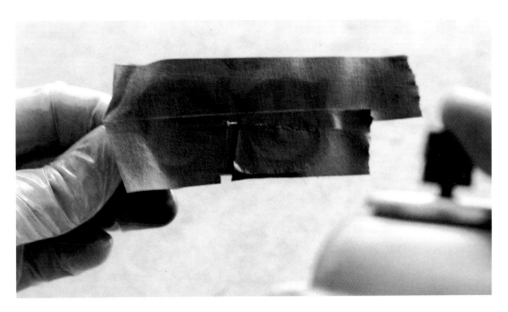

The rest of the emblem is masked off, and the "black" portion is exposed. We apply black enamel.

back into the holes. The barrel clips will snap the emblem back into place.

Now it's time to strip the badge of old wax, paint, grease, etc. Immerse the emblem in brake fluid or paint stripper (carb cleaner works equally well). Let the piece sit in the fluid for 24 hours. Note: If you decide to use paint stripper or carb/parts cleaner, take appropriate precautions. Be sure to use protective gloves and work in a well-ventilated area. Keep away from children and pets!

Remove the badge and wash in warm, soapy water. Then, clean it thoroughly with a wax and grease remover such as Acryli-Clean or Prep-Sol. If necessary, remove any residual paint with an old toothbrush. Dry with a lint-free cloth.

Using standard masking tape, completely cover the emblem.

We are now ready to create our first color mask. Using the handle of an X-Acto knife, burnish the raised portion of the type or graphic. Then, using a Number 11 or similar X-Acto blade, carefully cut out the surface of the letters or graphic you wish to paint first. Exert enough pressure to cut through the tape; do not press hard enough to scratch the chrome finish beneath. Most die-cast chrome finishes are tough enough to resist scratching from a small blade. Then, peel away the tape to expose the first area to be painted.

Use a good-quality enamel spray paint. There are several brands available; we use Plasti-kote fast-drying engine enamel. Reference books, color charts, or experiment with different paints to yield the desired color match. Using the manufacturer's directions for spray painting, cover the area to be painted with several smooth, even strokes. Do not use too much paint or "pooling" (and drying) will become a problem. Typically, two or three coats are enough. Let dry four to six hours.

Then, carefully peel away the excess tape, exposing the entire badge. We are now ready to create our second color mask. Mask off the area you have just painted. Be careful not to press the tape into the painted area, as the adhesive could pull off the fresh finish.

Using the X-Acto blade, cut the portion of the letters or graphic to be painted as you did before. Again, the key is to

We use paint thinner on a cloth very sparingly. The object is to wipe clean any paint that was sprayed onto the raised portion of the emblem.

use smooth strokes and not too much paint. You are trying to duplicate a factory appearance. Allow four to six hours drying time.

Holding the emblem by the mounting stems (to avoid fingerprints), carefully peel away the masking tape, exposing the area that we painted first. Both areas of the badge are now repainted, and the raised portion of the type or graphic may be covered with some overspray paint.

Using a lint-free cloth, dampen (do not soak) with paint thinner. Carefully rub the raised portion of the badge to remove the oversprayed paint.

An optional method of removing the oversprayed paint is to gently scratch it away with your fingernail. If you choose this method, make sure the paint is completely dry (at least overnight).

Reattach the emblem and head for the cruise-in!

Filling and Sanding the Body

 Time: Varies with the size and extent of the damaged area

 Tools: Block sander, grinder, air compressor (recommended), ball peen hammer (optional), sandpaper, grinding discs, towels, mixing sticks, dust mask, masking tape and paper

 Talent:

 Applicable years: All

 Cost: $100 for supplies

 Parts: Filler and hardener, primer/sealer

 Tip: Always wear a ventilated dust mask or respirator when performing bodywork. The airborne debris and toxic chemicals found in many products are extremely hazardous to your health.

 PERFORMANCE GAIN: Bodywork is all about looking good. Adding bodywork to the tool belt can pay off huge for many years to come (not to mention save lots of $$$).

COMPLEMENTARY PROJECTS: Project 10: Removing the Moldings; Project 11: Refinishing the Moldings; Project 12: Removing and Refinishing Painted Moldings; Project 13: Restoring Die-Cast Badges and Emblems

Bodywork can be a scary thing. Most of us would prefer just about anything over the painstaking task of hammering, filling, and endlessly sanding away on some slab of steel. Honestly, it just doesn't sound like fun, nor does it make your car go any faster. Still, the fine arts of bodywork and metal fabrication are always in high demand. Visit any reputable body shop and the lot is likely overflowing with work to be done. Bodywork can be extremely labor intensive and time consuming.

The forever-booming market continues to drive the price of almost anything (in any condition) over 30 years old up and out of the reach of the budget-minded car crafter. Unfor-

After grinding down the problem area, start with a block sander and some burly 36-grit sandpaper.

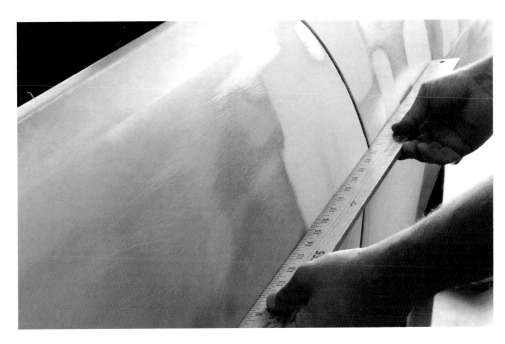

Using a straightedge, determine the severity of high or low spots on the panel.

tunately, this means many of us have to start with a heap of you-know-what just to get our hands dirty. So what better reason to roll up your sleeves and break some new ground? The big stuff is still probably best left to a pro, but with a little filler and some sandpaper, you can easily handle the minors.

If you're starting from scratch, remove any body moldings or trim items that will interfere with the work. Label your hardware and set it aside. Grinding is typically the first step in the preparation process. Using a power grinder and some 36-grit sandpaper, grind out an area on the body larger than the actual problem area to allow plenty of room to smoothly blend in the filler. After the area has been marked, use a wire wheel to thoroughly clean the surface of all debris and residue. It's important to have a clean, bare-metal surface to start.

Using some type of straightedge (a yardstick works well), examine the extent of the high or low spot on the body panel. This will help give you an idea of how much filler to mix up. Once you determine the amount, grab a clean pan or piece of cardboard and mix the filler/catalyst. Follow product instructions for the amount of hardener to use. If you are spot fixing a particular area, mask off the rest of the panel with masking tape and paper. Using a squeegee applicator, evenly distribute

Mix the filler and hardener on a clean surface. Once the two are thoroughly blended, waste no time in applying the mix to the body. The hardener tends to set up rather quickly.

43

BODY AND EXTERIOR

With the applicator, evenly distribute the mixture on and around the area of repair.

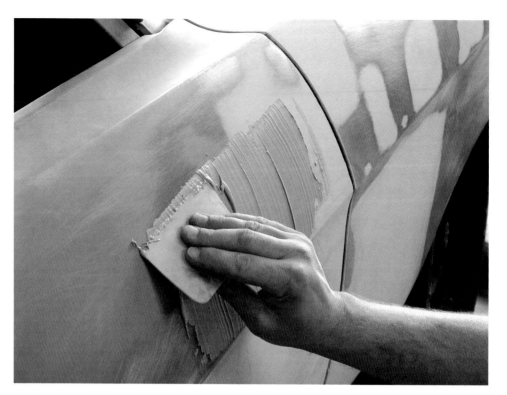

Use 36-grit paper to knock down the slightly dried filler.

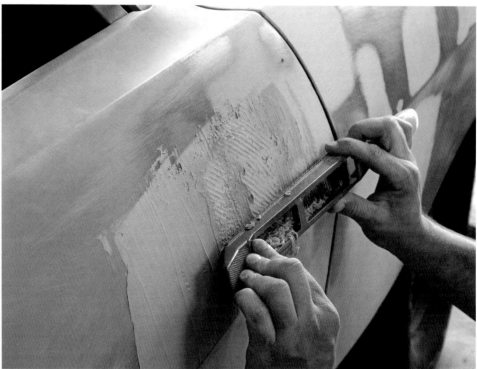

the filler on and around the area of repair. When the filler is almost dry (a slight drag is ideal), use a block sander with 36-grit paper to knock down the high spots in the filler. Be careful not to go too deep—about 1/3 of the way down is all you need at this point.

After the 36-grit, follow up with a finer 80-grit paper to smooth out the scratches from earlier. Sand back and forth across the treated area at 45-degree angles. Next, use an air compressor to blow off the sanded area and inspect the surface for any remaining ridges in the filler. If minute scratches still show in the filler, use glazing putty to fill and eliminate them. If ridges are left on the surface, they will also be seen in the primer and eventually the paint. Once the putty is dry, sand the entire area with a fresh strip of 180-grit paper. This will be the final sanding, so make it clean and smooth. While you're at it, slightly blend the surrounding areas with the 180-

44

Either by hand or with a sanding disc, carefully blend the surface with 80-grit sandpaper, periodically checking the finish.

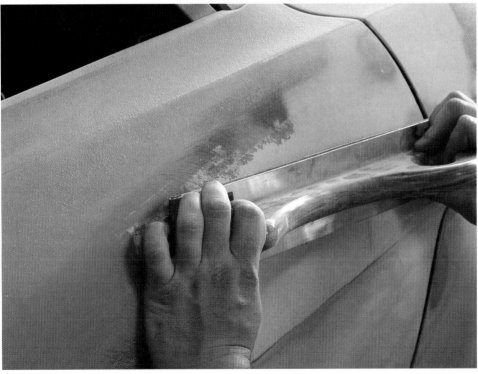

The final step in the sanding process requires a sheet of 180-grit sandpaper. This determines the actual finish of the panel prior to sealing.

grit as well to help transition the repaired section with the rest of the panel.

After the sanding is complete, repeatedly wipe down the metal surface with a clean towel and some wax/grease remover to rid the surface of any lingering contaminants. The restored panel is now ready for the sealer/primer of your choice. Consult a reputable body shop or body shop supply store for advice on which sealers and primers will best suit your needs.

Specialty tools play a big part in bodywork projects. The basics include block sanders, grinders, an air compressor, and a ball peen hammer. Most of these items are inexpensive and available at any supply store. Every car enthusiast should own an air compressor. It comes in handy and dramatically simplifies countless projects. If you decide not to purchase your own, compressors can be rented from parts stores and rental companies.

Wet-Sanding the Body

Time: Varies with the size of the area and repetition

Tools: Soft-block sanding pad, 1,000- to 2,000-grit sandpaper, garden hose or bucket, clean rags

Talent:

Applicable years: All

Cost: $20 for supplies

Parts: N/A

Tip: Choose an open, outdoor area that will allow you to run water continuously for extended periods of time.

PERFORMANCE GAIN: Properly wet-sanding your vehicle will make a night-and-day difference in the final presentation and sleekness of your paint job.

COMPLEMENTARY PROJECTS:
Project 12: Removing and Refinishing Painted Moldings; Project 17: Installing New Weather Stripping

Wet-sanding a vehicle after a fresh paint job is almost always mandatory. No matter how many hours you spend prepping and sanding the body before painting, the surface of the car will take on a somewhat coarse finish after the paint dries. Once the paint properly cures, the application of very fine sandpaper and water can make a huge difference in the final gloss and appearance of your machine. In fact, some shops make a habit of wet-sanding their paint jobs numerous times.

A new paint job can look absolutely stunning at first glance and from a short distance away. However, after closer inspection you begin to find small, circular dimples throughout the finish that closely resemble the pitted surface of an orange peel. Unfortunately, this is a common occurrence. Even veteran painters are plagued with the "orange peel" syndrome from time to time. In extreme cases, it can ruin the entire job, but most of the time, it's easy to fix with some sandpaper and a little finesse. Starting with 1,000-grit paper, the pros slowly and meticulously work every line and contour of the newly skinned metal. The process may be repeated for each grit of paper used, often all the way up to 2,000. You can bet the final finish is silky smooth and nothing short of awesome.

Although the art of wet-sanding is usually practiced in the body/paint shop arena, it can effectively be used to clean stubborn residue and gunk off your car's paint. Tree sap, bird droppings, and bug guts should be removed and cleaned as soon as possible. If left on the surface, these harmful (not to mention unsightly) agents are literally baked into the paint by the sun and can leave permanent markings and discoloration. If the standard soap-and-warm-water approach fails to budge and dissolve the gunk from the paint, try using a bug and tar remover. These products can be used safely on just about any painted surface and with positive results. After the grime has been cleaned off, lightly wet-sanding the area should remove any could-be-lasting marks.

The actual task of wet-sanding is pretty painless. It does not require much force or pressure to the surface in order to smooth the finish. Work in small, light passes around the problem area. Heavy swipes can dig into the paint and cause excessive scratching, which takes more work to fix than you originally bargained for. So go slow, and take it easy.

Grab some fine wet sandpaper in the grit of your choice (preferably between 1,000 and 2,000), a clean rag, and either a garden hose or a clean bucket of water. The most important thing to remember when wet-sanding is to keep the area very saturated. If the surface begins to dry out during sanding, you run the high risk of scratching and damaging the car's paint. One way to avoid this problem is to position and secure a hose to the particular area. Simply turn on the faucet and allow the water to continuously run over the paint and the sandpaper. If a hose is not available, a clean bucket of water and a rag will work in maintaining the desired effect. Sand a little; water a lot. Whether you have an entire body to smooth or perhaps just a small blemish, if you stick to these basic principles, the results will speak for themselves.

Above: A soft sanding block, superfine sandpaper, and plenty of water is all that it takes to get the job done.

Left: Lightly work the finish with the block while maintaining wetness with a clean rag or hose.

PROJECT 16

Adding Stripes and Body Graphics

 Time: 2 hours

 Tools: Small squeegee (supplied in stripe kit), ruler or tape measure, heat gun (optional), masking tape, degreaser/wax remover

 Talent: ♦♦♦

 Applicable years: All

 Cost: Stripe kits vary depending on car, $50–$150

 Parts: Stripe set

 Tip: To remove any unsightly air bubbles from your stripe, use a straight pin to puncture the bubble at its edge. Force the air out with your finger or the squeegee.

 PERFORMANCE GAIN: Nothing makes a muscle car look more authentic and original than a set of bold factory stripes.

COMPLEMENTARY PROJECTS:
Project 15: Wet-Sanding the Body

In fact, many stripe sets were painted on by the factory. In a way, it offered buyers a chance to slightly "customize" the cars to their liking. Along with the multitude of interior and vinyl top color options, the stripes and graphics packages allowed virtually any combination from mild to wild in the body of your choice.

Although some of the larger stripes were originally painted on the vehicle, many kits were made of vinyl and installed as decals. They were either "laid up" by the factory, or installed by the individual dealers. The kits could also be purchased over the parts counter. Later, stripe sets were often applied to entry-level models hoping to capture the bold, exciting appearance of a true muscle machine but lacking the brawn to back up the look. Even today, this is still a widely popular practice.

If your car is original and still wears its factory markings, they probably need replacement. As you can imagine, vinyl isn't exactly stunning after 35 years of baking in the sun, and stripes and/or body graphics are an important part of a muscle car restoration.

Let's start with the existing body—what kind of shape is it in? Typically, the best time to apply stripes is right after the car has been painted or at least while it's relatively new and fresh. Bold stripes on an old, faded paint job look out of place and weird. If you plan on painting the car in the near future, it might be a good idea to wait.

Clean the body thoroughly of all dirt and grease before applying any tape. Completely remove the old stripe from the surface if applicable. A fine sanding disc or solvents should safely remove the material from the body. Position the stripe on the car by applying small strips of masking tape to each end of the stripe. When laying the door and quarter panel pieces, be sure to leave a hem for the overlap into the door-jamb and around the back side of the door. Once you have determined the location of the stripe on the body, place a piece of masking tape vertically over the center of the stripe to create a "hinge." Remove the tape from one end of the stripe

In the late 1960s and on through the 1970s, car manufacturers and the public alike were obsessed with body stripes and graphics. Seemingly just about everything from Camaros to Gremlins sported some type of colorful body decoration. It actually started in the muscle car arena as a way to set apart the high-performance cars from the rest of the drab, mass-produced pack. And nothing screams performance like big and bold racing stripes. They could be ordered and installed in a variety of cool color combinations to match or offset the car's paint scheme.

Thoroughly clean the surface area with degreaser and a lint-free cloth before applying the stripes.

48

Carefully locate the final position of the stripe on the body panel with masking tape.

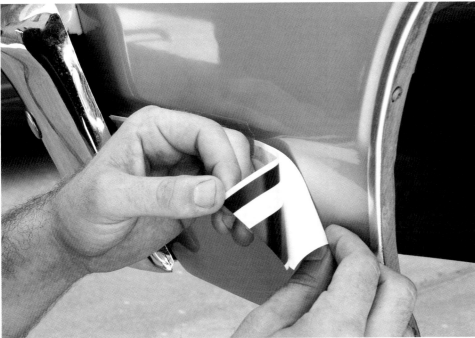

Peel off the adhesive.

and fold it back over the hinge. Carefully peel the backing from the stripe and cut away the excess.

Using the supplied squeegee, begin to apply pressure at the hinge of the stripe and slowly work your way toward the end. Support and "feed" the stripe to avoid preadhesion and the formation of air bubbles. After half of the stripe has been applied, remove the hinge and finish the rest of the piece in the same fashion. Now you can remove the outer protective layer of the decal from the installed stripe. Resqueegee the entire area of the panel to obtain maximum adhesion. The use of a heat gun may be beneficial in applying the hem flanges. With the stripe slightly heated, the material will bond to the surface even in the extreme bends and folds of the doorjamb.

There are other ways and methods to apply stripes and graphics. Some of this will depend on your car and the nature and design of the stripe package. Always follow the manufacturer's instructions on the specifics of the job and products.

Installing New Weather Stripping

Time: 30 minutes

Tools: Putty knife, utility knife, weather stripping adhesive

Talent: ▮

Applicable years: All

Cost: Varies, depending on seals or number of seals

Parts: New weather stripping

Tip: If you happen to break or lose a plastic retainer during installation, try using 3M weather strip adhesive in its place. The glue is tacky and forms a lasting, watertight seal.

PERFORMANCE GAIN: A quiet, weatherproof interior

COMPLEMENTARY PROJECTS:
Replacing the door glass; Project 6: Replacing the Window Regulator and Door Latch Assembly

When setting out on any restoration, we all know that new weather stripping is a must. It can make the biggest difference in the look and feel of your interior. It also serves as a barrier to keep out the harsh elements of the outdoors. If you have ever driven a car home from the paint shop with absolutely no weather stripping in it, you know what I mean. Unfortunately, the stuff is just plain ol' rubber and has no defense mechanisms against the sun, rain, or chemicals (not to mention time).

Lucky for us, replacing most weather stripping is a walk in the park. There are door seals, roof rail seals, window felts, quarter glass seals, vent window seals, and trunk seals. Most of these are readily available for just about any classic GM vehicle. Restoration parts houses usually offer these seals and

more in conveniently packaged and discounted kits. You can literally replace every rubber seal and bumper on your car for a few hundred bucks.

Removing old weather stripping typically requires little time and skill. Most seals can be removed by hand with the help of pliers and a gasket scraper. Old seals have a habit of cracking and breaking into pieces during removal. These should definitely be replaced. If the seals are to be reused, carefully remove the retaining clips and peel the weather stripping from the body. The old glue should be scraped clean from the sealing surface before installing the new weather stripping.

Door seals are some of the most commonly abused and replaced pieces of weather stripping. On hardtop cars, the door seals wrap around the body of the door in a large U-shaped form. Inside the seal are small, plastic push-in retainers that line up to predrilled holes in the door frame. On both ends of the seal are molded rubber "heads" with removable retainers. Starting at the front edge of the door closest to the dash, insert the retainers through the seal and into the frame. As you move down the door, lock each retainer into its corresponding hole. You may need to stretch the seal in some places for all of the retainers to properly line up. The seal will loop around the bottom of the door and back up to the other side of the window opening. Attach the head of the seal to the door frame and you're done. On post/sedan cars, the door and the window have a full frame. The seal works in a similar fashion, but is a one-piece "O" shape.

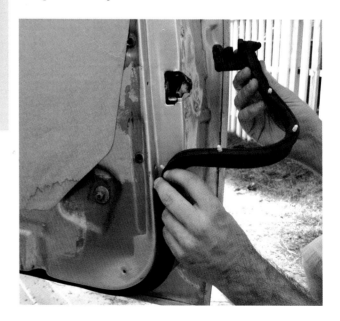

The plastic retainers in the seal simply insert into the factory-drilled holes in the door shell.

The quarter-glass weather stripping slides right up into the track of the window.

Lay down a little adhesive behind the roof rail seals.

Quarter glass seals are even easier. They use a small, vertical piece of weather stripping that measures approximately 12 inches in length. On one side of the seal is a molded groove/lip designed to slide up into the quarter glass window frame. The chrome vertical molding that adorns most quarter glass windows houses the track that the seal slides into. Although the seals essentially slide in and slide out, they can put up a fight. If necessary, the seals and the track can be lubricated with grease, oil, or hand soap to get them moving. After the seal is fully installed at the top of the track, there may be excess material at the bottom that needs to be cut off. The seal has a rounded taper at the lower end to allow it to enter into the quarter panel when the window is rolled down. If you need to hack the bottom of the seal off, you can do so easily with a utility knife. The seal should sit firmly in the track and overlap behind the door glass.

The roof rail seals complete the door opening/side window weather stripping. These seals are long, straight pieces of rubber with molded channels in the front and back sides of the seal. They fit into the upper run channel that both the door glass and the quarter windows roll up into. The channel starts in the forward opening of the door frame (just above where the front door seal head is installed). It follows the A pillar upward and continues along the roof to the rear of the quarter glass opening. The back side of the seal is channeled to mate with the roof rail track, while the front of the seal provides a recessed groove to cover the tops of the windows. Although the seal is pinched in place by the lips of the track, you should glue the seal with weather stripping adhesive.

The look and design of weather stripping will vary from car to car, but the overall approach is the same. Buy quality products and take your time installing them.

PROJECT 18

Repairing Sheet Metal (Replacing the Deck Filler Panel)

 Time: 8–12 hours

 Tools: Hammer, heavy flat-blade screwdrivers, work gloves, metal worker's chisel, window removal tool, grinding wheel, welder, mask

 Talent: ▮▮▮▮

 Applicable years: All

 Cost: Panel was regularly $150 from a salvage yard; for this project, ours was donated. (Lucky us!)

 Parts: Donor deck filler panel; new reproductions range from $60 to $120

 Tip: Like everything else, take your time and think this through. The hot ticket? The welds that hold the filler panel to the quarter panels are small and easy to break through with a hammer and chisel. Don't waste your time trying to cut them.

 PERFORMANCE GAIN: No more leaky rear window or trunk

COMPLEMENTARY PROJECTS:
Replacing the back window glass; Project 4:
Installing a Trunk Divider Board and Rear Seat
Shelf; Project 19: Restoring the Trunk

We use a hammer and heavy chisel to break the weld spots loose on either side of the filler panel, where it attaches to the quarter panels.

Right from the get-go, we won't mince words. This is a bodywork project that involves a certain level of skill, not to mention comfort level. If you're fairly familiar with bodywork, this may be the perfect project for you—nothing too radical (like cutting quarters off or floorpans out), and just small enough that it shouldn't take you more than a day to complete. If you don't own a welder, you can rent one at just about any equipment rental shop.

If you're a '68 to '72 GM A-body owner (Chevelle, Monte Carlo, Pontiac GTO/LeMans/Tempest, Olds Cutlass, or Buick Skylark), you're probably quite familiar with the rust-prone areas of your car. Due to original rear window design "flaws," these particular vehicles are very susceptible to rear deck filler panel cancer. The deck filler panel is the sheet metal that divides the top of the trunk and the bottom of the window. These panels are all different shapes, varying from car to car across the A-body lineup. If you haven't recently gone through a total restoration, and you think your car's deck filler panel is just fine, try this test. Carefully remove your rear window moldings and check out the area that the bottom of the glass sits in. Chances are you'll find rust, or maybe even worse, as in the case of our project car. Our 1969 Buick Skylark's panel is completely rotted through in this area, allowing moisture (let's face it—rain) to seep through into the trunk and the area directly behind the rear package tray (inside the car)—not a pretty sight.

Fortunately, reproduction deck filler panels are now available for most of these cars—most of them. Unfortunately for us, the '68 to '69 Skylarks haven't made the list yet. So, it's salvage yard time. Fortunately, we were "hooked up" by the nice folks at GM Sports Salvage in San Jose, California

We use a grinder to smooth out the stubborn bits of sheet metal that refused to break loose from their weld points.

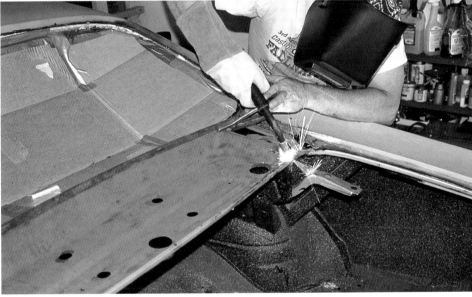

There are some residual holes, none larger than 1/8 inch, that require spot welding. Anything larger than that should be ground out and patched with new sheet metal.

(www.gmsports.com). They found us a relatively rust-free panel (it's almost impossible to find one with no rust at all), packed it up, and shipped it to us.

Since this project will be fairly time-consuming, we recommend that you park your car in a well-lit garage, out of the hot sun. Before we get under way, we disconnect the license plate light wiring and remove the trunk lid. Take care to mark the position of the bolts in relation to the hinges. You'll want to get that trunk lid in exactly the same position when it's time to reinstall it. We also remove the rear window, since the upper "skin" of the deck filler panel actually curves downward and into the rear package tray area.

Using the hammer and a heavy-duty chisel (made for sheetmetal work), we literally bust the original welds that attach the "skin" of the deck filler panel to the quarter panels.

The section at the base of the rear window is completely rotted away on our project car, so we are able to "peel" back the deck filler panel skin. (Check the bottom right corner of our first photo.)

We literally work the panel back and forth and pry the skin off its old base, using heavy-duty flat-blade screwdrivers and hammers. Be sure to wear heavy work gloves when you're working with sheet metal.

We use a grinder to burr down the rough sheet metal that remains on the deck filler base. The entire base panel is then sanded to remove any scaly rust. Note in the photo that we have fabricated a cardboard shield and taped it to the rear window opening of the Buick. This will prevent wayward sparks from finding the vulnerable vinyl and carpet inside.

Next, we hook up the welder and get to work. Grinding off the residual sheet metal and rusted out steel requires the attention of the MIG welder. Be sure to wear the welding mask and heavy gloves.

We apply the POR-15 rust-preventative paint.

The new panel is welded on at the flanges underneath. The original panel had five weld spots holding it to the quarter panel, so we've done the same. The new panel is also spot welded to the base of the original panel at several locations along the upper (window) and lower (trunk opening) portions of the panel, forming one complete unit.

After the deck filler base has been welded and sanded smooth, we use Marine Clean and Metal Ready to prep the panel (see Project 1). Then, it's time to treat the base to a coat of POR-15. The POR-15 "paint" literally stops rust permanently. We cover all areas of exposed metal, leaving out only the areas that are going to require welding when we install the new filler panel skin.

The last stage in our sheetmetal project is the installation of the new deck filler panel skin. Since the filler panel was shipped to us as a complete unit (the skin and the lower base were welded together), we have to break those welds and separate the pieces in order to use just the skin. This is much easier than trying to replace the entire panel, base and all. (The base of the deck filler panel connects to inner trunk supports and the trunk hinge bases.) The good news is that with the availability of many different deck filler panel reproductions, you can simply weld the brand new panel skin into place.

After the panel is welded into position, you'll need to have the seams resealed. Then, it's off to the paint shop.

Restoring the Trunk

 Time: 12–14 hours

 Tools: Wire brush, putty knife (scraper), scissors, pliers, portable electric pump, respirator, work gloves

 Talent:

 Applicable years: All

 Cost: $150

 Parts: Stripe set, Marine Clean (Industrial strength cleaner and degreaser), Metal Ready (rust remover, preprimer) POR-15 (rust-preventative paint), fiberglass patch kit, trunk spatter paint, clear coat

 Tip: Open the drain plugs in the lower portions of the quarter panels to let excess water drain. Mold the fiberglass patch to conform to the ribs in the trunk floor to blend the patch in perfectly.

 PERFORMANCE GAIN: Solid, virtually showroom-new-looking trunk.

COMPLEMENTARY PROJECTS:
Cleaning the spare tire; replacing the trunk harness

Ever notice the cars at the shows that don't have their hoods and trunks open? There's a good reason for that. Usually, the engine compartment hasn't been detailed, and the owner of that otherwise-gorgeous muscle car is pretty embarrassed about what's under the hood. Same goes for the trunk—some are just tired-looking, suffering from years of wear and tear. Others are downright frightening, sporting gaping rust holes, cracks, and virtually no signs of any original factory trunk paint or protectant. Not only can this be incredibly ugly, it can also be dangerous. Exhaust fumes can get sucked into the trunk through those nasty holes and eventually find their way inside the car's interior. The lowly trunk seems to be one of the most neglected areas during a restoration. You can simply shut the deck lid, hiding the horrors that lurk within—out of sight, out of mind. Well, when you get right down to it, there's

no good reason to let this mindset continue. We're going to show you how to give your trunk a new lease on life. It'll probably eat up the better part of a weekend, but the show-winning results will be well worth the trouble. Be sure to take before and after photos; you'll be amazed by the dramatic change. We'll take our tired old '69 Buick Skylark (a GM A-body car) and give it a total trunk makeover. Follow along with us.

Our trunk is somewhere in the middle—not a basket case by any means, but it certainly needs a lot of attention. The entire floor and the insides of the quarter panels are coated in a lovely shade of yellow–brown rust. One section is actually so badly rusted that the first layer of metal is missing altogether. Several smaller corrosion-induced holes (each about 1/8 inch in diameter) need attention. It looks terrible, but it's easily fixable.

First, remove the small circular rubber drain plugs in the lower portion of the quarter panels. You can access them from underneath the car. They simply pull out. We'll douse the trunk from time to time with cleaning solutions and metal-prep liquids, and the excess will need a place to drain. Next, sweep out the entire trunk cavity. Our trunk is filled with so much dust, dirt, and loose scaly rust that we actually use a respirator to avoid inhaling the nasty stuff. After the sweep-out, we take a heavy wire scrub brush and give the entire trunk floor a good scrubbing. In the section where the first layer of trunk floor has rotted out, we break off the rough edges with pliers. For your own protection, make sure you use heavy work gloves when working with sheet metal.

Next up, take a portable electric pump and "blow out" any remaining bits of loose rust and dirt. Get right down below the trunk floor and into the hollows of the quarter panels, blowing dirt out through the drain holes.

As described in Project 1, Marine Clean is a heavy-duty cleaner that helps wash away ground-in dirt and grime. Treat the entire trunk cavity to a good washing. The excess will run down and out the drain holes. After patting dry with shop rags and allowing to air dry, use the Metal Ready liberally throughout the trunk. Make sure to follow the manufacturer's directions on the label. Our trunk is pretty badly corroded, so we use several applications . . . .

Our next step is to apply the POR-15 rust preventative. Taking care to properly protect our skin, we brush coat the trunk. Not only do we cover the trunk floor and the insides of the quarter panels, we brush up under the deck filler panel and get into the trunk hinges as well. We allow about three hours drying time before applying a second coat. Work the POR-15 as deeply as possible into any rotted out sections.

After an overnight dry, it's time to address the gaping hole in our trunk. Out comes the fiberglass patch kit. Our hole measures about 4x10, so we cut our cloth accordingly, leaving at least 2 inches extra in all directions. Before mixing the resin and applying the cloth, we take 200-grit sandpaper and lightly

This neglected trunk features light, medium, and heavy rust accumulations. A portion of the floor has rusted through. In lieu of replacing the trunk floor with new metal, treat the rust, repair the damaged metal with fiberglass, and then coat the entire space with GM Spatter Paint. The pole on the right side of the trunk is holding up the trunk lid, as new trunk lid supports have yet to be installed.

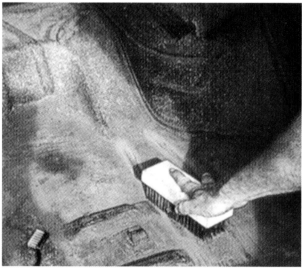

Flakes of rust and other chunks of dirt and debris are loosened up with a wire brush. A small wire brush works well to get into the corners and tight spaces.

All of the loosened debris must be removed. A dry paintbrush helps to gather the big stuff, and a vacuum cleaner will remove the remaining dust.

rough up the surface of the POR-15-coated area around the hole. This will give the cloth and resin a little more "bite." After mixing and brushing on the resin according to the manufacturer's instructions, we lay the cloth in place. To get a look consistent with the rest of the trunk floor, we actually mold (by hand) the resin-soaked cloth to simulate the floor's "ribbing." About two hours later, the resin has set up rock hard. Again, out comes the POR-15. Three coats of the black stuff over a few hours, and the "cloth" pattern has completely disappeared. Our trunk looks like one big black pit!

Now it's time to bring out the cans of trunk spatter paint. The label actually calls it "Reconditioning Paint," and it's manufactured exclusively for General Motors. Since our car is a '69 model, we're using the black/aqua combination. The '64

through '66 models use a gray-and-white "spatter" mix, while '67 through '77 GM vehicles use the black/aqua spatter paint. It takes five cans to coat the entire inside of the trunk, including the insides of the quarter panels. After approximately three hours of dry time, we use clear coat to seal the fresh spatter paint. A word of caution: Spatter paint is water soluble, so you'll need to protect it with plenty of clear coat. While the manufacturer indicates that one can is sufficient, we take no chances and use two.

There you have it—a once-rotten trunk compartment that's been completely transformed into a showpiece. It's a good idea to protect your new trunk with a genuine GM replacement trunk mat. You can pick up a two-piece set for $30 to $40 at any classic GM restoration parts supply company.

SECTION THREE

ENGINE (TOP END)

The top end components of the engine are responsible for big torque and power increases in your classic GM vehicle. The majority of the parts are readily accessible and easy to tune and adjust.

PROJECT 20

Converting to an Open-Element Air Cleaner

 Time: 30 minutes

 Tools: Standard wrenches

 Talent:

 Applicable years: All

 Cost: $50

 Parts: Open-style air cleaner assembly (with filter), carburetor-to-air-cleaner adapter plate (if applicable), valve cover breathers

 Tip: Using a drop-base air cleaner will allow for additional hood clearance and larger filter elements.

PERFORMANCE GAIN: Discarding the restrictive factory air cleaner for a deep-breathing open assembly will put a new "charge" into your engine's lungs and its performance.

COMPLEMENTARY PROJECTS:
Replacing the spark plugs; Project 26: Replacing the Distributor Coil, Cap, and Rotor

Swapping out the claustrophobic factory air cleaner assembly in favor of a deep, open breather is probably the most popular modification performed on any older vehicle. It's typically the first thing everyone does after driving a new project home. The car probably needs a lot of work, but you have to start somewhere, right?

Except for a chosen few, most factory motors were delivered in classic, choked-down fashion. Air restriction is a serious understatement—with a closed, unventilated air cleaner housing and small carburetor venturis, these motors stand very little chance of living up to their full power potential. Airflow makes horsepower, plain and simple. The more your engine can breathe, the more efficiently it will produce power. Refusing to feed high volumes of air into the motor while under heavy load is like trying to run a foot race while breathing only through a straw. Your performance dramatically suffers and total collapse is inevitable.

We all know that engine airflow can be improved a number of different ways.

More often than not, it means parting with a fistful of dollars. High-flow cylinder heads, aluminum intake manifolds, and custom-tailored exhaust systems make for great improvements in your engine's bottom-line performance. However, these modifications can require quite a bit of planning and time. One easy, sure-fire way to increase your car's breathing capacity is to open up the air cleaner assembly and install a free-flow element.

The procedure is about as simple as it gets, and it adds horsepower! First, remove the factory air cleaner lid, normally secured by some type of wing nut to the thread rod of the carburetor. Check around the entire diameter of the air cleaner housing and disconnect the vacuum lines. Be sure to look around the base of the carburetor as well. Label each line as to its designated location, and secure it out of the way. Remove the valve-cover-to-air-cleaner breather hose from both ports. Depending on your car, you may need to remove the stovepipe between the exhaust manifold and the underside of the air cleaner snorkel. Although these components are no longer needed for operation, it's a good idea to keep your original factory parts; you just never know when you might need them. At this point, the air cleaner base should be freestanding and ready for removal. Simply lift the housing up from the lip of the carburetor and set it aside.

Switching to an open-element cleaner is all about selecting the right base for your carburetor. If hood clearance is a concern, consider a drop-base air cleaner. These cleaners allow the filter element to sit slightly off the surface of the intake manifold and totally enclose the carburetor. Due to additional manifold accessories, you may not be able to utilize the drop-base without removing or rerouting some components. However, if the drop is only marginally too low, an air cleaner spacer can fix the problem. The spacers, designed to sit between the lip of the carburetor and the base of the air cleaner, can be found in a variety of sizes. The same approach can be taken with two-barrel carburetors, although an adapter plate should be used to provide the proper fit of the mounting surfaces. Two-barrel to-four-barrel adapter plates can be found just about anywhere for only a few bucks.

Factory systems can be quite miserly on allowing airflow, not to mention a messy clutter of breathing hoses and vacuum lines.

Choosing the right element is entirely left to preference. Plenty of aftermarket companies offer high-flow air filters, all of which promise startling results and have proven to flow more air than replacement paper filters. And they're reusable! Buy it once, run it, clean it, and throw it back in.

Breathers are an absolute must—your engine needs to breathe! Most factory valve covers are punched with at least one hole per cover (sometimes two on one side for a separate oil fill cap). Aftermarket covers come in a wide range of configurations. Simply choose the style that best suits your needs and decorative tastes. Only one hole is required to allow the engine to breathe. This port may also be used as your oil fill if necessary. Assemble the new air cleaner pieces and install them onto the carburetor. Follow the manufacturer's instructions on any prelubrication of the filter element.

Above: Making the swap is easy and only requires a few accessory items.

Left: Voilà! The new K&N air cleaner assembly looks great and is ready for the asphalt. Time to get to work on the rest of this engine bay.

PROJECT 21

Removing, Cleaning, and Reinstalling the Carburetor

 Time: 1 1/2 hours (depending on degree of accumulated grime)

 Tools: Adjustable wrenches, standard socket set, flat-blade screwdriver

 Talent:

 Applicable years: All

 Cost: Under $20

 Parts: Carb cleaner, toothbrush or soft wire brush, cotton swabs, compressed air

 Tip: Purchase a carburetor stand (not included in above cost) to provide a firm base while cleaning the carburetor out on the workbench.

 PERFORMANCE GAIN: Cleaner running engine, better throttle response

COMPLEMENTARY PROJECTS:
Project 20: Converting to an Open-Element Air Cleaner; Project 23: Adjusting the Metering Jets

A carburetor has to mix just the right amount of fuel with air so that the engine runs properly. If there is not enough fuel mixed with air, the engine will run lean, potentially damaging your motor. If there is too much fuel mixed with the air, your engine will run rich, which can lead to any of the following: flooding, smoking, bogging down or stalling, and very poor fuel economy. It's important that your carburetor stays in tip-top shape. Over the next several projects, we'll show you some basic tuning techniques. Once you grasp the concept of what the carburetor is supposed to do, everything else is pure experimentation.

Since the carburetor is to your car what your mouth is to your body, you need to take good care of it. In this section, we'll be working on a 750-cfm (cubic feet per minute) Holley four-barrel unit. We have replaced the stock Rochester Quadrajet carburetor with this better-breathing, infinitely-more-tunable marvel from the good folks at Holley.

As you probably already know, there are numerous aftermarket carburetors out there, some great, some good, and some not so good. We chose the Holley due to its overall bulletproof construction and the fact that you can tune this baby six ways to Sunday. Edelbrock, Demon, Barry Grant, and Jet carburetors are very good choices as well.

Now, let's get down to it. Crank open the hood, and get your tools out. In this first project, we're going to start out easy. We'll remove the carburetor, inspect it, and give it a thorough cleaning. Then we'll reattach it to your engine's intake manifold. First, remove the air cleaner. Spin the wing nut and pull off the lid. Disconnect any hoses that are connected to it (and attached to the valve covers). Put the whole unit in a safe place. Now, locate the throttle linkage, which comes up through the firewall and attaches to the side of the carburetor. Using a flat-blade screwdriver and a Crescent wrench, disconnect the throttle linkage from the carburetor.

Next, you'll need to disconnect the fuel line from the carburetor. There will be a little gas still left in the system, so be sure to pack a rag under the fitting to avoid a spill. Using a Crescent wrench, disconnect the fuel line. If your car has a vacuum advance line (a narrow-gauge hose that runs from the condenser to the carburetor), now is the time to remove it. It should just pull off by hand.

Using a socket wrench, remove the four bolts that secure the carburetor to the intake manifold and remove the carburetor. For ease of accessibility, place the carburetor on a carburetor stand. If you don't have one, any hard flat surface (workbench, tabletop, etc.) will do.

Cover the entire carburetor with a liberal amount of a good-quality carburetor cleaner. (We use Gumout for this session, but there are many others: Off, Gold Eagle, etc.). The goal is to remove any excess grease, grime, road dirt, and bugs. Using a toothbrush or soft wire brush, scrub off the carburetor body. Use cotton swabs to reach inside the venturis (barrels) down as deep as you can go. Take your time, and do a thorough job. Remember, the goal is for air and fuel to mix properly, not to be hindered by foreign objects. We won't disassemble the carburetor at this point, so it's important to get at all the visible spots. For the harder-to-reach spots, use compressed air (small cans are available at most stationery supply stores) to blow out deep-seated dirt. Turn the carburetor upside down and get the compressed air wand

Left: After removing the air cleaner, disconnect the throttle linkage with a flat-blade screwdriver and a wrench.

Below: Disconnect the fuel line. Don't forget to stuff an old rag under the fitting.

deep inside the barrels. Use the carburetor cleaner again, finishing off any areas you may have had trouble with previously. Then, wipe the entire unit down with a soft rag. Again, the compressed air will aid in blowing out and drying any cleaner that has pooled. By the time you're done, you should have a pretty nice looking carburetor. Best of all, you've done the base grunt work in getting your carburetor to start performing properly.

Now, you're ready for reinstallation. Bolt the unit back to the intake (replace the gasket if necessary), and reconnect the fuel line and throttle linkage. Don't forget about the vacuum advance hose. Congratulations! You've just completed carburetor basic training. If you want to move on and try some of the tuning projects that lie ahead, let's get to it! Keep that carburetor on the bench, and read on.

Right: Remove the carburetor bolts. In the bottom left corner of this photo, you'll see the condenser with a blue plastic cap attached. This is where the vacuum advance line will attach. If you have one, you'll need to remove it from the carburetor.

Below: A good soaking in carburetor cleaner will get that dirt loosened up.

Left: Use a toothbrush or light wire brush to get the tough stains off the body.

Below: Cotton swabs do a great job of getting into those tight spots.

Converting to a Dual-Feed Carburetor

 Time: 45 minutes

 Tools: Socket set, flat-blade screwdriver, small putty knife or scraper, adjustable wrenches (optional), rubber mallet

 Talent:

 Applicable years: All

 Cost: $100–$300

 Parts: Center-hung float fuel bowls (if needed), metering block and hardware (sold as kit), metering jets, replacement gaskets, dual-inlet fuel line

 Tip: Transfer the carburetor from the engine to a clean, open workbench. If you don't have a carburetor stand, simply slide four bolts of your choice through the mounting holes in the bottom plate and "nut" them up at the top. All you need is enough clearance for the levers and protruding linkage.

! PERFORMANCE GAIN: Increased fuel delivery and tuning accuracy

COMPLEMENTARY PROJECTS:
Project 23: Adjusting the Metering Jets;
Project 25: Installing Quick-Change Vacuum Springs

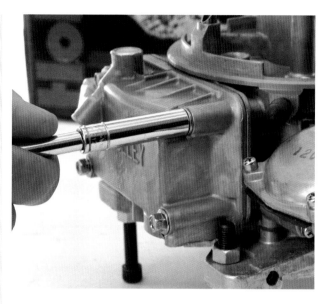

Start by removing the existing secondary fuel bowl (four bolts). Be careful not to tear the small, circular gaskets behind the bolt heads, as these are prone to leakage if damaged.

Whether you're working with an old, factory Holley or a fresh-out-of-the-box unit, making the switch to a dual guzzler can significantly boost your carburetor's performance. To avoid confusion, I am not talking about double-pumpers. Although they may reign supreme at the track, some of us simply must work with what we have in our pockets or what has been reluctantly handed down over the years.

For most mild street applications, just about any standard Holley 600- or 650-cfm carburetor (Model 4150 or 4160) should do the trick with minimal adjustment. These carburetors are engineered and built mainly for everyday economy and reliability with a little added performance on the side—not a bad route to go for the family truckster, but if you're serious about maximizing your engine's potential, a change or upgrade must be made.

First and foremost, let's take a look at the float bowl. Most of the smaller 4160 models share the same ill design of a side-pivot float. Mounted to one inside wall of the fuel bowl, these floats fail to control the proper level and flow that is needed under hard cornering. Think about it—if centrifugal forces push the fuel inside the bowl away from the float, the leverage to close the inlet valve is naturally decreased. In turn, this allows more fuel to enter the bowl than is really needed. The same goes for a turn in the opposite direction. This time, with an increase in leverage, the float is tricked into believing there is ample fuel present in the bowl, causing the inlet valve to close prematurely. Either way, it makes for pretty lousy performance.

In addition to the float flaw, 4150s and 4160s are equipped with somewhat problematic and restrictive fuel transfer tubes. This small 1/4-inch tube carries the fuel from the primary bowl down the side of the carburetor and into the secondary bowl. On each end of the tube is an O-ring seal. Nonreusable and stubborn to properly reseat, these gaskets

I recommend Holley's reusable, nonstick foam gaskets over the stock paper ones. Without the hassle of cleanup, projects like this are that much easier. Notice the secondary jets have already been placed in the block.

With everything back in its proper place, we now add the new dual-inlet fuel line. Braided stainless steel might be a little overkill for the low pressures this system will see, but it's nice just knowing it's there, and it looks great to boot.

can make something as simple as a jet change a true test of patience. This is about the last thing any of us care to deal with at the track, or anywhere for that matter. Luckily, there are plenty of upgrade kits available from Holley for just about anything you might be running. The swaps are fast and relatively straightforward.

With that said, let's get busy. We selected a stock 750-cfm vacuum secondary Holley (Model 3310) for the project. Factory equipped with dual, center-hung float fuel bowls, it only needed a secondary metering block and hardware (Holley Part Number 3413) to complete the conversion. The smaller models mentioned earlier would require the additional purchase of Holley Part Number 34-2, a pair of dual-inlet fuel bowls and their respective gaskets.

In our case, we start by removing the rear fuel bowl (see photo 1) to access the metering plate. The bowl is held in place by four small bolts and a gasket. Loosen the bolts and lightly tap the bowl with a mallet to break the seal. If your carburetor still has gas in the bowl, grab a rag or a small "catch cap" to keep from spilling. Once the bowl is off, carefully unscrew the metering plate from the carburetor's main body. There will

most likely be some leftover gasket material stuck on the mounting surface. If so, remove it with a small blade or scraping knife.

Replace the bowl seals with Holley's nonstick, reusable gaskets. They require no sealant or glue and install in seconds. The metering block and its jets follow suit and pop right into place (see photo 2). Similar to the front primary system, the addition of the metering block gives you total control of secondary delivery and allows you to tailor it to your application and needs.

Using the supplied longer bolts, simply snug the fuel bowl back onto the housing. Be cautious not to overtighten the bolts, which could tear or damage the seals. Tip: To keep track of your jet sizes, either front or back, write the numbers in a washable marker on your fuel bowl for quick reference.

Now, all that's left is slapping on the new fuel line. Regardless of the brand or style, all aftermarket fuel lines are similar in function and are made to easily adapt and fit your specific carburetor. If your local parts store does not carry what you need, try Summit Racing, Jegs, or any other major high-performance parts supplier.

PROJECT 23

Adjusting the Metering Jets

 Time: 1 hour (and plenty of testing time at the drag strip)

 Tools: Standard socket set, flat-blade screwdriver

 Talent: 👤👤

 Applicable years: All

 Cost: $5 to $6 for each jet. To save money, you can purchase a kit for $40

 Parts: Main metering jets (purchase individually or a complete set)

 Tip: Always log your jet changes to track improvements.

PERFORMANCE GAIN: Better full-throttle performance (but with sacrificed fuel economy)

COMPLEMENTARY PROJECTS: Installing reusable nonstick fuel bowl gaskets; Project 25: Installing Quick-Change Vacuum Springs

A balance of power: In most mild cases, if you choose the right carburetor to begin with, everything should be pretty much dialed in correctly from the factory. However, high-performance engines often require a little more attention to detail to maximize their power potential. One of the most common aftermarket adjustments is changing the fuel metering system. The correct way to do this is by experimenting with the main jets. It's worth your while to purchase a complete set of jets rather than drilling out existing ones. Again, we're working on a Holley for this project, and Holley rates its jets by flow capacity, not diameter.

"Proper" carburetor jetting is really formulated through compromise. Fuel economy is important, but so is wide-open, foot-to-the floor acceleration. It's a delicate mix—good gas mileage requires a certain degree of leanness, while brute horsepower demands a much richer air/fuel mix. "Correct" jetting is really just the combination that works best for you. Most carburetors are jetted at the factory to offer a good balance of performance and fuel economy.

Be warned: Although it's pretty simple to change your carburetor's fuel metering jets, you can lead yourself down a frustrating path pretty quickly. Each time you change out your jets you have to remove the fuel bowl(s): the primary and, if so desired, the secondary. Then it's off to the strip or a good stretch of road to see how you've affected engine performance, and at what cost. Sometimes it can feel like you're not making any progress at all or even adversely affecting performance (economy or power). Unless you happen to have a carburetor

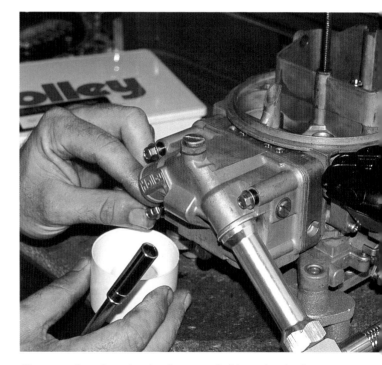

Place a small cup (or carburetor cleaner cap in this case) under the lower bolts to collect residual fuel.

The metering jets are easily accessible, and replaceable. Plan on doing a lot of this to get things just right. The photo shows the primary jets.

flow box to determine the precise fuel delivery curves, it's often wise to simply ask around at the racetrack to see what other drivers with the same carburetor and similar engine have done. It's nice if you don't have to reinvent the wheel.

Now, let's get to work. Set the carburetor on a carburetor stand. With a socket wrench, remove the primary fuel bowl. Don't forget, there'll be a small amount of gasoline left in the bowl, so place a cap or a rag under the bolt hole to soak it up. Our first photo shows the secondary fuel bowl being removed, and the next two photos show work on the primary metering block. Set the bowl aside in a safe place.

Now we have access to the fuel metering block and, of course, the jets. Removing the jets is very basic. Using a flat-bladed screwdriver, carefully unscrew them. Check the photo: The jets are on either side of the larger power valve. Place them in a clean plastic bag, taking care not to infest them with dirt or grime. You should also log their size for comparison purposes later on. Here's where you have to be careful—if you take a mild step up (one or two sizes, replacing two at a time), you may not feel any noticeable acceleration improvements at wide-open throttle. If you go full-out with a radical jet change, however, the detonation may be too lean, actually decreasing performance at full throttle.

Changing out your jets will not greatly affect your "street-cruising" gas mileage. The restricting orifice in the main jets controls the maximum amount of fuel flow, which only happens at full throttle. So, "getting on it" every once in a while won't kill you at the pumps. If all your driving is going to be a quarter mile at a time, however, go ahead and jump up to the larger bore jets. Experimenting with the primary and secondary metering jets can be very educational. Keep a log, recording your track times and the jet sizes that were used. Remember, there are many other variables that can affect your carburetor's (and your car's) performance. Type of fuel, elevation, ambient temperatures, and countless other

It's critical that you align the plunger on the bottom of the bowl correctly when reinstalling the primary fuel bowl.

variables can produce varying results. Just remember, with jet sizing, what's optimal for one person, may not be for another. To quote the pro who wrote the book on Holleys, Mr. Dave Emanuel, "Careful experimentation based on individual preference is the only method available to achieve that elusive ultimate compromise."

Once the replacement jets have been selected, install them into the metering block of the carburetor and gently snug them down. During the reassembly, be sure to check the fuel bowl gaskets. If they look at all ratty, get new ones and then reinstall the fuel bowls. When working on the primary bowl, it is critical that you align the plunger on the bottom of the bowl correctly. Do this before you secure the bolts. As described in Project 21, reconnect the fuel line, vacuum advance line, and throttle linkage.

Installing a New Accelerator Pump Cam, Discharge Nozzle, and Power Valve

ENGINE (TOP END)

Time: 1 1/2 hours (then test time at the drag strip)

Tools: Flat-blade screwdriver, Phillips screwdriver, adjustable wrench

Talent: ⚒⚒

Applicable years: All

Cost: Pump cam kits: under $20; discharge nozzles: about $11 each; power valves: about $7–$13

Parts: Pump cams, discharge nozzles, power valves, replacement gaskets

Tip: Think of these as three miniprojects to experiment with. Try them one at a time, and keep a log of your results.

PERFORMANCE GAIN: Better throttle response right across the rpm range (if done right!)

COMPLEMENTARY PROJECTS:

Complementary projects: Project 22: Converting to a Dual-Feed Carburetor; Project 23: Adjusting the Metering Jets

Now that you've got your metering jets dialed in properly, let's move ahead with some more basic carburetor tuning projects. This one is really three separate deals, but they're all fairly minor and can do wonders to help your street/strip performance.

First, we'll tackle the accelerator pump cam. Working on our 750-cc Holley, we have a nice choice of cams right out of the box. Actuating the accelerator pump with a plastic cam (instead of the typical lever and rod) affords a number of tuning opportunities. By changing the curve of the cam and the cam's position as it relates to the throttle lever, you can alter both your pump timing and the discharge volume. All of Holley's small plastic cams are color-coded and have a number embossed on them. Don't get too excited with visions of drastically increasing your "off-the-line" grunt here. Changing out a pump cam is easy to do, and the results are not huge. It is essentially one of the small steps that, done properly with other modifications, will add up to quicker track times. Switching the cam out to a more radical profile changes the accelerator pump fuel delivery timing as it corresponds to the throttle opening cycle, which causes minor changes in the volume of fuel when it comes out of the pump nozzle. Let's give it a shot.

As shown in Photo 1, use a flat-blade screwdriver and unscrew the small bolt that retains the plastic cam. Once again, we can go mild or wild. (Well, maybe not too wild.) Most street-driven cars should have a cam lift that is relatively slow. You want just enough fuel to be discharged early in the throttle opening sequence to avoid an "off-idle" failure. But there also has to be enough lift to achieve good part-throttle-to-full-throttle acceleration. At the other end of the spectrum, drag racers are after good fuel delivery later in the throttle cycle. Once they're off the line and the cam has done its job, drag engines no longer need the assistance of a pump cam. As you can see, you've got a few choices to make here. As a good starting point, use Holley's white plastic cam (stamped Number 218). It's a good "middle ground" cam and is probably Holley's most popular piece. Move up from there, experimenting with different cams until you get the desired effect. As we said, baby steps! The cam is held in place by one single bolt. Removal and installation is the same.

Now, we move on to the discharge nozzles. Officially, these are called accelerator pump discharge nozzles, sometimes referred to as "squirters" or "shooters." Like all the other variables on a Holley carburetor (most carburetor manufacturers make their units infinitely tunable), the discharge nozzles are available with different size orifices. The nozzles are individually stamped with a number indicating the orifice size. Here's how they work: The size of the nozzle and the pump cam shape work in unison to achieve a measured pump "shot." They time the fuel-delivery volume during

Remove the one screw that retains the accelerator pump cam and remove the cam.

This is a selection of available cams from Holley. There are lots of choices to fit your application and desired result.

various stages of throttle lever movement. The shot can be adjusted to be long or short and early or late (whatever works best for your application) in the throttle cycle.

Check out Photo 6. Here, we're using the Phillips screwdriver to remove the brass fitting that retains the nozzle. Photo 7 shows the nozzle removed, ready for replacement. Depending on your model carburetor, you may have two discharge nozzles. Vacuum-actuated versions only have one nozzle. "Double pumper" units have will have two. You can experiment with many combinations of nozzle sizes and pump cams. It's easy to get confused. Just make sure you keep

an accurate log of where you started (your benchmark) and where you're going. Again, make sure you're comparing apples to apples. Try to run your car at the same track and during similar conditions each time you try out the different combos.

Much has been written on the subject of power valves. By name alone, a lot of folks figure that by swapping a power valve out for a larger volume unit, they'll immediately shave a half-second off their quarter-mile times. Remember—baby steps. Swapping out a stock 6.5-inch for an 8.5-inch valve will bring an engine to maximum richness more rapidly, but that's about it. There are a lot of variables within the confines of a

Remove the brass fitting with the Phillips screwdriver. The fitting retains the accelerator pump discharge nozzle.

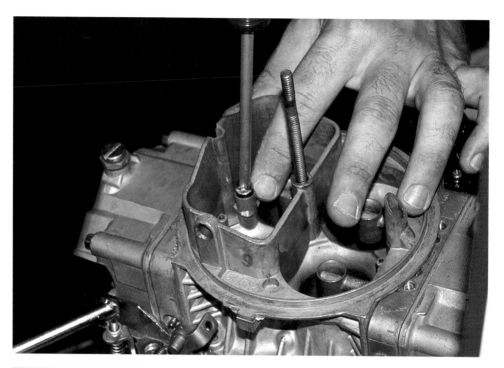

The discharge nozzle can be replaced with many different sizes. It's the perfect combination of these sizes, and the accelerator pump cam that makes the difference.

carburetor. Depending on how everything else is set up, upgrading your power valve could result in a noticeable improvement right out of the gate or offer no improvement whatsoever. In fact, you could start hurting gas mileage without the perk of extra power. Again, it's best to experiment. If you have everything else dialed in properly, installing a larger power valve should bring about an immediate out-of-the-gate acceleration improvement (for a second or two), but that's where it'll end. Once the valve is fully open, the amount of enrichment is the same regardless of the manifold vacuum figure at which the power valve operates. A word of caution: If you're after performance, stay away from the two-stage power valves. Originally designed for greater fuel economy, they restrict overall fuel flow.

Pull off the primary fuel bowl. After removing the fuel bowl (take the same precautions that we did in Project 23), use a flat-blade screwdriver to gently pry off the metering block. Make sure you do this the way the photo shows (in the middle of the block), as you can damage the block if you try prying it off from the side. Once the metering block has been freed, you can access the power valve. Use an adjustable wrench (to suit any application) and turn the valve out counterclockwise. Reinstall the new power valve and hit the track. You can experiment by changing out the valve in conjunction with the jets and pump cams. Remember, with a carburetor, it's all about trying different combinations 'til you get what works best for you.

Remove the primary fuel bowl. Take care to place a cap or rag under the bolt holes to catch the fuel still in the system.

Remove the metering block, taking extra care to pry it off gently. Split the two as shown in the photo to avoid damaging the block.

Remove the power valve gently, with a counterclockwise turn. Now it's experimentation time.

PROJECT 25
Installing Quick-Change Vacuum Springs

Time: 30 minutes

Tools: Small Phillips screwdriver

Talent:

Applicable years: All

Cost: $20

 Parts: Holley quick-change spring housing, vacuum secondary spring kit

 Tip: During the test and tune process, keep track of which springs help or hinder your carburetor's performance. They make it easy by color-coding the top of each spring.

PERFORMANCE GAIN: Ability to change and tailor your secondary fuel delivery in a matter of seconds

COMPLEMENTARY PROJECTS: Project 22: Converting to a Dual-Feed Carburetor; Project 24: Installing a New Accelerator Pump Cam, Discharge Nozzle, and Power Valve

We have all heard it a hundred times, yet it remains a back and forth issue with many performance enthusiasts—mechanical or vacuum secondaries? The answer really depends on your primary goals for the vehicle. If all-out performance and serious racing is your thing, I would opt for a mechanically actuated double pumper. These carburetors are virtually foolproof; they consistently deliver a greater volume of fuel every time you stomp on the pedal, whether they want to or not! However, if you prefer a combination of practical "streetability" and high performance, a vacuum-assisted carburetor might be your winning ticket. Although often disregarded as a true "performance" carburetor, the

We start by removing the four bolts of the original spring housing. Be careful not to snag or tear the diaphragm underneath when lifting off the lid.

72

Leave the old boot in place and realign the bolt holes if necessary. The new housing will drop right in on top (two bolts).

The quick-change lid uses the other two mounting holes. With a slightly recessed groove on the underside, the vacuum springs simply pop and lock into position.

vacuum secondary Holley is one of the most flexible and easily tunable units around.

As popular as it may be, the vacuum secondary carburetor is not without its own set of problems. The chief complaint has to do with the slow speed or late timing in the opening of the secondaries. Fortunately, the user-friendly design of these carburetors allows instant adjustments utilizing a variety of diaphragm springs, each with a different rate of resistance. By changing the spring inside the housing, the opening rate of the secondaries is greatly affected. The lighter the spring, the faster the bores will open and allow the fuel to be delivered. In contrast, a heavier spring will prolong the opening. Ideally, you want to use the lightest spring possible without causing your engine to stumble or bog out. Keep in mind that this depends entirely on the rest of your car (i.e., ignition timing and advance, cam profile, vehicle weight, rear axle ratio, etc.).

Needless to say, there are infinite possibilities. The only tried-and-true way to know for sure what works best is to hit the track. Make only one adjustment at a time and document your results. In addition to your own notes, save your time slips (even the embarrassing ones). You never know—they may serve as a helpful point of reference in the future.

To avoid losing any small parts or hardware, take an extra five minutes and remove the carburetor from the engine. As you see in the pictures shown, the whole swap is really three basic steps. In fact, only the lid of the original setup is substituted. By eliminating this single component and replacing it with the new, two-piece cover (See photo 3), you are literally able to change your carburetor's vacuum springs in seconds—perfect for crowded, busy days at the drag strip.

For a measly 20 bucks and 30 minutes, this quick-change kit is a no-brainer and easily adapts to any Holley vacuum secondary carburetor.

Replacing the Distributor Coil, Cap, and Rotor

ENGINE (TOP END)

 Time: 1 hour

 Tools: Flat-blade screwdriver, standard socket set

 Talent: ▮▮

 Applicable years: All

 Cost: $100–$150

 Parts: New coil, distributor cap, and rotor, purchased individually or in kit

 Tip: Key your spark plug wires to the correct terminals before removing them.

 PERFORMANCE GAIN: Excellent high-speed coil saturation for full power and higher rpm operation

COMPLEMENTARY PROJECTS:
Aftermarket ignition box upgrade; Project 28: Making Cut-to-Fit Spark Plug Wires

This is an extremely worthwhile upgrade that'll help you keep those candles lit. The procedure is fairly simple, and we'll get into it in a few moments. But first, a little primer . . .

General Motors' Delco-Remy HEI (High-Energy Ignition) is a breakerless, transistor-controlled ignition system. It was offered as an option with the 1974 model and was standard equipment by the time 1975 rolled around. If you're moving ahead on this project, you've already joined the legions of HEI converted. If you're still running an old points system, check out Project 27—you'll soon be switching!

Like other electronic ignitions, the HEI system uses a transistor located inside the ignition module that replaces the breaker points system. This transistor does the same thing that the points do in a conventional ignition: it switches the coil's primary current on and off at the appropriate time. So, although one system is prone to needing points replaced, and the other is "high-tech," they both essentially accomplish the same task. If you have reviewed and performed the next project (Project 27), you're already familiar with the benefits of installing an HEI system.

So, knowing what an HEI is all about, let's get down to our next project, a coil, cap, and rotor replacement/upgrade for your HEI. Step one involves a little precautionary work. You're going to remove all the spark plug wires, and you'll need to remember which wire goes where. Since we're dealing with many different makes and years of cars, space doesn't permit us to show the firing orders of all the engines. Before pulling off the plug wires, we suggest that you mark them and the terminals with something that will help you put it all back together again (color coded dots, masking tape, etc.).

After pulling the wires, we're going to remove the distributor cap. To do this, use a wide flat-blade screwdriver to "unhook" the three spring-loaded screws that secure the cap to the housing. Our distributor cap looks as if it has seen some serious abuse. Bent terminals (from yanking on the plug wires) and a small hole in the housing did nothing to enhance performance. This kind of damage can cause loss of electrical conductivity, resulting in poor firing or no firing at all.

Next, remove the coil cover. Once the cover is removed, remove the old coil. Use a flat-blade screwdriver to push out the terminal's ends. Now, we're going to install the new coil into the new cap. At this stage, you have a couple of different options. You can choose to simply replace your old HEI components with GM replacement parts, or you can opt for an aftermarket HEI kit. MSD Ignition offers the "Ultimate HEI Kit," and Pertronix carries many high-performance ignition parts. Both companies carry coils that offer much higher voltage generation that the factory stock replacements.

Push the terminals back into place, and be sure to ground the terminal with the coil screw. Before installing the new cap and coil, you'll need to fit the new rotor. Again, you have a choice. Both MSD and Pertronix offer rotors individually or as part of a kit. Or, you can simply go the stock replacement route. Just be sure to purchase a high-quality unit. Make sure the rotor is facing the same direction as the old one, and then reinstall the distributor cap and wires.

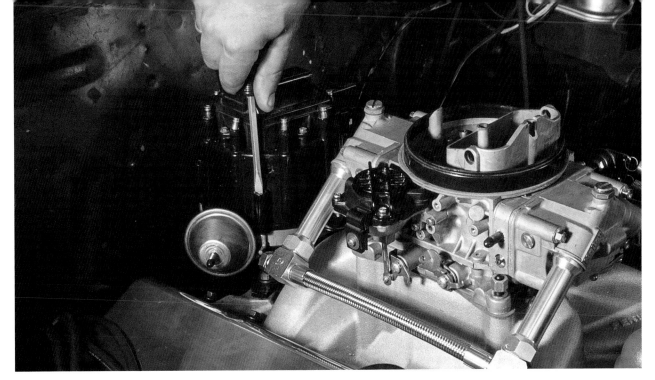

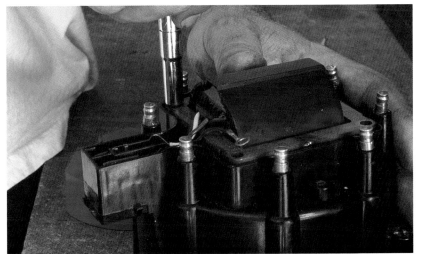

Above: After you've removed all the plug wires, release the three spring-loaded screws that fasten the cap to the distributor housing. Make sure that you keep track of what goes where.

Left: After removing the coil cover (three flathead screws), remove the coil and its terminals. Use a flat-blade screwdriver to push out the terminal ends.

Below: Install the new rotor. Make sure the rotor is facing the same direction as the old one.

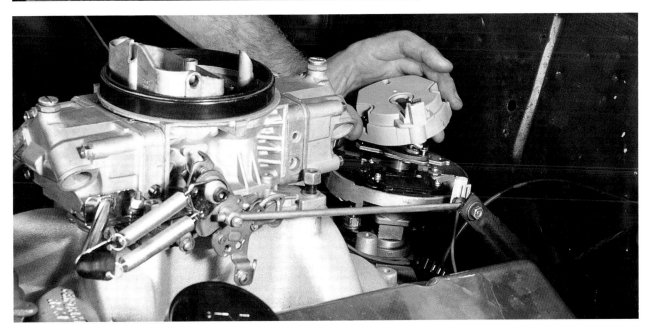

Converting to an HEI Distributor

 Time: 2 hours

 Tools: Standard wrench set, flat-blade and/or Phillips screwdriver, wire strippers/crimpers

 Talent: 👤👤

 Applicable years: All

 Cost: Varies by manufacturer—$175–$400

 Parts: HEI distributor (new, rebuilt, or used), HEI ignition lead connector, HEI style plug wires

 Tip: Label or mark the location of your spark plug wires on the distributor cap for fast, easy reference.

 PERFORMANCE GAIN: Increased coil saturation, higher spark output, more reliable performance

COMPLEMENTARY PROJECTS:
Project 28: Making Cut-to-Fit Spark Plug Wires

After removing the ignition coil, leads, and plug wires, the distributor is ready to come out.

The majority of cars produced during the 1960s and early 1970s were factory-equipped with a point-type ignition. Although not likely to be considered the greatest manager of spark, at the time there was no other option. It was not until the 1974 model year that GM offered the new HEI ignition system as an alternative. One year later, it became standard equipment for all, and with good reason.

The GM HEI, which stands for High-Energy Ignition, is a breakerless, transistor-controlled, inductive discharge system. It operates much like the conventional point-type ignition, but relies solely on a series of electronic signals to turn on and off the primary current, rather than the mechanical opening and closing of points. This task is routinely carried out by the switching transistor, located inside the ignition module. In fact, the ignition module, the ignition coil, the pickup coil, the magnetic pickup assembly, and the mechanical and vacuum advance units are all nestled tightly under the HEI distributor cap.

It is my assumption that anyone owning or driving one of these vehicles, at one time or another, has run into problems with the stock ignition system. Let's face it—points are not our friends. No matter what you drive in what application, points always seem to be in a constant state of tune, looking for that elusive, if not imaginary, sweet spot.

I finally found it, and it's called electronic ignition! Seriously, with so many other performance improvements that can be made to a car, who wants to spend their time adjusting the dwell angle of all things? Electronic ignitions such as the HEI are typically a little more expensive than the rebuilt "el cheapo" special at your local parts store. However, in the long run, the time and headaches you spare fiddling with your ignition will more than make up for the initial deficit.

By simply switching over to an electronic distributor, not only do you eliminate the aforementioned hassles of points, but you will also notice a significant increase in your car's overall performance. From crisper, off-idle throttle response to extra top-end pulling power, the gains from merely removing and replacing your stock distributor with a high-performance HEI are downright impressive.

And so this brings us to the garage. Any time you pull the distributor out of the engine, it's important to make note of a couple key elements prior to removal. First, detach the spark plug wires and the coil wire, and then remove the cap. Before loosening the distributor clamp and allowing the housing to

What a night-and-day difference between the two! The HEI distributor actually houses the ignition coil underneath that massive cap.

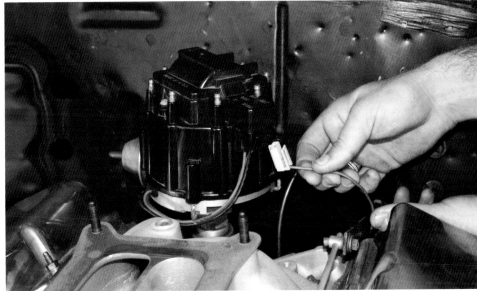

When reconnecting the new unit, you will need to purchase and splice in a single HEI terminal connector. This is your "hot" ignition wire coming from the engine harness.

rotate, mark the position of the housing as well as the vacuum advance unit and the rotor, all in relation to the engine block. Loosen the clamp and lightly lift up on the housing. (See photo 1.) If the engine is undisturbed while the distributor is out, installing the HEI is simply a matter of reversal at this point. Realign your markings and let it fall back in place. DO NOT force it. The teeth of the gears must properly mesh together in order to fully reseat. Once in position, hand tighten the single bolt and clamp to allow for slight adjustments when restarting the engine.

If the engine has been moved, you will need to locate its TDC (top dead center). One easy way to do this without removing the valve covers is to pull the Number 1 spark plug. Place a finger over the hole and rotate the engine by hand until you feel the compression. When the timing mark on the crankshaft pulley matches up with the "0" on the timing tab, you have reached TDC. Now, install the distributor with the rotor pointing at the Number 1 terminal on the cap.

With the ignition coil neatly tucked inside the HEI, the electrical hookup is a cinch. Splice the HEI connector (see photo 3) into the existing "hot" ignition lead. The connector then plugs into the cap at the "BATT" terminal. If you run an aftermarket tachometer, a second connector will be needed. It plugs in adjacent to the ignition lead at the "TACH" terminal. Points-type spark plug wires are not interchangeable with an HEI cap and vice versa. (See photo 2.) You will need to purchase a new set to match your distributor. Reattach the individual plug wires to their proper posts. Take your time and make sure you have them right.

With everything back together, reconnect the negative battery cable and fire the engine. Proceed to set the timing and secure the hold-down clamp. Check the timing once more to ensure the housing did not move while tightening. (For timing instructions, see Project 29.)

Making Cut-to-Fit Spark Plug Wires

 Time: 2 hours

 Tools: Wire cutters, crimping pliers, razor blade, permanent marker

 Talent:

 Applicable years: All

 Cost: $75

 Parts: Set of quality spark plug wires (boots and terminals included), white dielectric grease, wire socks (recommended), wire looms

 Tip: When cutting and installing a new set of wires, mark each end at the boot with its designated cylinder number. This will serve as a great quick reference in the future.

 PERFORMANCE GAIN: More reliable spark delivery to the plugs and a cleaner looking engine compartment

COMPLEMENTARY PROJECTS:
Installing plug wire protective socks and wire looms

Spark plug wires play an important part in the secondary ignition system. They deliver the voltage of the coil from the distributor cap terminals to the spark plugs. On systems with an external coil, there is also a small patch wire running from the coil to the distributor cap.

More often than not, an engine's spark plug wires are neglected. They always seem to fall last on the list of things to do or replace, like an afterthought. I have seen plenty of cars with a fresh engine and a nicely detailed engine compartment still running old, greasy, charred-out plug wires, and I've been guilty of it myself. Not only does this greatly detract from the finished look of a rebuilt motor, but it can also lead to a state of constant aggravation and poor performance—something many crafters struggle to associate with plug wires.

Heat is enemy Number 1 when it comes to plug wires. Forced to withstand extreme engine and air temperatures, a plug wire is only as good as its insulation. Most aftermarket companies today use heat-resistant silicone for the wires' outer insulation. In serious race applications, a second inner layer of silicone is used as well. If the insulation of any wire looks faulty or heat damaged, replace it—replace them all. A faulty wire will derail the voltage from the distributor and cause it to either ground or possibly jump to another nearby wire, thus creating a misfire. This is why it's important to use wire looms and/or rigid retainers when routing a new set of wires. Doing so will keep the wires off of the exhaust manifolds or headers and will maintain separation for the individual wires too.

Depending on the type and purpose of your engine, the first thing to do is select the right wire for the application. The popular favorite, and by far the most common, is the 8-millimeter resistance wire. Every ignition company under the sun offers a variety of sizes and colors to fit standard or HEI-type terminals. You'll also need to decide between straight and 90-degree boots on the other end.

Although you may be able to purchase precut wires to fit your engine, they are often not 100 percent accurate and can be more hassle to fit than bargained for. The easiest way to ensure the right fit and look is to tackle the job yourself. Before getting started, you first need to know the firing order of the engine. Whether you remove the wires one at a time or all at once, the location of the wire on the cap is crucial to cutting the correct length.

With the old wires removed, install the new wires on the spark plugs. Most cut-to-fit wire sets come with the spark plug boot already installed on the wire and have plenty of extra length to allow different routing options. You can now mock each wire up to its destination on the cap and make your mark. Using a pair of wire cutters, snip the wire and strip approximately 1/2 inch of the insulation back with a razor blade. Take it down to where only the conductor wire remains, and pin it against the outer insulation layer. (See photo 2.) Your kit should include standard and HEI-type connectors and boots. Position the wire in the proper connector with the inner conductor wire at the top. Firmly crimp the connector body over the wire to secure the conductor to the metal body. With the help of a little dielectric grease, slide the connector into the boot. (See photo 3.) Take your time and repeat the process for the remaining cylinders. Your wires will be clean, nicely tucked away, and safe from the harmful mishaps of life in the engine compartment.

To determine the correct length for each cylinder, install the wire on the spark plug and mark the other end at the cap.

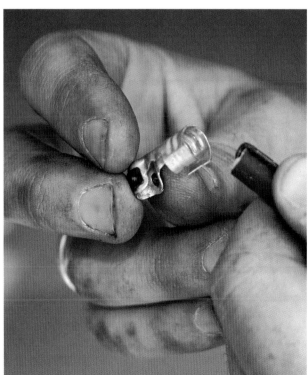

After the insulation has been stripped away, fold the conductor wire back and slide it into the connector to be crimped.

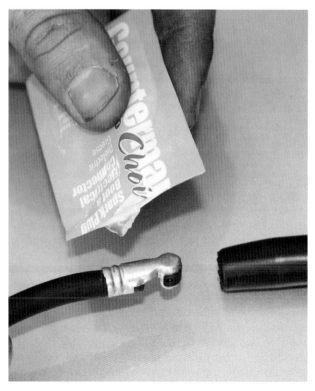

Be sure to apply plenty of grease to the connector before inserting it into the boot.

PROJECT 29

Adjusting and Setting the Timing (Initial and Mechanical Advance)

 Time: 1 hour (plus track test time)

 Tools: Timing light, flat-blade screwdriver

 Talent: ▮▮▮

 Applicable years: All

 Cost: $30–$150 for a timing gun

 Parts: None

 Tip: Adding tons of go-fast, bolt-on goodies to your engine is great, but remember what makes it all come together—the basic art of getting your timing just right.

 PERFORMANCE GAIN: With timing advance just right, you'll gain performance that you can really feel in the seat of your pants.

COMPLEMENTARY PROJECTS:
Replacing the spark plugs and wires

To put it simply, ignition timing is the measurement, in degrees of crankshaft rotation, of the point at which the spark plugs fire in each of the cylinders. Timing is measured in degrees, either before or after Top Dead Center (TDC) of the compression stroke.

Let's talk a little about initial advance. Even when your engine is at idle, the ignition spark has to be triggered before TDC (BDTC). The general specification for most V-8 engines usually falls between 6 and 12 degrees BTDC. This allows your engine to run smoothly and cleanly at idle without generating too much resistance during starting. Here's how it works: the distributor's shaft meshes with the camshaft, but the distributor's housing can be rotated independently to affect the amount of spark advance or retardation relative to the cam, which in turn affects the crank. Once you have established the initial timing, a distributor housing "hold-down" locks your housing in place.

We're going to start out by setting the engine's initial timing. To do this, the engine must be running at idle. First, connect the timing light (gun) to the car's battery (attach the gun's clips to the battery terminals). Then, insert the Number 1 spark plug wire (front, driver's side) through the timing gun's wire clip. The clip will take an impulse reading on how rapidly the spark plug is firing.

Photo 2 shows the timing tab and the notch (or marking) in the harmonic balancer. The notch corresponds to the position of the piston in the Number 1 cylinder. With the engine running (and the balancer rotating), turn the timing gun on and focus the strobe light on the notch in the balancer. (If you cannot clearly make out the notch, shut everything down and mark the notch with White Out or a light paint marking that will make the notch visible under the strobe.) You're attempting to read the initial timing at the timing tab. The strobe flash makes the notch on the balance appear to be standing still. (Certain models of timing lights feature a speed-adjustable strobe light, but this is not critical to setting timing.) Correct timing is indicated when the notch is visually aligned with the correct number on the timing tab. A word of caution: Do not stick the timing gun too close to the rotating fan. Remember, that strobe light may cause the fan blades to appear motionless.

To adjust the initial timing, remove the vacuum advance line (if so equipped) to prevent any distributor advance. This is the thin rubber hose attached to the small metal canister on the side of the distributor. Loosen the distributor base clamp locknut (or hold-down). Slowly turn the distributor by hand, holding it by the body (not the cap). Turn the distributor in the direction of the rotor rotation to retard (generally clockwise) or against the rotor's direction to advance (generally counterclockwise). Like most tuning procedures, the "correct" timing setting is how you feel your engine performs under all conditions. Remember, a good base line is somewhere between 6 and 12 degrees Before Top Dead Center (above the "0" mark on the timing tab). Experimentation is a must. After you've established your initial timing, secure the distributor with the locknut or hold-down.

To establish a mechanical advance, we're going to throttle up. All engines require additional timing advance as rpm increase—that's why a mechanical advance mechanism is built into most automotive distributors. This mechanism usually comprises two hinged weights affixed to a plate on top of the distributor shaft. They are retained by a set of springs. As the distributor spins faster, centrifugal force allows the weights to overcome the spring tension and they begin to swing outward. How does it all come together? The weights are affixed to a separate plate that mounts either the breaker points or the electronic pickup (either old-school points or

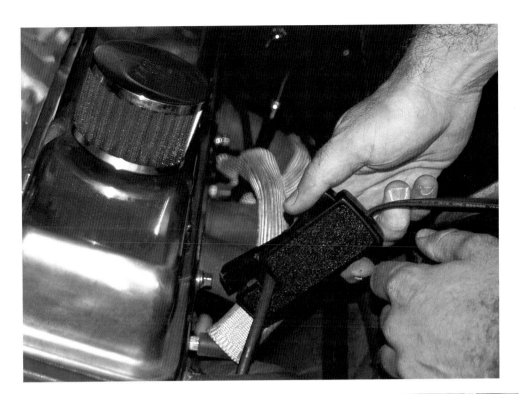

Left: Attach the Number 1 spark plug wire into the timing gun spark plug wire clip. This measures how rapidly the spark plug is firing.

Below: This is the timing tab and the notch on the harmonic balancer (use White-Out to see better in sunlight).

HEI). When the weights swing out, the breaker plate rotates a preset number of degrees, advancing the ignition timing. As with just about everything, tuning is the name of the game. Altering the tension of the springs or the shape and weight of the weights will change the rate of advance.

In Photo 4, we're setting the mechanical advance by manually throttling up and taking a reading (still at the harmonic balancer). By doing this, you can see where your timing is as your engine climbs into the high-rpm range (after your mechanical weights and springs have released). Again, it's all in the tuning. To achieve that optimal blend of perfect overall timing, you have to experiment.

Above: Manually adjust the timing (either retard or advance) by turning the distributor housing.
Below: Perform the final mechanical advance by adjusting the throttle in conjunction with taking a timing reading.

Installing a New Thermostat and Housing (Water Neck)

 Time: 30 minutes

 Tools: Standard socket set, flat-blade screwdriver

  Talent:

 Applicable years: All

 Cost: $20–$70 (depending on water neck cost)

 Parts: New thermostat, water neck

 Tip: Spend the extra cash on a good-quality, cast-iron water neck. Chrome looks great but can corrode quickly.

 PERFORMANCE GAIN: A good-quality, high-flow thermostat will open at the right temperature regardless of engine rpm, which keeps your car running cooler, even under race conditions.

COMPLEMENTARY PROJECTS:
Project 56: Installing a New Radiator and Hoses

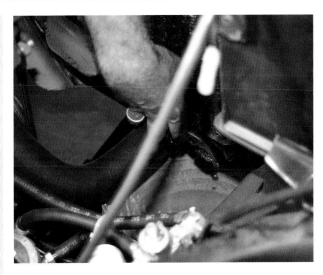

Open the drain cock at the bottom of the radiator. Once the coolant flow stops, you can remove the hoses attached to the water neck.

For an engine to keep cool it needs two things: airflow and water circulation. Too little of either will most certainly lead to overheating.

Many things can cause engine overheating. If there's overheating at speed, something is probably impeding airflow to the radiator. If overheating only occurs at slow speeds (say, less than 25 miles per hour), the fan isn't sucking enough air through the radiator. You can try installing a fan shroud or step up to a larger fan. Auxiliary electric fans are also a viable option. Be Cool now offers the Super Street Cooling Module Assembly, a total cooling system designed for super-high-performance engines.

Some electric fans move enough air to actually act as the primary fan.

If your vehicle is stock and has started to overheat, look for leaks in the hoses, radiator, and water pump. Also, check to see if the water is contaminated with blobs of oil. If it is, your head gasket has probably gone south. Excessive steam from the tailpipe and foamy oil (which indicates the presence of water) also point to a bad head gasket. If your car only overheats at slow speeds, check the fan clutch. With the engine warm and running, the fan should be spinning.

If you find your engine constantly overheating at any speed, it could mean that your thermostat is stuck. If the thermostat gets stuck in the closed position, it will severely limit the amount of water the engine circulates. It should be replaced right away.

The thermostat is a valve located in the cooling system. It remains closed when the coolant is cold and opens gradually in response to engine heating. It controls the temperature of the coolant and the rate of coolant flow. If you're going to upgrade to a new thermostat, it's one area where you shouldn't decide to save money. Go all out, and shop for a balanced, high-flow unit. Here's a little primer on thermostats: The cheap versions ($4.99 specials) actually increase their opening temperature as pressure builds. When your engine gets up into the higher rpm range, the water pump can actually generate 30 pounds or more pressure in the block against the outlet restriction of the thermostat. With that 30 pounds of pressure bearing down on a bargain basement thermostat, the "opening"

Use a socket wrench to remove the bolts that attach the water neck to the intake manifold.

With the water neck removed, you can see how the thermostat fits into its base. Make sure you install your new thermostat the same way. A thermostat that's placed the wrong way inside the water neck is useless—instant overheating. The "pointed" end should always face toward you (toward the front of the car).

temperature of a 185-degree unit can be raised to 199 degrees. A "balanced" thermostat has equal pressure on both sides of the sleeve, so the opening temperature is independent of the pressure coming from the outlet. There are a number of excellent thermostats on the market today. Mr. Gasket and Jet Performance offer balanced, high-flow units that retail for $10 to $13, easily worth the few extra bucks.

Now we'll show you how to replace your thermostat and, if necessary, your water neck (the housing that the thermostat resides in).

First, the car should not be running and should be cooled down to nonoperating temperature. We're going to drain some of the coolant out of the system. Get a large bucket (12- to 14-quart version) and place it under the drain cock at the bottom of the radiator. It may be necessary to jack the front end of the car up a little to get the bucket underneath. Open the drain and let the coolant flow. Only the coolant that is in the front of the system will drain (radiator, radiator hoses). Once it stops, you can get back to work.

Next, we're going to remove the water neck. Depending on your application, you may need to free the water neck from any retaining brackets. You should also remove the upper radiator hose from the water neck by loosening the clamp with a flat-blade screwdriver. Take note of how the thermostat is positioned in the water neck.

Also, you may want to upgrade your water neck at this point. Cheap chrome units (that usually sell for around $8 to $10) may look cool, but they are prone to rust, and rust means flaking. Not too healthy for your cooling system. Your best bet is a high-end, cast-iron unit. They can range in price anywhere from $13 for a replacement unit to $60 for an original-style unit.

Install the new thermostat into the base of the water neck (be sure to replace the gasket at this point), and install the whole unit. Reattach any brackets. Be sure to tighten the drain cock at the base of the radiator, and refill the system with coolant.

Start the car, let it run for a few minutes, and check the coolant level again. Top up if necessary.

Installing a New Intake Manifold

 Time: 3 hours

 Tools: Standard socket set, standard wrenches, flat-blade and/or Phillips screwdriver, putty knife or scraper, torque wrench

 Talent:

 Applicable years: All

 Cost: $100–$300

 Parts: Aftermarket aluminum intake manifold, high-performance intake gaskets, gasket sealer

 Tip: Before final installation, double-check the fit of your parts to make sure everything lines up and will work for your car.

ENGINE (TOP END)

! PERFORMANCE GAIN: A cooler, higher-flowing intake charge; aluminum manifolds typically drop 25 pounds off the weight of your engine

COMPLEMENTARY PROJECTS: Project 26: Replacing the Distributor Coil, Cap, and Rotor; Project 30: Installing a New Thermostat and Housing (Water Neck)

Swapping in an aftermarket aluminum intake manifold is one of the most popular engine upgrades of all time. It's easy, it's cheap, and the bottom line is it works. Not only does aluminum dissipate heat faster and more efficiently than cast iron, but it will also save you about 25 pounds in dead weight. The new aftermarket manifolds have an improved plenum design and will far outflow a factory cast-iron piece. In fact, most are dyno-tested and proven to yield power and torque increases throughout the entire powerband.

With any manifold swap, the first order of business is to remove all the attaching components—the carburetor, distributor, and thermostat and housing. Note: Be sure to fully drain the cooling system before disconnecting the upper radiator hose. For reference, the proper procedures for removal of these items can be found in this book.

Working in a zigzag-type fashion, loosen and remove all the bolts securing the manifold to the engine block. The number of bolts varies depending on the size and make of your engine. Using a long screwdriver or pry bar, gently lift up on the edges of the manifold. A little leverage should break the bond between the two pieces. You may need to unbolt the valve covers for adequate clearance and to keep from damaging them when prying the manifold up.

Before removing the old gaskets and silicone, lay a clean towel into the lifter valley to prevent any debris or contaminants from entering the engine. Use rags to plug the intake ports in the cylinder heads as well. With a small putty knife or

To bridge the gap between each intake gasket, lay down a thick, even bead of sealer across the block. Caution: If too much is applied, the excess may fall down inside the lifter valley when compressed.

scraper, remove the old gasket material from the mating surfaces of the head and the block. Follow up by thoroughly wiping down the areas with an industrial-type stripper or cleaner. This is a crucial step in ensuring a lasting, leak-free seal. All bolt holes should be inspected and properly cleaned out with a tap if needed.

When installing, first apply a thin coat of gasket sealer to the back sides of the manifold gaskets, and place them on the cylinder heads. This will keep them from walking around and sliding out of position when dropping the manifold into place. Using quality oil-resistant silicone, apply a thick bead of sealer across the front and back of the engine block. (Most intake manifold gasket kits include formed-rubber end seals for this purpose. However, they are terrible in sealing the manifold and should be discarded.) Be careful not to lay on too much silicone in any one area. When the manifold is installed and tightened down, the excess sealer can fall down inside the lifter valley and harden, leading to serious blockage and interference problems in the engine block.

With the gaskets and sealer in place, carefully lower the manifold into position. Apply a fair amount of thread sealer to the intake bolts and snug them down by hand. Depending on manifold selection, it may be necessary to purchase a longer set of mounting bolts. I recommend using ARP's line of stainless-steel bolts and hardware for just about any job. They are strong, durable, and provide the perfect finishing touch for any fresh engine rebuild.

Last, but definitely not least, is the final tightening of the manifold bolts. Using a standard foot-pound torque wrench, start at the center of the intake and work your way to each end in a cross pattern. To prevent warping or cracking the manifold, work in gradual steps with the torque wrench. For example, if your final torque specification is 20 ft-lb, torque all of the bolts first to 10 ft-lb, then 15 ft-lb, and finally 20 ft-lb. It's a good idea to check them once more after running the car and allowing the manifold to heat up.

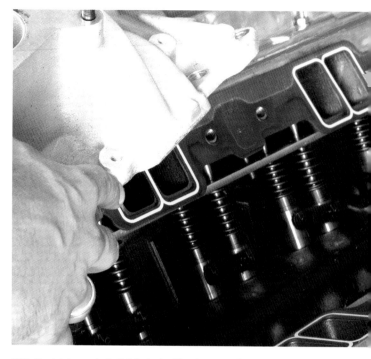

With the intake gaskets lightly tacked in place, carefully lower the manifold into position.

Torque the manifold down to manufacturer's specs, which will differ depending on the material used—cast iron versus aluminum.

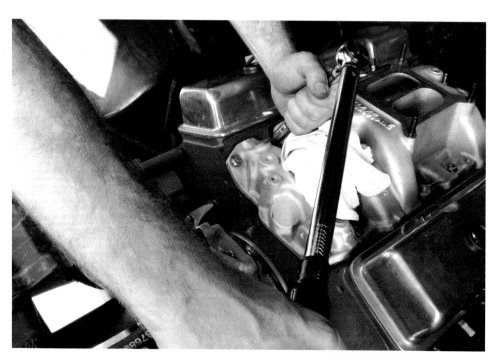

Installing Valve Cover Gaskets and Studs

 Time: 1 hour

 Tools: A pair of 3/8-inch box wrenches, putty knife, deep sockets and socket wrench

 Talent:

 Applicable years: All

 Cost: $35

 Parts: Valve cover gaskets, gasket placement glue, valve cover studs

 Tip: Periodic tightening of the valve covers will help prevent oil leaks.

PERFORMANCE GAIN: A clean, leak-free seal and ease of further installation (studs)

COMPLEMENTARY PROJECTS: Installing valve covers, engine breathers, and plug wire retainers

Nothing is more annoying than the constant dribble of oil running down the back and sides of your engine due to leaking valve cover gaskets. Not only does it burn off and smoke when driving, but it also makes a mess of your clean, white driveway at home. As long as you keep plenty of oil in the engine, there is no problem, but why take the slacker approach on something so easy and inexpensive to fix?

The first step is to remove the hoses, breathers, and hardware attaching to the valve covers. Loosen the valve cover bolts and retainers, and set them aside. Even if you replace them with studs, it's a good idea to hang onto old hardware for anything that may come up later. Every mechanic needs a random, leftover bucket o' bolts. With the valve covers off the heads, remove the old gasket material with a scraping knife and thoroughly clean the mating surface. This will play an important part in the proper resealing of the valve covers. The new gaskets will have a hard time resisting leakage if they are installed on an oily or dirty surface. Watch out for any gasket remnants or debris that may fall into the cylinder heads when cleaning. To avoid such contamination, place a clean rag just inside the head below the gasket mounting surface. This should catch any sludge or chunks that come off in the process. Carefully fold the rag inward and remove when completed.

Although replacing valve cover gaskets is a pretty simple task, it can often be a challenge to pull off properly. The gaskets never seem to stay in place long enough to install the covers and find the bolt holes again. Fortunately, the answer is simple—valve cover studs. They make the chore of gasket replacement

Using a small putty knife, remove the old gaskets and thoroughly clean the ridge of the cylinder heads.

Apply a small amount of gasket glue to the back sides of the gaskets and the mating surface if necessary.

To insert the stud, lock the two nuts together and turn clockwise.

about as simple as you can get. When screwed into the cylinder heads, the studs serve as the perfect placement locator for both the gaskets and the valve covers.

Installing the studs is equally basic. They are threaded on both ends with a small, machined section in the center as the stopping/starting point. You should be able to feed the majority of the stud into the head by hand. When it begins to stiffen, double-nut the upper half of the stud and drive it in with a wrench until the center section is close to flush with the cylinder head. If you have not installed studs or inserts before, allow me to explain the "double-nut" method: By threading two nuts (one on top of the other) onto the stud and tightening them to each other, you create a fixed point that is used to spin the stud into its insert. After it is fully seated, simply loosen and remove the nuts.

Most valve cover gaskets don't require the use of gasket sealer or silicone. The gaskets should make the seal by themselves. However, you should apply a small amount of placement glue to the back sides of the gaskets to keep them from sliding out of position when installing the valve covers. Gaskacinch works great for this kind of thing. It's thin, lightweight, and it sets up in a few minutes. With the gaskets stuck in place on the cylinder heads, lower the valve covers over the studs and onto the gaskets. Install the valve cover washers and nuts and evenly snug them down. Be careful not to overtighten. You can easily crush the gasket and end up with a bigger mess than you started with. A half to three-quarter turn past snug should do the trick. Fire up the engine, and check for any leaks; retighten as necessary.

In addition to the valve cover gaskets and studs, replacing your engine's valve covers can further aid in the cleaning up of your engine compartment. Most factory rocker covers are flimsy, stamped steel and are highly prone to bending and warping. Many aftermarket pieces are even worse. Look for a set with thick gasket flanges and good overall rigidity. You might pay a little more for this than the $19 chromed specials, but remember: Quality parts mean quality results.

Installing New Valve Springs, Locks, and Retainers

 Time: 3 hours

 Tools: Standard socket set, standard wrenches, valve spring compressor, feeler gauge, breaker bar, crankshaft socket, calipers, micrometer (optional), dial indicator (optional)

 Talent:

 Applicable years: All

Cost: $150–$250

Parts: Springs, locks, retainers, valves, and valve stem seals (optional)

Tip: Purchasing valvetrain components in a packaged kit will eliminate the hassle of trying to assemble unequal and incompatible parts

PERFORMANCE GAIN: The proper set of valve springs, locks, and retainers will maximize the capabilities of both your cylinder heads and your camshaft.

COMPLEMENTARY PROJECTS: Project 34: Installing Roller Rockers and Poly Locks; Project 35: Selecting and Installing Pushrods

The valve springs and their retainers play an integral role in the performance of your vehicle's valvetrain. Their primary function is to retain the intake and exhaust valves in the cylinder head and to control and dampen the valve's constant opening and closing motions. As your engine rapidly climbs in revolutions, greater valve spring pressure is necessary to keep the valves from floating in their pockets. This valve floating condition is especially common with large camshafts with long duration and high-lift profiles. The radical lobes or ramps of these cams often cause the lifters to overcome the retaining pressures of the valve springs and confuse the operation of the valves. The valve springs will compress and expand 100 times per second at 6,000 rpm. With the engine operating in this repetitive dysfunctional state, you not only lose significant horsepower, but also run the risk of damaging and breaking parts.

Using a valve spring compressor, compress the spring to release the tension from the valve keys. A large, leverage-style compressor may be necessary to fully compress the spring.

Stubborn springs and keepers sometimes warrant the use of the mighty hammer. Place a socket over the locks and tap the retainer with the hammer to jolt them loose.

First-time engine builders consistently overlook proper valve spring and retainer selection as mere details. This is a big mistake. The valve springs must be matched to the cam to produce the ultimate results in your engine. Most factory-style cylinder heads are equipped with a single coil spring and a flat inner ribbon spring. The inner ribbon provides added strength and helps control the valve spring's natural movement under load. This is not considered a dual-spring setup. For most mild applications, a single spring with a damper will do the job just fine. However, in high-performance engines with big cams, a true dual or triple spring assembly is required. These springs also use a flat ribbon spring to further dampen the vibrations.

Your choice of valve springs should depend on your engine's normal operating rpm range, maximum rpm, the aggressiveness of your camshaft, and the weight of the relative valvetrain components. Heavier pieces, such as stock valves and retainers, will require more spring pressure to stabilize the valvetrain during operation. Conversely, the lighter the components, the less pressure is required. Lightweight valvetrains also mean less friction and destructive wear of the moving parts and increased reliability and longevity. Contact your camshaft manufacturer for recommendations on the best overall package. Buying a matched set, including the springs, locks, and retainers, is often the winning ticket.

The removal and replacement of the valve springs can be performed with the cylinder heads installed or removed from the engine. If you plan on changing the intake and exhaust valves at the same time, the heads must be unbolted and set up on a clean workbench. To swap the springs only, you must force compressed air into each cylinder to keep the valve from falling down inside the bore when the spring locks and retainers are removed. One at a time, replace the spark plugs with an air fitting adapter and compress the cylinder. Make sure the adapter has a reliable inline gauge to determine the proper pressure. Each cylinder must be on its compression stroke in order to follow this procedure. On the compression stroke, the cylinder valves will be closed, allowing the air pressure to hold the valve in position.

You will need a quality valve spring compressor to remove the locks and retainers from the valve assembly. Start by placing the tool over the top of the spring retainer and compressing until the two valve locks or keys can be removed. It may be necessary to first jolt the locks loose using a hammer and a deep socket (see photo 1). With the valve springs fully compressed, carefully remove the keys from the tip of the valve (a small magnet sometimes helps remove the keys from their machined grooves). Slowly release the compressor from the valve and remove the spring. For valve replacement, the lower valve stem oil seal must be removed as well. These seals should always be replaced when removing and reinstalling the valves. At this point, the valves will freely slide out the bottom of the cylinder head. Number each valve in relation to its cylinder prior to removal.

When installing a new set of springs, it is absolutely crucial to take proper measurements of the valve springs being used (installed height, open pressures, seat pressures, and coil-bind height). For the installed height of your valve springs, first install the spring retainer and key onto the tip of the valve with the spring removed.

With the spring compressed, remove the valve keys from the grooved stem in the valve.

The springs are free to be removed.

Clear out the remaining seals, shims, and hardware to allow access to the valve.

Measure the distance between the underside of the spring retainer and the top of the spring seat. The readings can be taken using a micrometer or a pair of calipers. Repeat this process for each valve. With all of the valves measured, find the shortest installed height. This will become the installed height on your cylinder heads. Copper or steel shims can be placed in the spring pocket to obtain this height for the remaining valves (plus or minus 0.020 inch). Before disassembly, measure the distance between the underside of the spring retainer and the top of the valve seal. This measurement must be greater than the lift of the valve. If not, the valve guides in the head will need to be machined for adequate clearance.

The open and closed (seat) pressures of the valve springs are measured using a spring-rate checker and a pair of calipers. The seat pressure (when the valve is closed) is the amount of pressure on the spring seat at the installed height. The open pressure (when the valve is open) is the amount of spring pressure at the tip of the valve stem when the cam is at maximum lift. The coil-bind height represents the height of the coil when the spring is fully compressed. Again, this distance determines the amount of valve lift the spring is capable of handling. Coil-bind can be checked by fully compressing the spring in a bench vise and measuring its height. When the valve is completely open (spring compressed), there should be a

minimum of 0.060 inch clearance between each coil of the spring, both inner and outer.

In addition to the aforementioned clearances and measurements, the spring seats or pockets in the cylinder heads should be checked in relation to the outside diameter of the recommended valve spring. Machining the pockets may be required to achieve the appropriate diameter.

These measurements require the use of specialty tools that most of us don't have lying around the garage. However, they can be rented from most tool supply companies and are fairly inexpensive. In a last resort effort, any automotive machine shop could easily handle the chore for you.

Once you have selected and measured your parts, the reassembly is basic. If you removed the valves or are installing new valves, lightly coat the stems with clean engine oil and insert them through the guides in the cylinder head. Install the necessary shims, seals, and retainers. Using the spring compressor, compress the spring over the stem of the valve until the locks can be inserted. After the heads are fully installed, check for clearance between the valve retainer and the rocker arm. If necessary, this can be corrected with either different length pushrods or valves. Spin the motor over by hand with a breaker bar and a crankshaft socket, and double-check any tight clearances before starting the engine.

Installing Roller Rockers and Poly Locks

 Time: 3 hours

 Tools: Standard socket set, Allen wrench set, breaker bar, crankshaft socket, clean engine oil

 Talent:

 Applicable years: All

 Cost: $250–$450

 Parts: Set of roller rocker arms, set of poly locks

 Tip: Be sure to check all of your existing valvetrain clearances before purchasing new rocker arms.

 PERFORMANCE GAIN: By drastically reducing friction and heat in the cylinder heads, a quality set of roller rockers will almost always show significant power increases (10–30 horsepower advertised).

COMPLEMENTARY PROJECTS:
Project 35: Selecting and Installing Pushrods

Although compatible with the rest of the valvetrain, the two rocker arms have a distinctly different body from one another (note the machined roller tip on the right).

Rocker arms, in conjunction with the pushrods, actuate the opening and closing of the valves. As the camshaft rotates, the lifters continuously ride up and down on the ground lobes of the cam. Atop the other end of the lifter sits a pushrod. It serves as the bridge between the lower rotating assembly and the upper portion of the valvetrain. Naturally, as the lifter is thrust upward, so is the corresponding pushrod. Coming up through the bottom of the cylinder head, the pushrod engages the machined recess in the underside of the rocker arm. By translating this repetitive up-and-down motion, the other end of the rocker arm (placed at the tip of the valve) will open and close the valves accordingly.

There are three basic parts of the rocker arm assembly—the body, the fulcrum, and the tip. Each one plays a significant role in your car's valvetrain operation. Most factory rocker arm bodies are stamped steel. Although fine for stock or mildly enhanced performance applications, these units are prone to distortion and failure when mated with larger cams and heavy-duty valve springs. The results can be devastating. If you install a radical, high-lift cam, switching over to a quality set of aftermarket rockers is a must. Not only does the flexure and bending of stamped steel pose a serious threat to the rest of the valvetrain, but it also produces inconsistent ratios from one rocker arm to the next. To fix the dilemma, most aftermarket high-performance companies, such as Comp Cams, use high-strength, investment-cast chrome-moly steel, cast-aluminum, or even stainless-steel bodies for accurate readings and rigid strength.

The rocker arm fulcrum is the center pivoting point on which the rocker moves back and forth. As the arm slides down over the stud, the fulcrum ball and adjusting nut follow. Once in motion, the fulcrum becomes a concentrated area of intense friction and relies purely on engine oil for lubrication. In fact, most performance rocker arm kits come complete with upgraded, grooved fulcrum balls. The small passages grooved into the outside of the balls trap and retain oil to help reduce the friction. A full-roller rocker arm is

When using poly locks or any similar locking rocker nut, first tighten the nut itself followed by the setscrew. This keeps the constant vibration of the valvetrain and engine from backing off the rocker nut.

designed with a "rollerized" fulcrum consisting of needle bearings to further eliminate excess wear and heat.

The tip of the rocker arm is positioned to sit evenly on the top of the valve. However, over time, sloppy and inaccurate stock-style rockers can cause substantial damage to both the valve tips and the guides. This is where roller-tip rocker arms enter the picture. The roller tips of the rockers help reduce the constant friction and scraping of the valve ends. By replacing your factory rockers with a quality roller-tip version, you can preserve the life of your valvetrain and pick up more than a few extra ponies at the same time.

In addition to changing out the stock rocker arms in your motor, think about investing in a set of poly locks. Most engines with an adjustable valvetrain came from the factory with a standard rocker arm nut. This nut threads down on the rocker arm stud to locate and retain the arm in relation to the valve tip. Under load, the rocker nuts can work themselves loose and even come off of the stud altogether. Constructed of high-strength materials, poly locks are designed with a small jam screw in the top of the nut to place added tension on the stud. Again, if you run a high-lift cam, buy the extra insurance and protect your valvetrain from possible disaster. Poly locks are fast and easy for setting valve lashes as well.

When the time comes to decide on what style of rocker arms to purchase, think practical. What is the primary function of the vehicle? Not every motor will benefit from having the biggest, baddest (not to mention the most expensive) rocker arms on the market. You want the rockers to complement your existing camshaft and valvetrain without having to change everything around. Regardless of your car and engine, there are plenty of choices. Keep in mind that you have the option of increasing the rocker ratio. On a small-block Chevy with a stock 1.5:1 rocker ratio and a 0.500 lift cam, upgrading to a 1.6:1 ratio rocker arm with the same cam would yield a valve lift of 0.533—you basically trick the motor into believing it has a larger cam than it actually does. Although most performance engines would respond favorably to the swap, it does present a new set of concerns regarding clearances. In this case, technical hotlines of major valvetrain companies can prove to be extremely helpful and informative.

Now that we have a little bit more understanding of the components and how they operate, let's get to work. Up first are the valve covers and anything else that may restrict access to the inside of the cylinder heads. With a socket and wrench, loosen the nut and remove the rocker arm and pivot ball from each stud.

Always follow the manufacturer's specs on lubrication prior to installing the new arms. This is very important for the initial "break-in" of the new components. It is also recommended that you replace the pushrods when installing new rocker arms. Pushrods and rocker arms tend to wear together much like a camshaft and its lifters. Installing new rockers on old pushrods can result in premature failure. (We cover pushrod geometry and selection in Project 35.)

Install the new arms and pivot balls onto the rocker studs. Hand tighten the rocker nuts or poly locks to the body of the rockers and begin to set the required valve lash or lifter preload. If you have a solid lifter cam, the procedure for setting and adjusting the valves can be found in Project 36. For hydraulic cams and lifters, the steps are similar and equally straightforward. Turn the engine over by hand in the direction of rotation, using a breaker bar and a crankshaft socket. As the exhaust valve begins its upward travel, the intake valve is ready to be set. Slowly tighten the rocker nut while spinning the pushrod of the intake valve with your fingers. When you feel a slight drag or resistance in the rod, the clearance has been taken up, reaching the "zero lash" point. Approximately a half-turn on the wrench past this point will provide the proper preload for the valve.

On the exhaust side, turn the engine until the intake valve of the same cylinder reaches its highest point of travel. Continue to rotate the motor, allowing the intake valve to return three-fourths of the way back down. The exhaust valve can now be set to "zero lash" and snugged down a half-turn. This completes preloading the valves for one cylinder; repeat for all.

Selecting and Installing Pushrods

 Time: 3 hours

 Tools: Standard socket set, Allen wrench set (poly locks)

 Talent:

 Applicable years: All

 Cost: $50–$200

 Parts: Full set of pushrods, clean engine oil

 Tip: Double-check all valvetrain clearances by hand-turning the motor after the installation is complete.

 PERFORMANCE GAIN: Installing the correct length pushrod will not only allow for maximum performance of your engine, but will also protect and extend the longevity of the valvetrain.

COMPLEMENTARY PROJECTS:
Installing pushrod guide plates;
Project 34: Installing Roller Rockers and Poly Locks

ENGINE (TOP END)

The pushrod, and its role in the valvetrain, is an often over-looked yet vital piece in the puzzle of high performance. It is the translator of cam and lifter movement to the rocker arms and valves. Bridging the gap between the two, the pushrods are responsible for delivering the exact orders of the camshaft without flex or deviation.

Most factory-style pushrods were constructed with a welded-on ball tip on each end of the rod. At the tip of the balls is a small hole used for oil transfer and lubrication to the point where the pushrod meets the underside of the rocker arm. There have been numerous changes made by aftermarket companies to further improve on the design for specific applications.

Although basic in form, there are many facets to the selection of the right pushrod for any high-performance engine.

Let's first take a look at valvetrain geometry and its effects on the function and performance of your engine. When installing a new set of rocker arms or pushrods, it is crucial to obtain the proper working geometry in the valvetrain to maximize your engine's power potential and reliability. There must be ample clearance for all moving parts of the valvetrain.

In this case, the relationship between the rocker arm tip radius and the valve stem tip will determine the overall geometry of your valvetrain. Ideally, as the valves open and close, the tip of the rocker arm should be square on the tip of the valve stem through its full range of motion. This is not entirely possible, however, as the rocker arm tracks in a slight arc across the tip of the valve upon opening and closing. At zero lift (when the valve is fully closed), the rocker tip should sit just a tad offset toward the rocker arm fulcrum (intake side of the motor). At the midlift point, the rocker should reach its maximum travel across the stem centerline, this time on the exhaust side of the motor. As the valve continues to open, the tip of the rocker arm will then sweep back across the valve stem to near its original position. Although you may not be able to nail it exactly, use this as a general guideline when setting things up. Maintain the rocker arm contact point in the middle third of the valve stem tip. If the rocker repeatedly strays too far from the centerline of the valve, it can result in a number of serious problems, ultimately robbing power and destroying your valvetrain.

Just about any modification made to the existing top or bottom end of a stock engine could result in valvetrain problems. The most common potentially problematic modification is installing a larger camshaft. Many car crafters try to stuff the largest, craziest cam they possibly can into an otherwise stock or mildly built engine and expect everything to work seamlessly. Wrong! There are many factors and variables to take into account when selecting a camshaft, as it alone affects just about every other component in the system. In addition to cams, changing the head gasket thickness, installing longer valves, milling the block and heads, and changing rocker arm ratios can all easily modify the operation of your engine.

Fortunately, correcting such problems on a stud-mounted, adjustable valvetrain is fairly simple. With the help of aftermarket camshaft companies and the use of adjustable "checking" pushrods, pinpointing the right geometry angles for your motor has become relatively painless. By using a checking pushrod, you are able to adjust the length of the installed rod to see exactly where it places the rocker arm in relation to the valve stem tip (as well as other clearances). Once the correct length has been determined, you can select the pushrods needed for the job.

As you can see, the pushrod slips right down in its designated slot through the cylinder head, connecting the lifter to the rocker arm.

In certain high-performance applications, the use of pushrod guide plates is recommended. Under high-rpm load, pushrods tend to flex. Typically bolted underneath a screw-in rocker stud, the rigid guide plate slightly narrows the traveling channel of the pushrod. If the pushrod begins to flex, it will hit the guide plate and cease bending. Keep in mind this could create metal-to-metal contact inside the cylinder head. The use of hardened pushrods and guide plates is necessary to avoid an unwanted shower of metal shavings in your engine.

With all of the preliminaries out of the way, the actual removal and replacement of the pushrods is basic. They simply drop down the designated slot in the cylinder head and are seated on top of the lifter (see photo 1). Done! Always follow manufacturer's specs on the prepping and lubrication of any valvetrain component. Once installed with the proper valve lash or preload set, turn the engine over by hand, allowing the valves to fully open and close. Observe operation, checking for any problems or clearance issues.

PROJECT 36
Setting Valve Lash

 Time: 1 hour

 Tools: Standard socket set, breaker bar, crankshaft socket, feeler gauge

 Talent: 👨‍🔧👨‍🔧

 Applicable years: All

 Cost: Under $15 for feeler gauge; optional poly locks start at $70 a set

 Parts: None (but poly locks would be a wise investment)

 Tip: Ask 10 racers how they set valve lash, and you'll get 10 different answers. It's best to stick to this tried-and-true method.

 PERFORMANCE GAIN: Consistent performance throughout the entire rpm range

COMPLEMENTARY PROJECTS: Project 32: Installing Valve Cover Gaskets and Studs; Project 34: Installing Roller Rockers and Poly Locks

ENGINE (TOP END)

The method for setting valves is the same for a hydraulic lifter-equipped small block or a mechanical cam big block. Since all four-stroke engines open and close their valves in the same sequence, you want to set the lifter on the base circle of the camshaft. In this instance, we're going to work on a mechanical camshaft-equipped small-block. We'll tell you how to adjust a hydraulic lifter-equipped engine as we move along . . . .

Mechanical cams require a set amount of clearance to function properly. This clearance is measured between the rocker arm tip and the valve stem. Typically, the clearance is between 0.015 and 0.030 inch when you measure it with a feeler gauge. Simply put, you adjust the clearance by loosening the rocker stud nut. The clearance is referred to as a "hot" clearance because it allows for heat expansion when the engine is running at full operating temperature.

Turn the crankshaft clockwise by hand using a breaker bar and crankshaft socket. A bump-starter will work just fine, too.

97

Above: After watching the Number 1 cylinder exhaust valve reach its bottom-most point of travel, you'll see the valve start to open (upward travel). Stop. This will put the intake valve in position to be adjusted. Here we've loosened the poly lock with an Allen key.

Below: Slightly loosen the nut so that there is free play in the rocker arm. Insert the feeler gauge. A snug fit is all that is required. Tighten the nut back down again.

Following the steps outlined in the text, adjust the exhaust valve lash.

Before you begin, let the engine warm up to normal operating temperature. After a few minutes, shut the car down and remove both valve covers. In Photo 1, you'll see that we've elected to turn the engine by hand, using a breaker bar attached to the snout of the crankshaft. You can also use a "bump-starter," which is a momentary starter switch connected across the start and battery terminals of the starter solenoid. If you choose this method, make sure to disconnect the coil wire so the engine won't actually fire up.

We're going to start with the Number 1 cylinder (front of the engine, driver's side). Turn the engine over slowly until the exhaust pushrod begins to move, opening the valve. After you see the valve start to open, stop. You can now adjust the intake lash. Loosen the rocker stud nut slightly (in this case, we're using aftermarket poly locks*). Insert the feeler gauge between the valve stem and the underside of the rocker. (We're using a 0.018-inch gauge.) Tighten the rocker nut until there is a slight drag when moving the feeler gauge.

Now, it's time to adjust the lash on the exhaust valve. Turning the engine again, watch the intake pushrod. Wait until it moves all the way to its uppermost position and starts back down again. When it is about halfway back down, stop. Loosen the rocker stud nut on the exhaust valve, and insert the feeler gauge. Again, tighten the rocker nut until there is a slight drag when moving the feeler gauge. You want to be able to pull it

out but with a little effort. Repeat this for all cylinders. Some of the old-time hot rodders would use anything from a matchbook cover to a guitar pick as a temporary feeler gauge. Not totally accurate, but effective nonetheless . . .

You'll find the chart helpful in indicating which valve is which for your application.

To adjust the lash on hydraulic lifters, the procedure is essentially the same. Turning the engine by hand, watch for the opening and closing valves as described above. Instead of using a feeler gauge to determine lash, loosen the rocker stud nut, spin the pushrod between your fingertips, and slowly tighten the nut until there is a slight drag on the pushrod. Further tighten the rocker stud nut a half-turn. Your lash is now adjusted. Following the same procedure for both the intake and exhaust valves, move through the engine until you've tackled all cylinders.

*A word about rocker stud nuts: Most engines use a crimping or locking nut on the rocker studs. These end up pinching the rocker stud threads. Over time, the nuts will damage the stud threads, causing the nuts to lose their grip. There goes the correct valve lash! Poly locks are the answer; they use straight threads and an internal Allen jam. They're easy to adjust, and they won't back off. They work equally well on roller rockers and factory stock rockers. You can purchase poly locks from any cam manufacturer.

Removing and Replacing the Cylinder Heads

 Time: 3 hours

 Tools: Standard socket set, standard wrenches, breaker bar, small pry bar, gasket scraper

 Talent: ▮▮▮

 Applicable years: All

 Cost: $800–$3,000-plus (new)

 Parts: High-performance cylinder heads, quality head gaskets, thread locker

 Tip: When cleaning the engine block for new head gaskets, stuff a rag into each cylinder bore. The last thing you need is debris from old gaskets scratching or damaging the walls.

PERFORMANCE GAIN: Aftermarket cylinder heads can produce the biggest gains in horsepower and torque compared to any other engine upgrade.

COMPLEMENTARY PROJECTS: Project 31: Installing a New Intake Manifold; Project 46: Installing a Camshaft and Lifters; Project 53: Installing Aftermarket Headers

Making big horsepower is all about enhancing your engine's breathing. The more air that is forced into the engine, the more power it ultimately creates. Cylinder heads serve as a prime example of this theory. They are the lifeblood of your engine. Whether you run iron or aluminum castings, the cylinder heads determine the overall performance capabilities of your powerplant.

To remove the cylinder heads from the engine block, you must first loosen the exhaust manifolds, or headers. Total removal is not always necessary; you may leave them attached to the lower collector to simplify matters. In addition to the exhaust, the intake manifold and any accessory items should be cleared out as well. You will need complete access to the cylinder head bolts and enough room to heave the head out of the engine compartment when ready.

The exhaust will unbolt rather easily. Once loosened, tie the header or manifold back away from the engine to avoid banging the side of the cylinder head and snapping a spark plug. In some applications, removing the spark plugs is mandatory.

Using a large breaker bar and socket, gradually loosen the cylinder head bolts. Start with the outer bolts in the pattern and slowly and evenly work your way to the center of the head. When all of the bolts are removed, carefully pry the cylinder head from the block. Break the bond using a small pry bar or long screwdriver. Due to the gaskets, sealer, and extreme heat, it may take a little muscle to split the two mating surfaces apart. Use a small piece of wood or cloth at the point of contact to prevent damaging the sealing areas of the block or the cylinder head. With the seal broken, give the head a valiant tug and remove it from the engine bay. Cover the cylinder bores in the block with rags to keep out all contaminants, and thoroughly clean both surfaces of old gasket material and residue.

The installation is straightforward and requires only the bare essentials. Place the new gaskets on the surface of the block, followed by the cylinder heads. Gasket sealer may be necessary to hold them in place while setting the heads in position. Lightly coat each head bolt with thread locker and insert it into the head. Tighten the bolts in a cross-type pattern and torque them to the manufacturer's specifications. Reinstall the removed valvetrain pieces and the rocker covers. Keep in mind you will need to set the proper valve lash or lifter preload before final assembly.

Above: Unbolt the headers from the cylinder heads and remove the gaskets. It's a good idea to pull the plugs as well.
Below: Remove the head bolts with a breaker bar and socket.

Above: Remove valvetrain components such as the rocker arms and pushrods to free the heads of restraints.
Below: Clean the engine block of old gasket residue before reapplying the new gaskets.

Installing a Cowl Induction System

Time: 3–4 hours

Tools: Standard socket wrenches, Phillips screwdriver

Talent:

Applicable years: '70–'72 Chevelle

Cost: $700 for parts, roughly $300 for a cowl induction hood

Parts: Hood, cowl induction door assembly, hood screen, air cleaner spacer, cowl induction air cleaner assembly, A/C intake relay, A/C wing nut, vacuum actuator, vacuum actuator support, cowl induction wiring harness, firewall grommet, valve frame kit, air control switch and bracket, flow control valve, hood pins (if desired)

Tip: Whether you're using your existing cowl-equipped hood or a brand-new one, remove the hood from the car and place it upside down on a firm, level surface at least a foot off the ground. You can install the system with the hood still attached, but it's much easier when removed. Hood removal is very simple, and you will need two people to do it. Unscrew the four bolts that retain the hood to its hinges, and carefully lift.

PERFORMANCE GAIN: Nothing measurable in terms of acceleration, but you'll gain the legendary look and action of a cowl induction system.

COMPLEMENTARY PROJECTS:
Project 16: Adding Stripes and Body Graphics

ENGINE (TOP END)

Picture this: Two gorgeous big-block Chevelles parked side by side, packin' identical firepower. One's got the standard SS hood; the other's equipped with a cowl induction setup. What's the big difference, you ask—5, 10, maybe 15 more horses? Actually, the cowl induction system adds zero horsepower to your GM A-body. What's the point then? How 'bout a supercool flap that opens up under full-throttle acceleration announcing to the world that this car's not to be messed with? You'll love how easy it is to install one of these systems on your '70–'72 Chevelle or El Camino.

Whether your car was originally cowl-induction equipped or not, we'll show you how to install the complete system. In a few hours, you'll be flashing warning signs to all the other muscle on the street.

We're using parts from Original Parts Group in Huntington Beach, California (1-800-243-8355). Their part numbers are referred to in this project.

First, a few words of advice and precautions:

• A cowl induction system can be installed on any '70–'72 Chevelle that is equipped with a four-barrel carburetor, including 350, 396, and 454 engines.

• Prime and paint your hood before installing the cowl system. Be sure to paint the cowl door and screen body color.

• Be very careful working around the underside of the hood. It is stamped sheet metal and all the edges are very sharp.

• When reinstalling the hood, make sure you line it up correctly on its hinges. Lightly tighten the bolts, and then gently shut the hood to check for fit. Once you're satisfied, tighten all four bolts with a socket wrench.

In our first step, we insert the valve frame cage flap into the valve frame cage, using the three supplied retaining clips. We also insert the electric solenoid into its preattached retaining bracket. All the parts necessary for this step are included in OPG's "complete valve frame setup" (Part Number C15004).

With the cowl induction hood (Part Number PZ00653) placed upside down on a firm surface and raised off the ground, insert the assembled valve frame setup into the hood opening. Secure with the six supplied self-tapping screws using a 5/16-inch socket wrench.

Next, we insert the firewall grommet (Part Number C634000) into the prestamped hole in the hood and feed the tan wire from the wiring harness (Part Number CWH8922) through the grommet. Then, we attach the tan wire terminal to the solenoid. You will access the solenoid through the large air cleaner hole in the center of the hood.

Now, we will assemble the hood door. Attach the two door supports (one at each side of the hood door) using the supplied bushings and pivot screws. The cowl induction hood door assembly kit is available from OPG (Part Number KC1502). Even with the screws fully tightened, the door supports will feel loose and not firmly connected to the hood

103

The cowl induction system on this Chevelle is straight out of 1970. You can see the valve frame setup in the hood opening.

door. This is normal, as the hood door must be allowed to open and close freely.

Now that the hood door is assembled, we're going to install it into the hood. Lay the hood door into the prestamped hole in the hood, and attach it by screwing four (two each side) 3/8-inch self-tapping bolts through the hood door supports. Note: Due to irregularities in metal stampings, you will need to shim the door supports (using washers) in order to properly align the hood door. Look under the hood (actually, on top of the hood) and shim the door so that it sits flush with the hood surface.

Before you tighten down the door supports, make sure the hood door is able to open and shut freely. There should be at least 1/16 inch of clearance between the door and the actual hood. Don't forget to take into consideration the thickness of new paint.

Next, insert the vacuum actuator (Part Number PZ00417) into the vacuum actuator support (Part Number PZ00418) and fasten it to the hood using 4 1/4-inch self-tapping bolts. Then, attach the vacuum actuator "throw" to the cowl hood door using the supplied screw.

Now that we have all the hood hardware in place, we're going to attach the cowl hood screen (Part Number 7CCH116) to the rear of the hood opening, using eight self-tapping screws. This will keep out those pesky leaves and unusually large bugs.

Don't freak—because there's no vacuum in the system yet, the door will remain in its open position.

You may be wondering why your '70–'72 A-body has three big gaping holes in the cowl grille area (just below the windshield). They're obviously for airflow, but for some strange reason the factory left them open and unprotected. To keep out leaves and extraneous junk, you may want to invest in a set of cowl grille inserts (Part Number CHV4510 without A/C or Part Number CHV451B with A/C). They simply snap into place.

Reattach the hood to the car. Have a friend help, and take your time to make sure both sides of the hood align properly with the fenders.

Now, we're going to get the whole system activated. If wire routing and switch installation intimidate you, you're in for a treat—this is a pretty simple setup; just follow along.

Attach the air cleaner intake valve relay assembly (Part Number PZ00419) to the firewall, using a Number 10 self-tapping screw. This unit sends a "hot" signal from the wiring harness to the cowl induction solenoid.

There's a black "plug" located in the firewall just behind the engine's valve cover. Pop it open and insert the pink and brown leads from the wiring harness and the braided section of wire. The pink and brown leads will feed down and attach to the air control valve solenoid switch, which we will install at the gas pedal. The braided section of the wiring harness will also feed down and attach to the car's existing wiring harness. At the gas pedal, you will need to remove the existing retaining plate.

Attach the air control valve solenoid switch (Part Number PZ00415) to its bracket (Part Number 7CCH119), using the

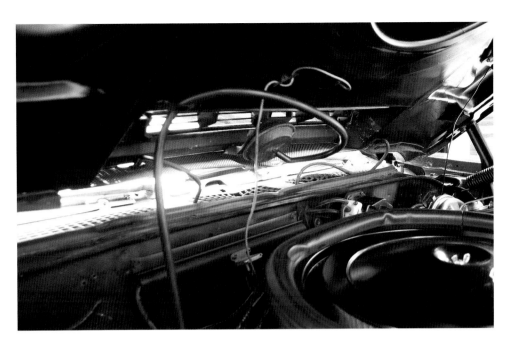

The 1/4-inch rubber hose attaches to the vacuum actuator. The other end routes to the vacuum port on the intake manifold, just behind the carburetor.

At rest, the hood door is supposed to stay open, because there's no vacuum in the system.

supplied screw. Now, fit the bracket to the existing holes where you removed the retaining plate. The protruding post on the side of the solenoid switch will press against the gas pedal linkage upon full-throttle acceleration, actuating the vacuum and opening the cowl hood door.

Attach the pink and brown wire leads to the terminals on the solenoid switch (proper fit will be obvious), and attach the braided section to the existing wiring harness under your dashboard. This last connection will provide power to the cowl induction system.

Back in the engine compartment, plug the two remaining short wires into the air cleaner intake valve relay assembly. (Again, the proper fit will be obvious.) Now, route the tan wire (that attaches to the electric solenoid we installed at the beginning of this project) through the wiring sheath on the firewall to protect it.

Place the cowl induction spacer assembly (Part Number SM436SP) on top of the carburetor. This ring simply sits atop the carb and allows the air cleaner to sit up a little higher into the cowl hood.

Attach the cowl induction air cleaner flange and seal kit (Part Number KC1500 black lid or Part Number KC1501 chrome lid).

Now, fit a 1/4-inch rubber hose (not included in the kit, but available from any auto parts supply store) to the vacuum actuator. Route the hose to fit the other end to the vacuum port located on the intake manifold just behind the carburetor. The vacuum port is standard on all Chevelles, as it is used for other vacuum-operated accessories.

Fire it up and grab a few shifts. Watching that cowl door open under full throttle makes it all worthwhile.

105

Port Matching the Gaskets

ENGINE (TOP END)

 Time: 3–8 hours

 Tools: Power drill or air compressor, various carbide cutters, polishing attachments

 Talent:

 Applicable years: All

 Cost: $50–$75 for materials

Parts: Intake gaskets, layout dye

 Tip: Avoid using shafts that measure over 4 inches in length, as they tend to wobble or break at operating speeds.

 PERFORMANCE GAIN: Greater airflow, increased power

COMPLEMENTARY PROJECTS:

Project 31: Installing a New Intake Manifold, Project 37: Removing and Replacing the Cylinder Heads

The most basic principle in creating horsepower is airflow. The more airflow your engine has, the more power it produces. Cylinder heads are largely responsible for the flow potential of your engine. The intake and exhaust ports on the cylinder head allow the air to enter and leave the engine with as little drag as possible. Air is fed into the engine through the intake ports of the manifold and cylinder head. The exhaust ports of the cylinder head discard the spent gases out through the exhaust manifolds or headers. Due to the rough and often misaligned castings of the heads, the rapid flow of air is restricted or disturbed during its course, and this causes the engine to lose power. A simple fix to this common imperfection is to port match the intake manifold/gasket/cylinder head interface and create a smooth, seamless path for the air to travel.

The practice of port matching adjoining components has been around and widely used for quite some time, and it makes perfect sense. If two connecting ports are different in size, shape, or diameter, the internal transfer of air from one port to the other will be disrupted. There is literally nowhere else for the air to go but around the surface of the port. By gasket matching your cylinder heads and your intake manifold, you can streamline the path and improve power across the entire rpm band.

Port matching requires the use of specialty tools, such as a grinder and various burring attachments, a polishing kit, and layout dye. You can use a power drill or an air compressor to do the grinding, but always wear protective safety glasses or a shield.

To start, remove the intake manifold and the cylinder heads from the engine and set them aside on a clean workbench. Disassemble and thoroughly clean the heads before breaking out the grinder. Unless you previously knew the port size of the cylinder heads, it's necessary to first remove the heads to see what size intake gaskets you will need. Purchase the gaskets that allow the amount of port opening desired.

Once the heads are clean, lightly coat the surfaces with the spray can layout dye. This creates a clean, uniform finish on the heads that will make the scribe marks easier to read. When the dye has fully dried, center the gasket over the ports of the cylinder head as a template, and mark the flange surface with a scribe. Remove the gasket to determine the amount of material you need to grind out of the cylinder head. Although there may be no difference whatsoever between the gaskets (left and right), it's best to keep them together with the proper head.

The porting process begins with slow circular movements around the opening of the port. Carefully work your way out toward the scribe line, stopping just shy of the border and concentrating on the high spots in the surface. As you approach the outer rim of the port window, start blending the flange surface of the head into the intake port. Be sure to leave enough raw material for final smoothing and polishing.

It's important to work from various angles when porting and removing material from a cylinder head or an intake manifold. The smoother that the casting is made, the more airflow that is permitted through the ports. All rough edges and sharp corners should be rounded out and blended into the surface. Also, start out with a shallow port depth and gradually work your way deeper into the pocket. The main area of focus is at the mouth of the port. However, when polishing, use the reverse approach. Start deep into the port and blend your way out.

Porting and polishing require time and practice to produce quality results. These methods can be applied to cylinder heads, intake manifolds, and even exhaust headers. The tools may vary from one piece to another, depending on the type of material being ground. Cast-iron parts require the use of different burrs with fewer flutes than aluminum burrs. Since aluminum is softer than iron, an iron flute would quickly become loaded up with excess material if used on aluminum surfaces.

Cylinder head porting begins by lightly blending the rough edges of the casting.

Different sized and shaped carbide cutters are used to cover and reach the contours of the pockets.

Additionally, be sure to lubricate the burr with some type of oil or fluid to reduce the buildup of heat when cutting aluminum. If the burr gets too hot, it can deeply gouge the metal and remove more material than intended. The key is to always keep the burrs moving in a consistent pattern, stopping periodically to inspect the surface with your eyes and your fingers. It may be necessary to backlight the ports to gain a better look at the inside surfaces.

After the grinding and polishing are complete, clean all parts again before piecing the engine back together. Blow out each port and opening with compressed air to ensure that no metal shavings are left inside. Install the head gaskets and the reassembled cylinder heads on the block and torque them to specification. Align the intake gaskets on the cylinder heads and carefully tack them in place with a small amount of gasket sealer. Position the manifold onto the gaskets and torque evenly.

Installing a Nitrous Oxide System

Time: 3–5 hours

Tools: Standard socket set, standard wrenches, power drill and drill bits

Talent:

Applicable years: All

Cost: $250–$550

Parts: Nitrous kit with bottle, electrical connectors

Tip: Use electrical relays for close control when increasing the flow and size of the nitrous solenoids.

PERFORMANCE GAIN: Big, indisputable horsepower and torque

COMPLEMENTARY PROJECTS:

Project 31: Installing a New Intake Manifold; Project 41: Installing a Mechanical Fuel Pump and Fuel Pressure Regulator; Project 71: Installing a Powertrax No-Slip Traction System

Installing a nitrous kit may not be the immediate answer to the horsepower question for a lot of people. It's complicated, dangerous, and has a nasty habit of grenading engines, right? We have all heard the rumors and the horror stories. Although many may indeed be true, nitrous does have a solid, track-proven reputation for producing serious horsepower on the cheap. Bar none, it's the biggest bang for the buck you can get.

Nitrous oxide is a molecule comprised of two nitrogen atoms and one oxygen atom. When nitrous oxide is compressed in a sealed tank above 750 psi, the nitrous gas is transformed into a liquid. When the liquid is released, the natural pressure drop causes the liquid to return to its former gaseous state but

at a much cooler temperature (-127 degrees Fahrenheit). This rapid transformation is one of many advantages of nitrous oxide. When activated, the cool gas enters the intake manifold and reduces the inlet air temperature by as much as 65 degrees.

Once the nitrous molecules arrive in the combustion chambers, the extreme heat of the chambers separates the oxygen and nitrogen atoms from each other and allows more fuel to be burned. In fact, nitrous oxide is 36 percent oxygen by weight. The more oxygen that is forced into the combustion chambers, the more power that is created and put to the rear wheels.

To maintain the proper air/fuel mixture when injecting nitrous into the engine, additional fuel is necessary. If the engine fails to receive the much-needed fuel, the combustion chamber temperature skyrockets and can actually produce enough heat to melt the piston dome. To avoid such violent disasters, most nitrous systems are intentionally jetted on the rich side of 11:1 (air/fuel) or greater.

Needless to say, the application of nitrous is a very delicate matter. Nitrous systems, much like conventional carbureted fuel systems, use jets to control the amount of nitrous and fuel delivered to the combustion chambers. Since nitrous bottle pressures average around 1,000 psi, an electric solenoid is used as a regulator to apply nitrous pressure to the engine. A second solenoid is used on the fuel side to initiate the nitrous/fuel mixture. The electrical solenoids of the nitrous system are highly important in protecting your engine against fatally lean conditions. If the nitrous solenoid fails to open, the excess delivery of fuel simply causes the engine to run rich and stumble. On the other hand, a faulty nonoperating fuel solenoid creates an abundance of nitrous in the system and can instantly kill the engine.

Most entry-level nitrous kits use a plate system. These kits supply the recommended nitrous and fuel jets to prevent the first-time user from leaning-out the engine. They serve as a safe, yet highly effective, introductory course to getting started with the famed power booster. For these types of single-stage systems, the horsepower advantage generally ranges from 100 to 200 horsepower. Multistage kits offer greater adjustability and the opportunity to custom-tailor the power curve to your liking. For example, a two-stage kit may initially release a 100-horsepower shot to launch the car, followed by a second 100-horsepower shot moments later. The calculated timing of multistage nitrous systems makes it easier to maintain traction at the rear wheels and increase acceleration down the track.

To handle the added load of the nitrous kit on the engine, both the fuel and ignition systems need to be modified. The fuel system especially should be tested for adequate fuel pressure before engaging and releasing the nitrous. Depending on the type of kit being used, the required fuel pressure will vary. Replace the existing fuel pump with a high-volume unit to ensure the pressure is sufficient and capable of performing in extreme conditions.

Above: The entire nitrous system (minus the bottle) installs neatly around and underneath the carburetor.
Below: The nitrous plate and spray bar sit between the intake manifold and the carburetor.

The fuel pressure regulator ties into the system and controls the pressures to the solenoids.

Always mount the nitrous bottle with the top facing the front of the car and the outlet line facing down.

The ignition system is also placed under heavy load as cylinder pressures increase. Greater voltage is required to jump the gap of the spark plugs and ignite the nitrous mix. Reducing the gap on the plugs is one way to boost the ignition and overcome this problem.

Another method is to use colder, short ground-strap spark plugs that narrow the path of heat to the head of the plug. This helps eliminate the problem of backfiring, commonly associated with nitrous.

Ignition timing is yet another factor in the equation of nitrous power. Nitrous burns at an accelerated rate inside the cylinder, requiring the ignition timing to be retarded to compensate for the difference. The higher the nitrous load, the less total timing is needed. A rough estimation on recommended timing versus nitrous load is 2 degrees every 100 horsepower.

Every nitrous kit will have its own set of recommendations and guidelines. They are heavily researched and engineered to work in a particular manner. Follow them intently and do not cut corners. The results of a sloppy assembly could be catastrophic. Be safe and enjoy!

110

SECTION FOUR

ENGINE (BOTTOM END)

The lower rotating assembly supports and strengthens the remainder of your vehicle's powertrain. The bottom end creates a solid foundation for the performance of the cylinder heads, intake manifold, and carburetor.

PROJECT 41

Installing a Mechanical Fuel Pump and Fuel Pressure Regulator

 Time: 2 hours

 Tools: Standard socket set, adjustable wrench, flat-blade screwdriver, Allen wrench set

 Talent:

 Applicable years: All

 Cost: $100–$150

 Parts: Fuel pump and mounting gasket (supplied), fuel pressure regulator and gauge, 3/8-inch fuel hose and clamps, NPT pipe fittings

 Tip: When rerouting new lines, closely measure all of your lengths beforehand to avoid last-minute miscalculations.

PERFORMANCE GAIN: Superior fuel flow over stock pumps (80–130 gallons per hour), and the pressure adjustability to ensure the right mix

COMPLEMENTARY PROJECTS: Replacing the fuel filter; installing new fuel lines; Project 23: Adjusting the Metering Jets

When reinstalling the pump, use a small screwdriver to carefully hold the pushrod up and out of the way.

With everything back in place, the only thing left to do is securely mount the regulator to its bracket and attach it to any rigid surface. In this case, we will most likely use the inner fender well.

When it comes to cars and our beloved spontaneous combustion engines, fuel and plenty of it is the name of the game. Regardless of size or design, all engines rely solely on fuel being pumped in from an outside source, such as the tank. And to this we look no further than the workhorse we know as the fuel pump.

Fuel pumps come in a variety of forms and can be mounted in several locations. Today, most late-model vehicles utilize an electric pump, which is typically installed inside the tank. However, the older, and by far the most common, design is the mechanical fuel pump. Mounted on the side of the engine block, these pumps use the age-old method of a single pushrod to get things flowing. The fuel pump pushrod is driven by the camshaft to actuate the pump's rocker arm, much like the valvetrain in the cylinder heads.

Supplying the fuel to the pump is an automatic process. Basically, there is a main line, either 5/16 inch or 3/8 inch, running front to back (the length of the car) between the fuel tank and the pump. This is the suction line. The spring-loaded rocker arm is actuated up and down by the rotation of the cam, creating a vacuum in the system and drawing fuel in from the tank. On the outlet side of the pump is the pressure line, which then feeds the fuel into the carburetor's bowl(s). Install a quality fuel filter between the tank and the inlet of the pump to keep the gunk and debris in the tank from entering your fuel pump and, more importantly, your engine.

Installing a New Water Pump and Pulley

ENGINE (BOTTOM END)

Time: 2 hours

Tools: Standard socket set, standard wrenches, gasket scraper, long screwdriver or pry bar

Talent: ▮▮

Applicable years: All

Cost: $75–$250

Parts: New performance water pump and gaskets

Tip: Never reuse old coolant. Over time, it can chemically break down and actually harm and attack the internals of your cooling system.

PERFORMANCE GAIN: A lighter (aluminum), more reliable, higher-flowing cooling system

COMPLEMENTARY PROJECTS:

Installing deep-groove engine pulleys; Project 30: Installing a New Thermostat and Housing (Water Neck); Project 56: Installing a New Radiator and Hoses

Old gasket removal is critical to obtaining a good, leak-free seal. Using a putty knife, lightly scrape the water pump mounting surface until the bare metal of the block is clean.

Along with the radiator, the water pump serves as the focal point of the cooling system. Without its vital contribution, there would be no water/coolant flow through the engine. In fact, the water pump acts as the instigator in the system, immediately initiating the flow of coolant when the engine is fired up. The impeller inside the pump draws in coolant via the lower radiator hose and pushes it through two passages into the engine block. Once inside the block, the coolant circulates around each of the cylinders on both sides, picking up heat along the way. Working in a front-to-rear fashion, it then moves upstairs into the cylinder heads where it continues to cool the valve pockets and guides, exhaust ports, and combustion chambers. The intake manifold and its thermostat are next. Depending on the operating temperature of the engine, the thermostat will allow the coolant to reenter the radiator to be cooled and recirculated through the system.

After many years of service, this system and its hard-working components slowly deteriorate and fall victim to negligence; it's amazing they last as long as they do. When it comes to water pumps in particular, the most common failure is typically the impeller. Although your stock water pump may appear to be fine and show no signs of leakage, the impeller could be in serious trouble and unable to pump the required volume of coolant. Why? Slowly but surely, coolant in the system becomes acidic and will eat any form of metal in its path, including impeller blades. Whether yours is a daily driver or a drag strip demon, this is highly unacceptable. The water pump and its counterparts are readily accessible at the front of the engine and require minimal effort (and a small wad of greenbacks) to upgrade.

Using either the radiator drain plug or the lower hose, carefully drain and empty the old coolant into a large

The water pump is safely secured to the rest of the engine by four bolts. One at a time, snug the bolts down evenly; then, return to tighten.

Most aftermarket aluminum pulleys are deeply grooved to reduce engine weight and to allow the fan belt to fully seat into position.

container and dispose of properly—DON'T reuse it. Spend the extra 10 bucks and refill the system with clean fluid. When the system is finally empty, remove the radiator hoses to allow for better access to the fan and water pump.

Next up are the water pump accessories. Starting with the fan and working back, remove all necessary brackets and attaching hardware from the pump. If this is your first time, keep track of what goes where to avoid confusion or mix-ups later.

Held in place by four 3/8-inch bolts, the water pump can now be removed. Even after the bolts are out, you may need to smack it a couple times with a rubber mallet to break the bond. Take a look at the passages in your old pump—this gunk has been flowing throughout your engine for years!

Before simply slapping a gasket down and installing the new pump, take the time to thoroughly clean the mating surface (see photo 1). If you are unable to remove the old material with a scraper, stuff a rag in the ports and use a power drill with a small-diameter wire wheel attachment. Often overlooked, this is a crucial step for a long-lasting seal.

Using a small amount of gasket sealer, apply the new gaskets on the block and install the pump. Let the sealer briefly set up prior to installation to prevent the gaskets from slipping out of place. As seen in Photo 2, tighten the water pump mounting bolts slowly and evenly. Remember, aluminum has a higher thermal expansion rate than cast iron, so be careful not to overtighten. It's always best to follow the manufacturer's torque specs when possible. In addition to the water pump, we also decided to purchase an aftermarket aluminum deep-groove pulley. These work great for positive belt retention in high-performance engines, and they save weight.

The rest of the reassembly is self-explanatory—just reverse your steps to complete. If you have any questions regarding the finishing procedures (setting fan belt tension, properly refilling the radiator, thermostat placement, etc.), refer to the appropriate projects in this book.

Installing a New Fan and Fan Belt

Time: 1 hour

Tools: Standard socket set, standard wrenches, long screwdriver or pry bar

Talent:

Applicable years: All

Cost: $40–$70

Parts: Replacement or aftermarket engine fan, aftermarket fan spacer (if needed), fan belt

Tip: Always be careful of loose clothing, jewelry, or hair when working around engine fans. Keep an eye out for any loose wiring as well.

PERFORMANCE GAIN: Increased airflow and cooling capacity, horsepower gains from lack of drag on the engine at high rpm

COMPLEMENTARY PROJECTS:
Installing deep-groove engine pulleys;
Project 56: Installing a New Radiator and Hoses

The new fan is made of heavy-duty steel with lightweight stainless blades to allow for flexing out at high engine speeds.

ENGINE (BOTTOM END)

Although many complain of the power loss and drag created by engine fans, they are highly necessary in just about every application. Some enthusiasts swear by the rigid, fixed-blade stock fans. Some prefer thermal and nonthermal clutch-type fans. And others exclusively use high-speed flex fans for their cooling needs. The possibilities are endless. It's just a matter of finding the right combination of components that will complement your engine and meet its cooling requirements, and that's the hard part.

Before running down to your local parts house and buying whatever is hanging on the wall, spend a little time researching different fans and their characteristics. Call the technical support hotlines of the manufacturers. Tell them what you have and what you are looking for. The more

information you obtain on the subject, the better equipped you will be to make the right selection for your engine.

We decided to swap out our old stock-style fan with a new 18-inch heavy-duty flex fan from Flex-a-lite. These fans are designed with a greater blade pitch to move more air faster at low-rpm speeds. Since the car is often used in daily driving situations in city and freeway traffic, we figured it would be a good investment for the cooling system. In addition to the increased low-speed flow, the fan blades literally flatten out at higher rpm, reducing the overall drag on the motor.

Due to tight clearances between the front of the fan and the radiator, it may be necessary to first remove the radiator and its shroud in order to access the fan. Trying to pull a tightly nestled fan without removing the radiator can prove to

While prying the alternator up into position, tighten the bracket bolt with your other hand to set the load on the belt.

be bloody brutal on the fingers and knuckles. Those fins are sharp, and there's no escaping them. If you have to do it without removing the radiator, wear protective gloves.

All engine fans are secured to the front flange of the water pump by long-shaft bolts that tie the fan clutch (if applicable), the fan, the pulley, and the water pump together. Priority one is to loosen and remove the four bolts from the front of the fan. You can now access the fan belt directly. To release the tension from the belt, loosen the alternator's slide bracket adjusting bolt. Removal is not necessary—back the bolt out just enough to push the body of the alternator toward the center of the engine. This will give the belt plenty of slack to be removed from the water pump and crankshaft pulleys.

With so many different manufacturers and endless part numbers, the best bet for correct belt replacement is to use what you know will work. In other words, don't throw out your old one just yet. Take it with you to the parts store and have them match it up. That way, there are no surprises and everything goes back together the way it should.

To install, slip the new rubber (right side up) over the pulleys and grab your biggest, meanest screwdriver. A thin pry

bar will also work. Leverage the bar under the alternator and force it to slide up and outward (opposite of the way it was loosened). When the alternator is back in position, tighten the slide bracket adjusting bolt to hold it in place. Check for proper tension by depressing the belt midway between the two pulleys. The belt should deflect about 1/2 inch if the distance between the pulleys is 12 to 16 inches, or 1/4 inch if the distance is between 6 and 10 inches.

Depending on the type of fan you select, the mounting procedure may vary slightly. In certain cases, aftermarket spacers are needed to position the fans closer to the core of the radiator. Regardless, the fan will mount into the front flange of the water pump as before. Hardware should be included with most fan kits. Make sure you tighten everything down snugly. The motor produces intense and constant vibration and can cause bolts to loosen and back out if not sufficiently tightened. Double-check any tight clearances around the fan and the shroud before turning the engine over.

At this time, start the engine and check for any slippage in the belt(s). If it screeches when you fire the ignition, it is too loose and needs to be adjusted.

Removing and Replacing the Harmonic Balancer/Damper

 Time: 30 minutes

 Tools: Harmonic balancer puller, adjustable wrench, balancer installer, torque wrench, timing tape (optional), clean engine oil

 Talent:

 Applicable years: All

 Cost: $75–$300 (new balancer), $25–$75 for tools

 Parts: New harmonic balancer

 Tip: Although most specialty tools can be rented these days, damper pullers and installers are essential to engine building and should definitely be added to the tool collection.

 PERFORMANCE GAIN: Excessive engine vibration can be a silent killer. It can rob plenty of precious horsepower as well. High-performance balancers/dampers constantly fight the evils of these vibrations and keep the moving parts of your engine running smoothly and in harmony.

COMPLEMENTARY PROJECTS:

Replacing the timing cover; Project 45: Removing and Replacing the Timing Chain

The balancer removal tool is an absolute must.

Harmonic balancers and dampers are designed to minimize and control the intense vibrations generated from the engine and the crankshaft. The balancer is installed directly onto the front snout of the crank through the timing cover. Over the life of your engine, harsh vibrations can destroy bearings, seals, and even the crank itself. Having the right balancer on your engine is essential to increasing its longevity and performance.

Changing your harmonic balancer is an easy project. However, when not equipped with the proper tools, it can be a real nightmare. The first thing to do is purchase both a damper remover (harmonic balancer puller) and an installation tool. This will simplify life tremendously and produce the best results.

Whether you plan on tackling the project with the engine in or out of the car, the approach is basically the same. Starting with the accessories, loosen and remove the fan and pulley assembly from the water pump. Although not totally necessary, this allows a little more room to access the crank pulley and the balancer. The belt must be removed regardless. The crankshaft pulley is the next to go. Back out the mounting bolts from the balancer and set them aside, along with the pulley. On some early model vehicles, the balancer/damper is press-fitted onto the front of the crankshaft without a retaining bolt and can be removed directly with the proper tool. However, if there is a damper retaining bolt, it must first be loosened in order to free the balancer. If the bolt is too tight to break loose without spinning the engine, apply a liberal amount of penetrating oil to the bolt and allow it to soak for a few minutes. If this doesn't do the trick, there are other devices

Once the tool is installed on the damper, drive the floating shaft into the snout of the crankshaft.

Notice the key on the shaft of the crank that mates to the inner housing of the balancer.

and tools with which to lock the crankshaft or flywheel in place while removing the bolt.

With that out of the way, let's proceed to the balancer. Using the removal tool is simple and very effective. It attaches to the front of the damper using the same mounting holes as the crankshaft pulley. The four-slot design of the yoke will work with both two- or three-hole applications. As you turn the threaded shaft through the center of the yoke and into the snout of the crank, you will slowly and evenly pull the balancer off the shaft.

After the balancer is removed, you will notice the grooved key slot in the hub for proper installation on the crankshaft. Also pay attention to the surfaces of the mating parts. The inner area of the hub and the outer area of the crank could have built-up corrosion on them, making the job a lot harder

than it has to be. If corrosion is detected, brush over the surface with steel wool and moderately lubricate with clean engine oil.

To install, the procedure is really not much different. However, you will use a separate installation tool this time around. Before installing the balancer, lightly coat the back of the unit that will be in contact with the front timing cover seal with clean engine oil. Align the grooved slot with the key on the crank and slide the balancer onto the shaft. Do not hammer the balancer into position. The installation tool will slowly draw the hub down the shaft, similar to the removal process. The damper retaining bolt may also help in positioning the unit. Once the hub is fully seated, tighten and torque the retaining bolt to the manufacturer's specifications and reinstall the pulley.

PROJECT 45
Removing and Replacing the Timing Chain

 Time: 3 hours

 Tools: Standard socket set, standard wrenches, crankshaft socket, breaker bar, gasket sealer, torque wrench, clean engine oil

 Talent: 🔧🔧🔧

 Applicable years: All

 Cost: $75 (chain and gaskets)

 Parts: New timing chain, timing cover gasket

 Tip: Before getting started, check the clearance between the oil pan and the crossmember to see if there's enough room to remove the pan while the engine is in the car.

⚠ PERFORMANCE GAIN: Consistent performance and reliability

COMPLEMENTARY PROJECTS:

Installing a new timing cover and seal; replacing the oil pan gasket; Project 46: Installing a Camshaft and Lifters

After removing the timing cover bolts, gently pry the sides of the cover to release it from the block.

Although replacing the timing chain in itself is a simple task, the multitude of steps one must take to access this area of the engine can be quite involved. If the engine is already out of the car and perched nicely on an engine stand, most of the dirty work is done. However, if it's necessary to perform the deed with the engine still in its cradle, the job may be slightly more challenging, but don't be discouraged. This is how we all learn, right?

We first need to access the timing cover. That means all accessories blocking the path to the cover and chain must go. Remove all braces, brackets, and hoses that may interfere as well. The more room you allow yourself, the better. Be sure to fully drain the cooling system prior to removing the water pump, thermostat housing, and any cooling lines. You may find it beneficial to pull the radiator for extra clearance, too.

With the front of the engine disassembled, move down below to the oil pan. The timing cover is designed in such a way that it requires the removal of the oil pan to replace. Raise and securely support the car with a pair of jack stands. Drain the engine of its oil and remove the pan. Depending on the type of oil pan used and the clearance between it and the crossmember, you may not be able to remove the pan entirely without loosening the engine mounts and slightly hoisting the engine. If this is the case, you should consider pulling the engine out completely. True, it's a little more work than you may have expected, but it makes the project a lot easier and cleaner once the engine is out. Besides, there's always plenty of other stuff you can accomplish when the engine is sitting on a stand. Either way, the pan needs to come off.

Using the proper removal tool, loosen and remove the pulley and the harmonic balancer from the front of the

Loosen and remove the oil pan for complete access to the timing cover.

Using a crankshaft socket and a breaker bar, spin the engine in proper rotation to align the timing marks on the two sprockets.

crankshaft. You should now have full access to the timing cover. The cover is secured to the engine block by a series of small, 1/4-inch-20 bolts. Remove the bolts and the timing pointer, if separate. The cover will most likely be stuck to the block by old gasket material and sludge. Gently pry the sides of the cover with a screwdriver or similar instrument.

With the cover removed, examine the location of the upper and lower sprockets in relation to each other. Using a crankshaft socket and breaker bar, turn the engine over by hand in the direction of rotation. Align the timing marks on both sprockets to face one another (see photo 4). When the sprockets are in this position, the Number 6 cylinder is at TDC. To achieve TDC of the Number 1 cylinder, simply turn the crankshaft one full revolution. The camshaft timing mark will now be at the top of the sprocket. In reference to the marks, there will be a small circle machined on the surface of

The two marks should be facing each other prior to removing the sprockets or chain.

each sprocket. Remove the bolts attaching the upper sprocket to the camshaft. This will allow you to slide the sprocket away from the cam and release the tension on the chain. They can now both be removed from the engine.

While the timing cover and chain assembly is dismantled, consider replacing any additional components that may be problematic or on their way to failure. Common replacements may include a timing cover oil seal or even a new timing cover assembly. The front oil seal is well known for its leaky tendencies and can be damaged, torn, or become corroded quite easily. The seals are cheap and take no time at all to replace. Using a small screwdriver or pry bar, carefully remove the oil seal from the timing cover. Clean out the inner lip of the cover to ensure a clean, leak-free seal. To install, first support the underside of

the cover to prevent warping or damage. Lubricate the new seal with clean engine oil and place it into position. The open end of the seal should be facing the inside of the timing cover. Carefully drive the new seal into the cover using the proper installation tool.

Timing covers themselves can often be the culprit behind a nasty oil leak. Most factory timing covers were made of stamped steel. Although they are superior to the aftermarket stamped steel pieces you find today, they still have their weaknesses. The thin, outer flange on a stamped steel cover bends and distorts when you tighten the cover bolts. This causes the underlying gasket to "walk" around on the surface and possibly break, guaranteeing oil leakage. Fortunately, there are plenty of quality aftermarket aluminum timing covers to prevent such messes. Most are machined with thick, rigid flanges that will not flex under load and provide deep channels for the gaskets to fully seat and seal.

To reinstall the chain and sprocket assembly, first make sure the crankshaft timing mark is facing upward at the top of the sprocket. Insert the new chain on the camshaft sprocket with timing mark facing downward at the bottom. Slip the chain underneath the crank sprocket while positioning the upper cam sprocket at the end of the camshaft. Make sure the marks are aligned, once again facing each other. Insert the upper sprocket bolts and tighten to manufacturers' specs.

Prior to reinstalling the cover, thoroughly clean the mating surfaces of all old gasket material and residue. Apply the new gasket to the block with a small amount of sealer on both sides. Proceed to install the cover and the mounting bolts. If you removed the oil pan completely, use a new gasket. I highly recommend one-piece rubber oil pan gaskets. They seal far better than the conventional cork gaskets with bridge seals. They may not be available for all applications, but it's worth checking into. Install the new gasket and the oil pan, and refill the crankcase. Be sure to fill the cooling system as well with new or clean fluid.

First, remove the mounting bolts of the sprocket to loosen and disengage the chain.

PROJECT 46
Installing a Camshaft and Lifters

Time: 3 hours

Tools: Standard socket set, standard wrenches, assembly lube, thread locker

Talent:

Applicable years: All

Cost: $175–$600 for cam and lifters; up to $800 for a complete kit

Parts: Cam and lifters

Tip: When reinstalling the camshaft sprocket and bolts, apply a small amount of thread locker to the threads to help secure everything in place.

PERFORMANCE GAIN: Camshaft upgrades yield big power increases. When applied as a total package, the results are awesome!

COMPLEMENTARY PROJECTS:

Project 33: Installing New Valve Springs, Locks, and Retainers; Project 34: Installing Roller Rockers and Poly Locks; Project 35: Selecting and Installing Pushrods; Project 45: Removing and Replacing the Timing Chain

Installing a high-performance camshaft is one of the most drastic power improvements you can make to your engine. The cam is like the heartbeat of the motor. Its unique design is machine-ground to fit and perform in a very concise and calculated manner. Manufacturers spend countless hours researching and developing specific profiles to work in just about every application imaginable. Many offer complete camshaft packages that include lifters, valve springs, and timing chain assemblies. This is done with very good reason.

Changing the profile of your camshaft will directly alter each individual component of the valvetrain and the geometry of the moving parts.

Most aftermarket cams have a substantially greater lift than a factory-ground cam. This puts added pressure on the valve springs and can lead to "coil-bind" before the cam reaches full lift. Therefore, it is crucial to thoroughly research your camshaft prior to purchasing or installing. Coil-bind of the springs can be checked by inserting a feeler gauge between the coils when the valve is at full lift. You should read a minimum of 0.050 inch. Typically, the cam manufacturer will recommend a specific valve spring to work in unison with the cam to prevent such problems.

Camshaft selection should be practical in every sense. It's easy to get carried away with high duration numbers and giant lift. Who doesn't want more horsepower? However, unless the rest of the motor is engineered specifically for those radical components, you are wasting your time and your money. In fact, mating a high-horsepower camshaft with a lesser valvetrain can result in significant power loss and poor drivability. The best approach is to map out a plan according to your needs. Select the parts that will work cohesively with your existing setup. If necessary, contact the camshaft manufacturer and explain in detail the specifics of your engine, the application, and your desired gains.

Removal of the camshaft is rather simple. Whether you choose to perform the swap with the engine in or out of the car, the process is basically the same. First, remove any and all pieces that block or restrict access to the timing cover and the intake manifold. The valve covers should be pulled off as well. Loosen and remove the rocker arms and pushrods from the cylinder heads. Unbolt the intake manifold and remove the lifters from the valley. If you plan on reusing the same cam and lifters again, mark the lifters in relation to their designated bores. The two must be installed and operated in the exact same order and fashion. The top lobes of the camshaft are now visible through the lifter bores in the engine block. This will serve as a visual guide in removing and installing the cam.

The timing cover and chain are the next to go. Prior to removal, you must first align the upper and lower timing marks on the sprockets. The smaller crankshaft sprocket will be facing upward at 12 o'clock. The larger cam sprocket will be facing down at 6 o'clock. This ensures the Number 1 cylinder is in position at top dead center (TDC). Remove the upper sprocket bolts and the timing chain. The bolts or sprocket may be reinstalled to the front of the camshaft to aid in the removal. Gently roll the camshaft out of the engine block. Excessive force is not required. If the shaft does not move or slide freely, stop and check for any obstructions. Do NOT force it—you could very easily damage the cam bearing journals.

Once removed, inspect the old camshaft for any signs of unusual wear or scarring. This will be a good indication of the

ENGINE (BOTTOM END)

Pull the lifters up and out of their bores in the valley.

Slowly turn and roll the camshaft through the bearing journals and out of the engine block.

condition of the remaining parts. The new camshaft can now be installed. Coat the distributor gear and each lobe of the cam with the supplied assembly lube. Coat the cam bearing journals with clean engine oil. Reinstall the cam sprocket or bolts to the front of the new shaft and slowly roll it into position in the engine block. Be careful not to allow the assembly lube to be wiped off during the process. At this point, you may want to consider the replacement of the timing chain and sprockets if needed. Position the sprockets to once again face

each other (timing marks). Reattach the chain and tighten the cam bolts to the proper torque specs. Install the new lifters into the bores and insert the pushrods. Assemble the remainder of the engine and set the required valve lash or lifter preload.

Installing a new cam takes a lot of planning and blueprinting. Every situation is a little different. Take the time to check for proper piston-to-valve clearance, rocker arm and pushrod geometry, and valve spring heights and pressures before firing the engine.

Removing and Replacing the Engine

 Time: 3–5 hours

 Tools: Standard socket set, standard wrenches, engine hoist, engine stand or cradle, floor jack (if needed), heavy-duty chain and/or lifting plate

 Talent:

 Applicable years: All

 Cost: If renting an engine hoist, $40 per day

 Parts: n/a

 Tip: If you pull the engine and transmission out together as one unit, invest in a transmission tail plug to avoid trans fluid pouring out the rear of the case during removal.

PERFORMANCE GAIN: Hopefully, you're pulling the engine to either freshen up what you have or to stuff a monster, fire-breathing big block in its place.

COMPLEMENTARY PROJECTS:

Replacing the engine mounts; repainting the engine compartment; Project 62: Removing and Installing the Flywheel/Flexplate; Project 98: Painting the Engine

Pulling the motor out of a car is something every car builder or mechanic must do. It's a rite of passage. It clearly shows that you are serious about the performance of your vehicle. For whatever reason, the time has come for you to uproot the powerplant and seek alternatives. It can be intimidating for the novice, but if you take it slow and make a sound game plan, you will find there is nothing to it.

To perform the swap with ease, you will need space. The engine hoist is not exactly petite and requires plenty of open floor room to move around. It always helps to have an extra set of hands for this project. Although you can do it by yourself, it really is a two-man job, especially if it's your first time. If you don't currently own a hoist, you can rent one from any tool rental company or parts store for about 40 bucks. Most are collapsible and easy to transport in a pickup. This is not something you will use every day in the garage, so renting is really not a bad option and saves you the storage space at home. An engine stand, on the other hand, is something you should definitely consider buying for yourself. Once the engine is out of the car, it needs to go somewhere. Whether for storage or rebuilding, engine stands serve as perfect, mobile alternatives to an old tire sitting on the floor. And they're cheap! You can spend $50 on a quality, 1-ton engine stand that lasts forever.

As you can imagine, there are quite a few preliminary steps to take before the engine can actually go anywhere. Some people prefer pulling the transmission out with the engine, regardless of the situation or the cause. They feel it's easier to remove and replace as one complete unit than it is to align the engine to the frame and to the transmission bell housing all at the same time. I would have to agree. The transmission is a good centering point in the assembly and helps balance the weight of the engine on the hoist. The engine is mounted to the frame with a rubber mount on both sides of the block. The only rear support it receives comes from the transmission mount at the rear crossmember. Therefore, that rear mount naturally centers the engine where it needs to be in relation to the frame. It takes a little pushing and shoving to get things just right, but that's normal. It really comes down to a matter of preference and what you feel comfortable with. You can do it either way without too much hassle.

First, disconnect the battery and completely drain the cooling system. Not only will this reduce the overall weight on the hoist, but it will also make the removal process much cleaner without spills. Remove the front engine accessories, such as the alternator, power steering pump, water pump, and AC unit, as well as their various brackets and pulleys. Detach the fuel line at the fuel pump and clamp it off. Keep track of and label the hardware for each component. It may be a long time before everything is actually reassembled.

Moving to the top of the engine, remove the carburetor and the air cleaner assembly and all attaching hoses and brackets. Disconnect the throttle linkage from the firewall and set it aside. Remove the distributor, ignition coil, and the plug wires. You want the engine to be as short as possible to allow for maximum lifting clearance under the hood. If you have a high-rise intake manifold, pull it off. You can use the manifold holes in the cylinder heads to chain the engine and pull it out. Be sure to disconnect any wiring harness connectors, temperature sensors, and oil pressure fittings from the manifold, cylinder heads, and engine block.

On four-speed cars, disengage the clutch linkage from the ball stud coming out of the engine block. Remove the springs,

We chose two opposite intake manifold holes in which to chain and harness the engine.

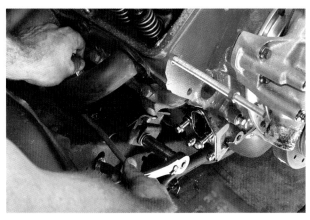

Using a boxed wrench and a socket, loosen and remove the two engine mount bolts.

The idea is to slowly lift the engine and roll the hoist back, allowing it to exit and swing out over the front of the fender.

rods, and the Z-bar assembly. If you choose to remove the transmission along with the engine, unbolt the shifter and the shifter handle. The same applies for automatics. Any obstructing floor or column shift linkage should be removed.

Engine compartment space will vary for each car. Some will require the removal of the radiator, spark plugs, exhaust manifolds, starter assembly, and headers. In fact, aftermarket headers can prove to be a real pain in this situation. You may need to disconnect them at the collector as well as the cylinder head and allow them to move freely as you pull the engine up and out. This is where the extra set of hands comes into play. For some vehicles and engines, hood removal may be required.

If the transmission is staying in the car, unbolt the bell housing from the back of the block and support the front of the transmission with a floor jack. On automatic-equipped vehicles, you will need to remove the torque converter from the flexplate. Be sure to note their relation to each other before unbolting the converter. Automatic transmission cooler lines should also be disengaged. If you decide on the shoehorn method, unbolt the transmission from the mount at the crossmember. Use the floor jack to support the transmission until

it is lifted out. Disconnect the speedometer cable from the side of the transmission and pin it back out of the way. It may be necessary to loosen and remove the rear crossmember once the transmission is unbolted for added clearance.

Unbolt the motor mounts from their frame brackets and secure the engine with heavy-duty chain and hardware. Try to pick two symmetrical points on the motor to help balance the weight, once it's in the air. If necessary, use a floor jack to lift the engine up to meet the hoist in order to minimize any unwanted swag in the chain. Attach the hook of the hoist to the center of the chain and slowly bring it up. Have a friend watch and guide the rear of the engine and/or transmission as it comes up and out of the engine bay.

Lower the assembly to a safe working area and remove the transmission and/or the remaining components. Attach the mounting brace of the engine stand to the back of the block and slide the brace into the stand. You can now lower the hoist and remove the chain.

Although it sounds like a lot, it's really not that difficult— one time, and you've got it down. The installation is essentially the same in reverse. Take your time, be careful, and have fun.

PROJECT 48

Installing a New Oil Pump and Pan

 Time: 1 hour

 Tools: Standard socket set, standard wrenches, long screwdriver or pry bar, gasket scraper, torque wrench

 Talent: ▮▮

 Applicable years: All

 Cost: $50 for pump, $50–$250 for pan

 Parts: Pan and pump, oil pan gasket, gasket sealer

 Tip: When working with an engine on a stand, make sure it's on a flat, level surface and the rotation lock pin is in place.

 PERFORMANCE GAIN: Swapping on a high-volume oil pump and an aftermarket pan can produce a 10- to 15- horsepower gain on some engines.

COMPLEMENTARY PROJECTS: Project 45: Removing and Replacing the Timing Chain

A mere afterthought to most, the lower oiling system is crucial to the strength and longevity of any high-performance engine. The oil pump, in particular, is responsible for providing adequate lubrication to all moving parts inside the engine as well as maintaining consistent pressure throughout its operating range. If any one part in the system fails, the results can be catastrophic.

As you might have guessed, you're going to need the engine out of the chassis and mounted on a 360-degree engine stand. That way, you can easily turn the motor upside down and access the pan and pump. Make sure you completely drain all engine oil from both the crankcase and the filter. The cooling system should be dry as well. With the motor rotated 180 degrees and secured in place with the engine stand lock pin, unbolt the oil pan from the block. You may need a little help from a rubber mallet or pry bar to separate the two surfaces. Remove the pan and set it aside along with the hardware.

At this point, the oil pump is right on top and ready for removal. Unbolt the pump at the base where it mounts to the rear main bearing cap. There may be dowels in the cap to locate and secure the pump. (See arrows, Photo 1.) The pump should disengage from the driveshaft and lift cleanly off. Remove the driveshaft and inspect for any unusual wear or damage.

To remove the oil pump, loosen the bolt that connects the pump base to the rear main bearing cap.

127

Align the pump to the inner tang on the shaft when reassembling.

The new pump will install in the same fashion. Be sure the upper end of the extension shaft is fully mated to the lower end of the distributor driveshaft when reassembling. The oil pump must also align with the tang on the lower end of the extension shaft. (See photo 2.) Once the new pump is in place, tighten the mounting bolt to the proper spec.

Before reinstalling the pan, clean the mating surface of the block with a gasket scraper and engine degreaser. Oil leaks (commonly from the pan) can make your driveway a mess and drive you crazy. Make sure everything is clean and dry before applying the new gasket. The heavy-duty, one-piece oil pan gaskets work great if you can find them for your application. If not, use a quality gasket sealer to help with the bridge seals and in the corners.

Contrary to popular belief, all oil pans are not created equal. Most factory-style pans are made of thin stamped steel that will distort or warp from tightening or overtightening the oil pan bolts. They are somewhat limited on oil capacity, too. If you run a serious, high-performance mill, consider an aftermarket deep-sump pan with internal baffling and a screened windage tray. These designs offer rapid oil return to the sump without the power-robbing splash-back effect. Often, the lower rotating assembly will sling the oil against the solid, factory-style tray and cause the oil to bounce back into the moving parts, ultimately losing power. Deep-sump pans are not exactly cheap, but they are well worth the extra insurance and horsepower. Reinstall the pan and tighten the bolts down evenly in stages.

PROJECT 49
Removing and Replacing the Crankshaft and Main Bearings

 Time: 2 hours

 Tools: Standard socket set, crankshaft socket, breaker bar, feeler gauge, torque wrench

 Talent: ♦♦♦♦

 Applicable years: All

 Cost: $50 for bearings and supplies

 Parts: Replacement main bearings, Plastigage

 Tip: If you plan to remove the crankshaft while leaving the rod and piston assemblies in the bores, attach a rubber band to a bolt on each rod and to a reinstalled oil pan bolt. This will keep the rods off to the side and prevent them from banging into the block when pulling the crank out.

PERFORMANCE GAIN: A stronger, longer-lasting bottom end

COMPLEMENTARY PROJECTS: Project 50: Removing and Replacing the Connecting Rods and Rod Bearings; Project 51: Installing New Pistons and Piston Rings

The process of removing the crankshaft and replacing the main bearings is very similar to that of the connecting rods and rod bearings. Although it may be possible in some applications to do so with the engine still in the vehicle, I do not recommend it. It's best to have the engine out of the chassis in a clean and well-organized working environment.

The oil pan and pump must first be removed to access the crankshaft and the main bearing housings. Follow the procedures listed in Project 50 on the disassembly and removal of the connecting rods and their bearing caps. With the rods out of the way, start by unbolting the main bearing caps from the engine block. Depending on the design of the block, there will

Start by removing the main bearing caps from the cylinder block.

129

Underneath the rear cap, you will find both the rear main oil seal (shown at right in the typical two-piece version) and the crankshaft thrust bearing (left).

The crank can now be hoisted from the engine block and the upper main bearings removed from their saddles.

be two or four bolts per main cap. The four-bolt blocks were used in most factory special high-performance engines for extra strength and rigidity. Be sure to mark the location and direction of the main caps prior to removing the crankshaft. Also note the position of the keyway in the crank so it may be installed in the same orientation.

Like rod bearings, the main crankshaft bearings consist of two halves, or shells—one in the recess of the cap, and one in the block. When properly tightened, the two halves come together to create a seamless casing around the crankshaft journal. Check both the upper and lower halves of the bearings for any irregular wear or scoring. Always replace the two shells together, even if one side still appears to be in good shape. For the proper gauging procedure of the main bearings, again refer to Project 50 and follow the steps described. Once the bearings have been installed, recheck all clearances. Spin the crank by hand to check for any excessive drag in the rotation. Torque all of the main bearing caps to the proper specification, excluding the thrust bearing cap.

On a typical small-block Chevy, the thrust bearing is located under the Number 5 main bearing cap (the furthermost rear cap). This bearing is designed to handle and minimize forward-thrusting loads coming up from the transmission. High plate pressures and thrust of the torque converter often cause the deterioration and failure of the thrust bearing, especially in high-performance applications.

To align the thrust bearing and the crankshaft end play, first hand tighten the thrust bearing bolts at the rear main cap. Using a clean pry bar, pry the crankshaft to its extreme rearward travel. Follow this by prying the crank to its extreme forward travel. This is to ensure the upper and lower thrust bearing surfaces are fully seated and aligned with each other. With the crankshaft still in the extreme forward position, tighten and torque the cap to the proper spec. To check the crank's end play, measure the gap between the lip of the crankshaft and the front of the rear main bearing with a feeler gauge. End play may also be measured at the thrust bearing. Acceptable tolerances generally range between 0.003 and 0.010 inch.

130

Removing and Replacing the Connecting Rods and Rod Bearings

 Time: 3 hours

 Tools: Standard socket set, rubber mallet, crankshaft socket, breaker bar, feeler gauge, torque wrench

 Talent:

 Applicable years: All

 Cost: $50 for bearings and supplies

 Parts: Quality set of rod bearings, Plastigage, 3/8-inch rubber hose

 Tip: To avoid scratching or damaging the cylinder walls when removing or installing the piston and rod assemblies, cut two short lengths of 3/8-inch hose and slide it over the rod bolts.

 PERFORMANCE GAIN: Smooth, reliable operation from the lower rotating assembly

COMPLEMENTARY PROJECTS:

Project 48: Installing a New Oil Pump and Pan;

Project 51: Installing New Pistons and Piston Rings

Rebuilding an engine takes time, patience, attention to detail, and plenty of room. The first thing you need to do is clear out some space in the garage, enabling you to work in an efficient and orderly manner. At this point in the game, organization is everything. There are too many small parts to label and keep track of to work in a messy shop.

First, the engine needs to be thoroughly degreased and mounted on a sturdy, rotation-style engine stand to allow for easy access to the lower rotating assembly. Before flipping it over, however, the intake manifold and cylinder heads should be removed from the top of the engine. Remember to drain the engine oil prior to disassembly. Slowly turn the engine block over so the oil pan is facing upward. Remove the retaining bolts and the pan, and label the hardware. In addition to the oil pan, disengage the oil pump and extension shaft, and set them aside for added clearance. You now have a clear shot at the connecting rods and their caps. The rods are attached to the crankshaft by two bolts and a cap. Grooved inside both the connecting rod and the cap is a precisely machined bearing. The bearing rides directly on the surface of the crank, reducing friction and minimizing wear.

Before removing any components from the rotating assembly, stamp and label the parts in relation to each other to simplify the installation process and guarantee proper fit. Mark the connecting rod cap for each cylinder to its respective rod with a scribe. Each cap must be reinstalled on the correct rod in the correct direction. Loosen and remove the rod bearing cap and the rod bearing.

With the caps and bearings removed, slide the rods and pistons out of the cylinder bores. Coat the cylinder walls with clean engine oil to protect the inner surfaces and ease the pistons out. It may be necessary to lightly tap the ends of the rods

With the oil pan removed, loosen the connecting rod caps from the crankshaft.

The connecting rod and its cap are stamped with the proper cylinder designation.

Once the nuts are removed, the rod bearing caps can be pulled off the crankshaft journal.

with a mallet to initiate the process. Once the rod and piston assembly is removed from the block, reconnect the proper cap and nuts. Again, label the rod and the piston in relation to its designated bore in the engine block.

Now, it's time to replace the rod bearings. The connecting rod bearings consist of two halves, or shells, that are interchangeable in both the rod and the cap. With the bearings in position, the ends will extend slightly beyond the rod and cap surfaces to ensure proper seating when tightened down.

It's important to closely inspect the bearings once the rods and caps have been removed. Any flaking or scoring in the surface indicates excessive wear, and the bearings should be replaced. Be sure to check for proper clearance on the crank journal as well. If the crank shows any signs of ridging or damage, the crank must be replaced or reground and fitted with undersize bearings.

The best way to check for the correct rod-to-crankshaft bearing clearance is to use Plastigage. After cleaning the bearing shell and the crank journal, place a piece of the gauging material lengthwise along the bottom center of the lower bearing shell. Install the cap with the shell, and torque the nuts to spec. Be careful not to turn the crank while the material is in the bearing. Upon removing the cap, the material will be flattened and stuck to either surface. Using the scale provided with the product, measure the material at its widest point (in thousandths of an inch). Check the manufacturer's specifications for the desired clearance for your engine. You may need to purchase undersize bearings in order to achieve the specified gap. When this is accomplished, reclean the journals and install the new bearings. Be sure to coat the bearings, the cylinder walls, and the crank journals with clean engine oil prior to reinstallation.

One at a time, insert the rod and piston assemblies back into the engine block. The direction of the piston, the rod, and the cap should be identical to the breakdown. The notch in the top surface of each piston should be facing the front of the engine when installed. The rod bearing caps should remain loosely fitted on the crank journal until all piston and rod assemblies have been installed. Finally, check the clearance between the sides of the rods and the crankshaft using a feeler gauge. Make sure everything is within factory recommended spec. Proceed to reinstall the oil pump and pan.

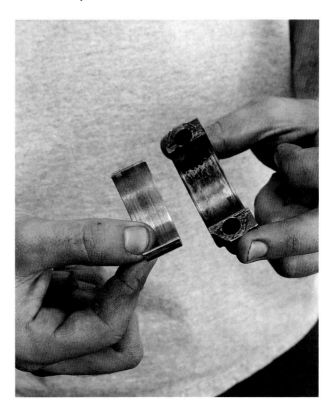

The bearing shell slips right into the recess of the cap.

132

PROJECT *51*

Installing New Pistons and Piston Rings

Time: 5 hours

Tools: Standard socket set, standard wrenches, breaker bar, crankshaft socket, piston ring expander and compressor, calipers (optional), micrometer (optional), snap ring pliers, feeler gauge, torque wrench

Talent:

Applicable years: All

Cost: $200–$500

Parts: Pistons and rings

Tip: Before removing the piston and rod assembly from the block, check the bore for any ridge in the surface that may worsen or damage other components in the process.

PERFORMANCE GAIN: Increasing your compression ratio with new pistons and rings will instantly boost the output of your engine.

COMPLEMENTARY PROJECTS:

Project 50: Removing and Replacing the Connecting Rods and Rod Bearings

Whether you are starting from scratch or merely rebuilding your existing engine, the removal and installation of the pistons and rings is inevitable. The piston assemblies are responsible for creating and maintaining the engine's compression. As the crankshaft turns in rotation, it forces the rod and piston assemblies through the cylinder bores to the top deck of the engine block. With both the intake and the exhaust valves closed, the tightly fitted piston travels upward and compresses the air/fuel mixture in the cylinder into the combustion area. In fact, if you ever wondered how to calculate the compression ratio, this is it: the cylinder volume with the piston at BDC (bottom dead center) versus the cylinder volume in the combustion area with the piston at TDC (top dead center) represents the cylinder's compression ratio. If the volume of the cylinder is 10 times the volume of the combustion area, your compression ratio would be 10:1.

Increasing the compression in the cylinders is a sure-fire way to boost your horsepower numbers. There are several approaches to raising compression, including piston selection, the size of the combustion chambers in the cylinder heads, engine block deck height, and cylinder head gasket thickness. However, changing any or all of these components will create a serious calamity in your engine if not handled and blueprinted properly.

The pistons are by far the first item on the list when it comes to increasing your engine's compression. There are seemingly countless piston designs available from aftermarket companies, all of which cater to exact applications. Your piston selection should depend on both the structural and performance needs of your motor. The idea is to find the set of pistons capable of raising your compression ratio as much as possible within the practical limits and boundaries of detonation. Keep in mind that alteration of other pieces may be necessary if the piston slugs are too radical. Although highly important, the pistons are just one piece in the puzzle of high performance.

The combustion chamber size of the cylinder heads is another vital piece to consider. The larger the combustion chamber, the more volume is added to the cylinder, which lowers the compression ratio. Conversely, smaller chamber sizes yield higher compression. On a typical 8.5:1 compression engine, replacing the stock 76-cc chambered cylinder heads with a pair of aftermarket 64-cc heads will raise the compression to 9.5:1. Milling the surface area of the cylinder head will also decrease combustion chamber sizes. The heads should be inspected by a machine shop to determine how much material can safely be removed. Small-chamber heads tend to restrict the use of large-diameter valves. If math is not your strong point, have a reputable shop thoroughly examine your clearances and discuss your options.

While you're at the machine shop, the deck height of the engine block in relation to the pistons at TDC should be checked and possibly resurfaced. Usually, blocks with a zero deck height yield the best results. Zero height simply means the pistons are flush with the deck of the block while in the TDC position. Again, by removing material and decreasing the size of the combustion area, you simultaneously increase the cylinder's compression. The amount of material that is

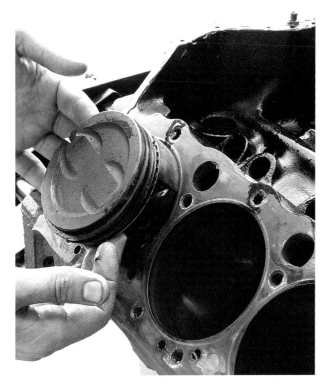

Carefully slide the piston and rod out of the cylinder as one assembly.

machine shop for the favor. Others are simply secured by snap rings, which are easily removed with a pair of snap ring pliers.

Prior to assembly or installation, check and set the piston ring end gap for the new rings. Using larger-than-required rings will dampen horsepower and lead to a shortened engine life. To set the proper gap, install the new rings one at a time into the cylinders with clean engine oil. Position the rings approximately 1 inch below the deck surface of the block. Measure the end gap of each ring with a feeler gauge and compare it to the recommended spec. Remove the rings from the cylinders and set the appropriate gap. Have this done by a machine shop for guaranteed accuracy; otherwise, you can do it yourself with a fine file and a bench vise.

Always follow the manufacturer's instructions on the correct order and procedure for installing the rings in the pistons. With the pistons assembled and reattached to the rods, thoroughly lubricate the piston rings and the wrist pins with clean engine oil before installing them into the block. Double-check the end gap location of the rings and carefully install the ring compressor over the assembly. Make sure the rings don't slip out of the grooves during the process. Slide the connecting rod into the bore and firmly seat the compressor against the deck. Using a rubber mallet or a hammer handle, slightly tap the piston down into the block. If you meet any resistance along the way, stop! Do not force it. Check for a ring that may have slipped out of its groove, or maybe the rod bolts are hitting the crank on the other end. Proceed slowly and guide the rod to its dedicated journal on the crankshaft. Repeat the steps for each cylinder and torque the rod bearing caps to spec. After each rod is reattached to the crank, rotate the assembly by hand using a torque wrench to measure the required force. Readings should not vary by more than 5 ft-lb per piston/rod assembly. Check for any unusual or excessive wearing on the walls of the cylinders.

available to remove will vary in each application. The main thing to consider is leaving enough material for proper piston-to-head and valve clearance. These measurements should include the compressed head gasket thickness.

A thicker head gasket will add volume and decrease the compression ratio, whereas a thinner gasket will increase it. Always measure the gasket in its fully compressed form. Most gasket manufacturers provide this data to help you in the selection prior to purchasing.

After you've selected your winning combination, it's time to get down to business. Refer to the connecting rod removal process (Project 50) to get the pistons safely out of the block. A piston ring expander is necessary to properly remove the rings from the slug. If the pistons are to be reused, carefully clean the grooves with the correct tool and wash with solvent. Do not use a wire brush or any type of acid to clean the pistons.

It is crucial to match the size of the pistons (new or old) with the cylinder bores. Using a micrometer or a telescoping gauge, measure the diameter of the cylinder bore at the piston wrist pin location (approximately 2.5 inches below the top of the deck). Secondly, measure the diameter of the piston perpendicular to the wrist pin. Clearance between the two should fall within factory or manufacturer's tolerance. Slightly boring the cylinders and the use of oversize pistons may be necessary to achieve the desired fit. If the difference does not require boring, finish honing of the cylinders is probably all that is needed.

Depending on the type of wrist pin, remove the pistons from the rods. Some engines utilize pistons with pressed-in pins, which must be removed with a press. Hit up your local

Removing and installing the piston rings requires the use of a ring expander.

PROJECT 52

Performing a Cylinder Leakdown Test

 Time: 1 hour

 Tools: Cylinder leakdown tester, standard socket set, standard wrenches, air compressor

  Talent:

 Applicable years: All

 Cost: $65

 Parts: n/a

 Tip: Chart the numbers of your leakdown testing every time the cylinders are checked. Periodically perform the same test to look for any signs of excess wear or failure.

PERFORMANCE GAIN: Increased combustion pressure and horsepower

COMPLEMENTARY PROJECTS: Project 26: Replacing the Distributor Coil, Cap, and Rotor; Project 55: Breaking in the Engine

The leakdown tester is an invaluable tool for maintaining consistent cylinder pressures in your engine.

It's important for every engine, stock or race, to fire and run on all cylinders. Although this may seem like a no-brainer, many are oblivious to the signs and effects of pressure loss in the cylinder bores. Pressure loss can be traced back to a number of different sources, including leakage past the valves, piston rings, or even the head gaskets. Whenever leaks are present in the system, the combustion pressure is naturally reduced. There is less force on the piston's stroke; therefore less power is created from the engine. It is possible for all cylinders to wear and leak evenly, but most of the time the problem lies with just one or two individual cylinders.

There are a couple different methods for checking the combustion pressure of the cylinders. The age-old approach to pressure testing is to remove each spark plug, one at a time, and insert a threaded gauge into the spark plug hole. As you spin the motor with the starter, the present pressure of that cylinder reads on the face of the gauge in psi. This may get you close or give you a rough idea of the pressure balance between the cylinders, but a more accurate, reliable alternative is to use a leakdown tester. As the name implies, a leakdown tester reads both the input pressure and the pressure loss in the cylinder. This is accomplished by feeding compressed air into the cylinder and measuring the percentage of loss. The tester is not able to determine the whereabouts of the leak, but at least it indicates the current state of affairs inside the cylinders.

Starting with the Number 1 cylinder, bring the piston up to the TDC location. Make sure the piston is on the upstroke so that the rings are fully seated in position. Remove the spark plug from the cylinder head and insert the threaded hose end into the open port. By removing only one plug at a time, you help prevent the compressed air from blowing the piston back down into the cylinder bore. The opposite end of the hose (male air fitting) attaches to the female air fitting on the body of the leakdown tester. The compressed air inlet line plugs into the air fitting at the pressure regulator. The regulator controls the amount of air that is forced into the cylinder through the spark plug opening.

The proper method used to load and read the cylinder pressure may vary between manufacturers, but by comparing the readings from the two different gauges, you will discover the percentage of blowby or loss found in that particular cylinder. Keep track of the pressures for each cylinder and repeat the process for the remaining bores. Be sure to locate each piston in the top dead center (TDC) location before initiating the leakdown.

Acceptable blowby or leakage in the cylinders depends on the type of engine. Race motors tend to yield extremely low levels of blowby due to the fact that they are rebuilt after every race. However, street engines have a much wider tolerance when it comes to acceptable levels of pressure loss. Anywhere from 6 to 14 percent blowby is common in most street-driven engines. Exceeding this mark (over 20 percent) shows significant signs of wear and possible failure of the piston rings or head gaskets. In addition, the cylinder-to-cylinder blowby percentage should fall in the range of 5 to 10 percent from one cylinder to another.

PROJECT 53
Installing Aftermarket Headers

Time: 3 hours

Tools: Standard socket set, standard wrenches, gasket scraper

Talent:

Applicable years: All

Cost: $100–$600

Parts: Set of application-correct headers, header and collector gaskets

Tip: After the installation, you may need to change your spark plug wires to accommodate the new headers. Although 90-degree boots are by far the most common, 135-degree or straight boots are sometimes necessary.

PERFORMANCE GAIN: Installing aftermarket headers and a free-flowing exhaust is the Number 1 external horsepower enhancer. You may see increases up to 30-plus horsepower.

COMPLEMENTARY PROJECTS:

Installing a performance muffler

Everyone is familiar with headers. They have been around since the beginning, and for good reason—the realistic horsepower gains from aftermarket headers can make a big difference in your vehicle's performance. When paired with a high-flow exhaust system, aftermarket headers will yield significant improvements in throttle response, acceleration, and fuel economy. They will cause other performance components such as intakes, carburetors, camshafts, and ignitions to reach their fullest potential as well.

Think of your engine as an oversized air pump. Naturally, the faster the air is able to flow through the pump, the more power it creates. Headers offer an improved and more efficient way to scavenge the exhaust gases and draw clean, fresh air into the cylinders. Headers are also designed to balance the pressures found between the intake and exhaust systems.

Unfortunately, just about every muscle car of the era rolled off the assembly line with a highly restrictive "pea-shooter" exhaust system. Stock cast-iron manifolds, small-diameter pipes, and a single outlet was the norm, even on some high-performance models. Therefore, installing aftermarket headers and a free-flow exhaust system is one of the most popular external engine upgrades.

When it comes to selecting headers and your new exhaust, think practical.

Primarily, you will be switching from a single pipe and exit system to a dual. Along with a cross-over tube or balance pipe, this will literally open up a world of difference in your engine's characteristics. Choose the headers that will most closely meet your driving and performance needs, not the biggest and loudest pipes you can stuff into your engine bay. A well-tuned, complete package is the key. Do not hesitate to call manufacturers' technical support lines and ask for advice. They are product specialists and can definitely steer you in the right direction.

Although many exhaust manufacturers now offer all-inclusive kits with pipes, clamps, and mufflers, your local muffler shop can handle the minor fabrication of the pipes and collectors. Be sure to request the use of aluminized tubing. Its corrosion resistance and longevity are far superior to the factory steel pieces. Mufflers are basically a matter of preference. From loud and crazy to sweet and low, there are seemingly endless options on the market today. Simply select the one that delivers your desired tone and flow.

Installing a pair of headers is never fun. With so many variables on each year, make, and model, the installation process fails to provide any regularity. In other words, be prepared to make adjustments. You will need the car in the air, on either a lift or a sturdy pair of jack stands. You may need to remove the hood for additional clearance. In some extreme cases, you may need to remove the engine from the chassis to fit the headers into position. You can install them from the top or the bottom of the car, wherever clearance allows.

First, loosen and remove the spark plugs and the exhaust manifold bolts from the cylinder heads. Disengage the bottom of the manifold from the collector pipe. Unbolt the muffler and its hanger from the rear of the vehicle and remove the exhaust pipe. Thoroughly clean the gasket-mating surface of the cylinder head before installing the new header gaskets. Paper header gaskets are often included with the headers, but they lack rigidity and are prone to breaking and leakage. Spend the extra money and purchase a set of quality, steel-reinforced gaskets. They will far outlast the paper gaskets and can be reused. Install the headers as necessary, and torque them to manufacturer's specs. Some headers will require slight

With the engine slightly hoisted, we first unbolt and remove the right side header from the top of the vehicle to allow extra clearance to maneuver the left header up and around the clutch linkage.

modifications to the primary tubes in order to clear suspension control arms, accessory brackets, and the frame of the vehicle. There are a number of ways to create the correct dimple in the headers without damaging them or compromising their structural integrity. First, test-fit the header, and mark the location of the needed dimple. Secure the header in a press or a bench-mounted vise, and carefully apply heat from a small propane torch. Squeeze the tube until the desired dimple is formed. This may also be accomplished with a steel bar and a hammer. Heat the tube and use the bar and hammer to create the extra clearance.

At the bottom end of each header is a collector-mounting flange that will mate the header to the collector and the exhaust pipes. The collector and the pipes, along with the mufflers, should be welded by a professional. After running the car, retighten the bolts periodically to guarantee a tight seal.

PROJECT 54
Oil Change and Correct Jacking Procedure

 Time: 45 minutes

 Tools: Floor jack, jack stands, socket or boxed wrench, oil filter wrench (optional), wheel chocks

 Talent:

 Applicable years: All

 Cost: Under $25

 Parts: Oil filter, engine oil

 Tip: If you plan on doing all of your own oil changes, purchase a catch basin and buy your oil by the case.

 PERFORMANCE GAIN: Prolonged engine life and reliability

COMPLEMENTARY PROJECTS:

Installing a magnetic-tip drain plug

Changing the oil is about the most important thing you can do for your muscle car, or any car for that matter. Oil is your vehicle's life blood. Without proper and regular oil changes, all the performance upgrades in the world won't mean a thing. There's one sure-fire way to ensure that your hot small block or your fire-breathin' big block keeps on rollin' year in and year out: CHANGE YOUR ENGINE OIL FREQUENTLY.

Maintaining fresh oil in your engine is critical because it reduces the amount of friction on the engine's internal moving metal components, preventing them from overheating. As time passes, motor oil loses its viscosity, breaking down and

Here we've used the floor jack directly underneath the front skid plate.

accumulating particles that will damage engine parts. We've all heard various intervals at which we should change our oil, but a good rule of thumb is the tried-and-true every 3,000–4,000 miles. Check your owner's manual; somewhere you'll probably find the words "change your engine oil more often if you operate your vehicle under severe driving conditions." You may think, "I don't drive my car under severe conditions!" Chances are, if you live in a major city or on dusty back roads, you are driving under severe conditions. If you drive in stop-and-go traffic day in and day out, shoot for the 3,000-mile mark instead of 4,000. With synthetic oils, you can safely stretch it another 1,000 or so before your time's up.

If you've never changed you engine oil yourself, you're in for a treat. It's very simple and, best of all, you'll never again have to wait in line at the local quick lube. Park your car on a flat, level surface (preferably your garage floor, out of the hot sun). It's best if the engine has been warmed up a little at first to allow the old oil to flow out of your oil pan more freely. Set the car in park, or in gear if you have a stick-shift. Set the emergency brake and make sure to turn the engine off. For added safety, use wheel chocks to block the rear wheels. Raise the front end of the car about 18 inches off the ground. Most do-it-yourselfers use a floor jack and a pair of jack stands or ramps to accomplish this. If you use ramps, make sure they are rated to carry the load of your particular vehicle. We place our jack stands directly under the vehicle, just behind the front wheels.

With the vehicle safely in the air, slide yourself under the oil pan. If you own a creeper, you'll save a lot of wear and tear on your clothes. With a catch basin in place to collect the old oil, remove the engine oil drain plug. Make sure you're

Place solid, high-quality jack stands under the front frame rails. If your car does not have frame rails at this location, there will be a solid flange or lip to place the jack under. If in doubt, check your owner's manual for correct jacking locations. Do not try to support the car's weight by positioning the jack stands under body cladding or ground effects.

directly under the engine. Further back is the transmission, and you don't want to drain that by mistake.

While the old oil is draining, check the threads on the drain plug. If the threads are stripped, you should replace it. If there's dirt and grime caked in the threads, take the time to wipe the plug clean with an old rag.

When the oil has almost stopped draining, take an oil filter wrench and remove the old filter. In this instance, the owner of the car has hand tightened the oil filter. If you choose to do this, make sure you tighten the filter as firmly as possible when replacing it. Be prepared for more oil to run out of the hole in the engine block where the filter was. Take some rags or paper towels with you when you slip under the car.

Once everything has drained, prep the new filter for use in your engine. Then, install the new oil filter. If you choose to muscle it in, tighten it securely. Otherwise, screw the filter in hand tight, then give it a 3/4 turn with the oil filter wrench. With an old shop rag, wipe the drain plug opening clean. Don't forget to reinstall the drain plug firmly with a socket wrench.

Add the fresh oil, get your car off those jack stands and take it for a drive—a mile or two will do. Then, check the oil level with the dip stick, and top off if necessary. Check under the car for any leaks. Double-check that you tightened the drain plug and the filter properly. After you change your oil a couple of times, you'll feel like an old pro. Just don't let your neighbors talk you into opening your own oil changing business!

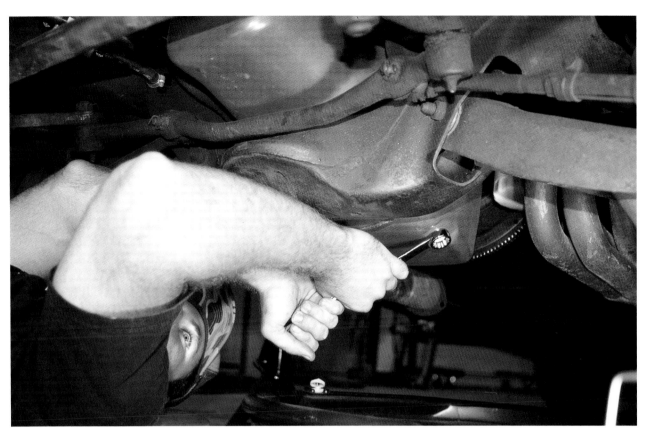

Above: Set the catch basin under the oil pan's drain plug, and remove the drain plug with a socket or boxed wrench. Take care not to "round" or strip the head of the drain plug.

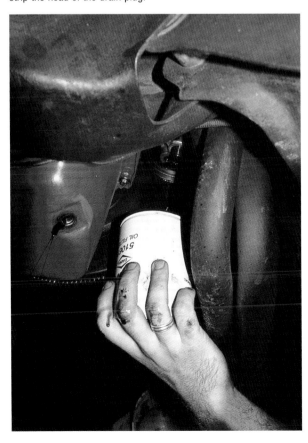

Remove the old filter. You can use an oil filter wrench or brute strength.

Right: Prepare the new filter by pouring a little oil in it and then rubbing a light film of oil around the filter gasket. Moistening the gasket helps create a good seal and prevents the filter from sticking to the engine block when the engine heats up.

Below: Refill the engine oil through the port in the valve cover. Use a funnel to avoid messing up your otherwise spotless engine. Be sure to check your engine's oil capacity first, making sure you have enough oil to do the job.

PROJECT 55

Breaking in the Engine

 Time: 2 hours

 Tools: Crankshaft socket, breaker bar, oil primer shaft, power drill

 Talent:

 Applicable years: All

 Cost: $50 for supplies

 Parts: Fresh engine oil and oil filter

 Tip: Use quality engine oil and filters that are well suited to your needs.

! PERFORMANCE GAIN: The correct break-in of an engine is just as important as its components and assembly. Without taking the necessary steps, the performance and longevity of your engine is severely compromised.

COMPLEMENTARY PROJECTS: Project 29: Adjusting and Setting the Timing (Initial and Mechanical Advance); Project 36: Setting Valve Lash

Now that you finally have your engine back together and ready for serious street/strip action, it's highly important to follow some basic guidelines to break it in smoothly. Many freshly built engines have been destroyed due to a lack of knowledge on properly firing and running a new engine.

After the engine is mounted back into the frame of the vehicle, add the required amount of oil to the crankcase. Refill the cooling system with clean fluid and water, and check for leaks as you go. Be sure all clamps and plugs are securely tightened before starting the engine and pressurizing the systems.

Setting the valves is next on the list and is a must to fire the engine. Refer to Project 36 for the play-by-play procedures. Once the valves and lifter preloads have been set, pressure-lube the engine with a power drill and a priming tool. The shaft of the distributor slips down inside the rear of the intake manifold and engages and drives the oil pump. The priming tool serves as a dummy distributor shaft and is rotated by the drill. If possible, have a friend rotate the engine by hand while priming the oil pump to ensure full coverage on the lower rotating assembly.

Next, locate the top dead center (TDC) position of the Number 1 cylinder. To determine the piston's location, remove the spark plug and cover the hole with the tip of your finger. Turn the engine by hand with a crankshaft socket and breaker bar until you feel air pressure at the opening. Continue to turn the crankshaft and align the timing marks on the harmonic balancer and timing tab at "zero." The Number 1 piston is now at TDC.

Install the intake manifold and distributor. With the Number 1 piston in position, mark the distributor housing at the Number 1 terminal. Remove the cap and line up the rotor with

your mark. You may need to slightly (and carefully) turn the gears of the oil pump with a long screwdriver to align the teeth of the pump and the distributor shaft. Loosely clamp the distributor housing to the manifold to allow for adjustments later. Install the plug wires to their dedicated terminals on the cap.

Place the carburetor and gasket onto the manifold and bolt them on. If the bowls of the carburetor are dry, use a small funnel to fill them. When the discharge nozzles squirt fuel down into the venturis, the carburetor is fully primed. Operate the throttle linkage by hand and check for any binding. Next, turn the idle mixture screws all the way inward (clockwise). Then turn them out (counterclockwise) 1.5 to 2 full turns to prevent a low idle when you first start the engine and ensure the fuel flow is sufficient. Plug all of the vacuum ports on the carburetor and the intake manifold and disconnect the vacuum advance line from the distributor.

With everything reconnected, it's time to run over the checklist. Inspect all fuel, water, and oil lines and their connections. Double-check the firing order of the engine and the supply of 12 volts in the starting system. When you are finally ready to execute the initial firing, have an assistant inside the car with the keys. You will want to watch for any problem under the hood. The engine should fire and run within a few revolutions.

Once the engine is running, vary the break-in rpm between 2,000 and 2,500 for about 20 to 30 minutes to properly run the camshaft in. You might need to roughly alter the ignition timing by hand at the distributor housing to find the smoothest operation. It's important not to let the engine idle during this time. Above-idle engine speeds splash oil on the new cam and provide

Having a great-looking and strong-performing engine comes from attention to detail.

the necessary lubrication for break-in. Reset the idle speed, idle mixture, and ignition timing for normal operation.

Now it's time to hit the road. Vary your engine speed and load for the first 20 to 30 miles, avoiding high-rpm accelerations. Moderate highway cruising is safe (55 to 65 miles per hour). Drive the next 500 miles normally, but without redlining the engine or subjecting it to heavy loads, such as climbing steep grades or towing. Change the oil and filter prior to and after the 500-mile break-in period to rid the engine of any assembly contaminants.

ENGINE COMPARTMENT

A clean and orderly engine compartment always sets off any classic car. The underhood area requires planning and organization to pull off correctly. These projects also tie into other systems of the powertrain and are helpful in any restoration.

Installing a New Radiator and Hoses

ENGINE COMPARTMENT

Time: 2 hours

Tools: Standard socket set, standard wrenches, flat-blade screwdriver, utility knife

Talent:

Applicable years: All

Cost: $250–$800, depending on radiator

Parts: New or re-cored radiator, upper and lower radiator hoses, new hose clamps (optional), new coolant/antifreeze (recommended), new radiator cap (recommended)

Tip: When installing a new radiator, don't forget about the cap. Use a cap with a built-in pressure-relief toggle valve at the top to bleed the system of any trapped air without removing the cap under pressure.

PERFORMANCE GAIN: A more efficient, reliable cooling system

COMPLEMENTARY PROJECTS:
Project 30: Installing a New Thermostat and Housing (Water Neck); Project 42: Installing a New Water Pump and Pulley; Project 57: Installing a Transmission Cooler

Along with the water pump, the radiator is one of the most vital components in the cooling system. Its primary function is to cool the passing fluid from the engine before circulating it back through the water/coolant passages in the engine block and cylinder heads. Often, crushed or clogged radiator fins create a block in the flow of coolant. When the radiator is unable to deliver the necessary volume of cooled fluid, the motor begins a rapid and fatal climb to boil. As fundamental as it is, we still seem to neglect this part of the cooling equation and just run the poor thing until it gives up and dies. Unfortunately, radiators don't like to go alone. In fact, they have a nasty habit of taking the whole system down with them.

Depending on the materials used in the construction of the radiator, prices can vary drastically. However, the function and design are basically the same. Consider the cooling needs of your engine and its general operating climate. For most performance street applications, a high-flow four-core copper/brass unit will work just fine. If weight (or lack thereof) is an issue, consider aluminum as an alternative. Either way, make sure your new radiator includes a full warranty against defects in workmanship and materials.

Removing and replacing the radiator is a simple, yet involved process. Before getting started, you first need to properly drain the system of all its fluid. Open the small valve at the bottom of the radiator to allow the coolant to exit the system in a slow, controlled manner. Next, loosen and remove the lower radiator hose clamp, and pull the hose from the radiator tank. Have a bucket in position to catch the remaining fluid. If your hoses are stubborn in removal, try cutting a small slice down the length of the hose at the neck. You should be able to unwrap the hose from the opening without tweaking or breaking anything else at the same time. Proceed to the upper radiator hose. If you currently use an overflow tank in your system, disconnect the line from the radiator and remove the tank from the engine bay. Remember to dump the old fluid out of the overflow reservoir before reinstalling.

With everything disconnected and disposed of, pulling the radiator is a matter of removing a mere four bolts from the core support. One at a time, loosen the bolts, and carefully lift the radiator from its housing. If your car has a fan shroud or a radiator cover plate, you will need to remove these items prior to the radiator. The tanks will most likely have a small amount of fluid left in them. Tilt the radiator core back to keep the excess fluid from running out of the necks and onto the engine during removal.

Over time and under extreme engine temperatures, radiator hoses begin to crack and deteriorate. They tend to lose their premolded rigidity and can easily kink or be sucked shut when subjected to the high pressures of the cooling system. For this reason, most lower radiator hoses come with a metal spring inside to prevent collapsing. If your hoses start to feel abnormally soft and pliable, replace them with a quality hose that fits your application.

The new radiator, if it's a stock replacement, should go back in the same way it came out. Some aftermarket pieces require minor drilling and new brackets to fit. If that's the case, follow the manufacturer's specs on the installation. Otherwise, simply reverse the removal process and refill the system with clean water and coolant. Although water has a higher boiling point than coolant, it is typically best to run a 50/50 mixture of

Drain the tanks by opening the small, threaded valve at the bottom of the radiator core.

There are just four bolts (two upper and two lower) that secure the radiator to the core support.

both (use distilled water to avoid rusting the internals of your cooling system and engine). With the radiator cap off, the coolant level should be just below the bottom of the neck. Start the engine and allow it to reach normal operating temperature. When the upper radiator hose begins to warm, the thermostat has opened and the engine is at temperature. You can now install the cap. Running the engine before installing the cap allows any pockets of trapped air to fully escape from the system. Run the car under pressure with the system closed, and check for leaks. Allow the system to cool and recheck the fluid level.

147

Installing a Transmission Cooler

ENGINE COMPARTMENT

Time: 2 hours

Tools: Standard wrenches, small flat-blade screwdriver, razor blade

Talent: 🔩🔩

Applicable years: All

Cost: $50

Parts: Transmission cooler and installation hardware (included in most kits)

Tip: Allow the transmission to completely cool before attempting to drain the fluid or disconnect any lines under pressure.

PERFORMANCE GAIN: A cooler, more efficient transmission capable of handling increased loads and horsepower

COMPLEMENTARY PROJECTS:
Project 43: Installing a New Fan and Fan Belt; Project 56: Installing a New Radiator and Hoses

An automatic transmission generally uses the radiator to cool its circulating fluid or oil. These fluid-driven transmissions tend to operate in the temperature range between 150 and 250 degrees Fahrenheit. On the back side of the transmission case toward the tailshaft, you will find a pair of fittings with steel lines attached. These are the transmission cooler lines. If you follow their path, they will lead you to the fittings in the lower radiator tank at the front of the vehicle. Warm fluid from the transmission is forced under pressure through one line to the radiator for cooling. The fluid is then circulated through a series of coils or fins and returned back to the transmission in the opposite line.

Most automatic-equipped vehicles have this type of built-in transmission cooler inside the radiator. They work well for most stock applications, but in the demanding world of high-performance, they come up a little short.

Due to time, extreme temperatures, and the relentless use and abuse of the transmission, the cooler assembly can take quite the flogging. Installing an external transmission cooler is one of the best policies of insurance you can throw at your transmission. The cooler will help guard and protect your transmission from excessive overheating due to pulling heavy loads, mountain driving, sustained high speeds, and racing. Whether or not you run the cooler in series with the factory cooler, the installation is straightforward and only requires a few basic hand tools.

The first thing to consider is the location and placement of the cooler. There are several possible approaches depending on your application and the space available. The preferred location is in front of both the radiator and AC condenser (if applicable). This configuration (the cooler is the most forward component) will produce the highest efficiency in overall cooling. If, in fact, you do have an AC condenser, a second option is to install the cooler between the radiator and the condenser. As a last resort, the install can be made with the cooler behind the radiator; however, you would lose approximately 40 percent of its cooling capacity by doing so.

Determining oil flow direction before installing the cooler or modifying the lines is a must. With the exception of the TH-350 and the TH-700-R4, most GM transmissions utilize the upper fitting on the case as the oil return line. Double-check the flow direction of the oil just to be sure using one of the following methods. Start the engine and put the transmission in gear to heat the oil. Shut the car off and feel the temperature of both cooler lines. The warmer line will be the pressure line, which delivers the oil from the transmission to the radiator. Another sure-fire way to tell pressure from return is to disconnect either cooler line at the radiator. Place a small rubber hose over the exposed fitting and start the engine. Put both line ends into a container and see which one yields fluid. If the oil comes from the cooler line, it's the pressure side. If fluid exits the radiator, it's the return side.

As you probably know, there's no shortage of aftermarket companies selling transmission oil coolers. Each one may vary slightly in appearance or design, but the principal function remains the same. Regarding the actual installation, follow the manufacturer's instructions. The mounting methods and hardware may be different from what is shown here. Select the one that best suits your performance needs and cooling requirements.

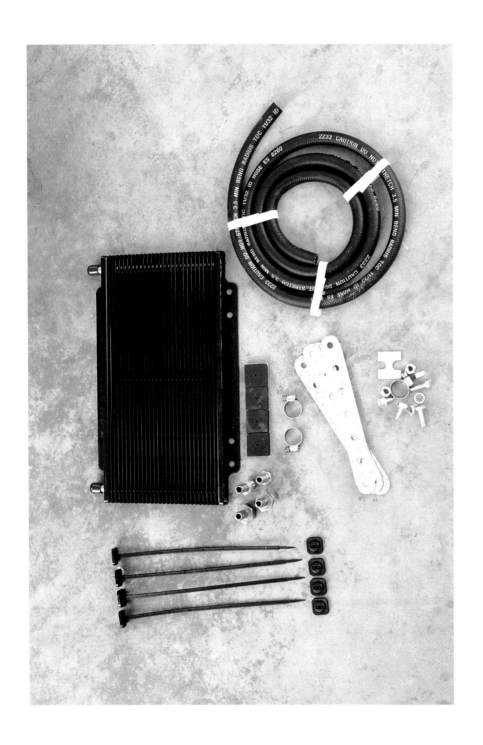

Most transmission oil coolers come complete with the proper mounting hardware and instructions.

Installing a Coolant Recovery System

ENGINE COMPARTMENT

Time: 1 hour

Tools: Flat-blade screwdriver, socket set, drill

Talent:

Applicable years: '64–'70

Cost: Under $20

Parts: Coolant overflow bottle (sold in a kit with mounting hardware), 5 feet of hose

Tip: Purchase more hose than you think you'll need.

PERFORMANCE GAIN: No more "topping up" the coolant level, and no embarrassing overflow

COMPLEMENTARY PROJECTS:

Project 30: Installing a New Thermostat and Housing (Water Neck); Project 56: Installing a New Radiator and Hoses

New coolant recovery systems come in many shapes and sizes.

Theoretically, your 1960s-era muscle car shouldn't belch out a quarter-cup of coolant every time you shut the engine down, although many of them do. Engines that run too hot, radiators in poor working order, and driving under any number of extreme conditions can cause coolant to overheat and spill out through the overflow tube. Not only is it embarrassing to have the green stuff seep out whenever you pull up to park, it can be downright expensive, too.

The purpose of a coolant recovery system is to prevent the loss of coolant due to overheating. Simply put, as the coolant boils, it is collected in the bottle. When the engine cools, the coolant is recovered by the radiator.

By the 1970s, GM cars and trucks rolled off the assembly line with a full coolant recovery system already installed. If your vehicle doesn't have one, we're going to show you step by step how to remedy the situation. It's very simple and takes less than an hour.

Make sure the engine is off and has completely cooled down. Pop the hood, and get your tools and new coolant recovery system ready. First, find a good location to mount the recovery tank. Coolant recovery systems come in a wide variety of designs, ranging from full-on plastic tanks (like the one we've chosen) or sleek cylindrical tubes that can be installed right alongside your radiator. Rest assured they all accomplish the same feat.

Follow the manufacturer's instructions to install the recovery tank. In this instance, we're drilling two small holes to mount the coolant tank holder. Our radiator's coolant overflow tube is attached to the far side of the radiator, near the battery. We're going to route the coolant hose from the overflow tube fitting on the radiator neck to the new coolant tank. Since we don't want an unwieldy length of hose dangling around the engine compartment, we'll need to properly secure the hose. Using a socket set, we're going to remove the upper radiator supports and the shroud attached to them.

The plastic hose that came with our coolant recovery system was very thin in wall thickness and proved to kink very easily. At our local auto parts store, we purchased 5 feet of 1/4-inch coolant hose. Much heavier, the new hose does the trick just fine. We attach it to the overflow tube fitting on the radiator neck and route it in between the radiator and the core support.

The new hose snugs in perfectly and attaches to the plastic fitting at the bottom of the coolant tank—no more

Drill pilot holes to attach the coolant tank holder (per the manufacturer's directions). The tank beside the drill is the windshield washer bottle.

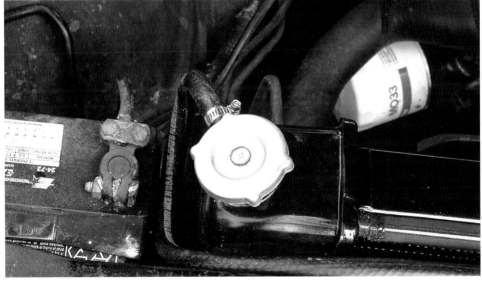

Left: The new overflow hose attaches to the fitting on the radiator neck and tucks in neatly behind the radiator.

Below: Connected to the new coolant recovery tank, we're ready for any rise in coolant temperature.

overflow problems. The last step is to reattach the upper radiator supports and the shroud.

The new coolant recovery tank will have coolant level markings inscribed on its side. The coolant level should be near the "add" or "full cold" mark when the system is cold. At normal operating temperatures, the level should be above the add/full cold mark or, if applicable, between the add/full cold marks and the "full hot" marking. Only add coolant to the recovery tank as necessary to bring the system up to the proper level.

A word of caution: Never add coolant to a hot engine unless it is running. If it is not running, you risk cracking the engine block.

You should pressure-check your cooling system at least once a year. If the coolant level is consistently low or rusty, it should be checked for leaks. Have your entire cooling system flushed and refilled with fresh coolant at least once every two years.

151

Installing the Heater Core and Hoses

Time: 3–4 hours

Tools: Standard socket set, standard wrenches, putty knife, flat-blade screwdriver

Talent: ▮▮▮

Applicable years: All

Cost: $75

Parts: Heater core and gasket set

Tip: Flush the cooling system prior to installing the heater core to get rid of any loose debris that could clog or damage the new part.

PERFORMANCE GAIN: Efficient and reliable interior heating

COMPLEMENTARY PROJECTS:

Project 30: Installing a New Thermostat and Housing (Water Neck); Project 56: Installing a New Radiator and Hoses

Although we spend a lot of time and effort trying to eliminate heat from our engines, transmissions, and passenger cabins, sometimes a little warmth and comfort in the right places can go a long way. The heater core is chiefly responsible for supplying the interior with heat. It is tightly nestled inside the heater box under the dash carrier. The heater box mounts to the inside of the firewall with the inlet and outlet ports of the heater core extending into the engine compartment. The heater core cover is attached to the opposite side (engine compartment) of the firewall and houses the blower motor and fan. The heater hoses attach to the ports of the core on the firewall and extend to the water pump and the intake manifold.

The heat/climate control system works as follows: hot coolant is picked up through the engine and delivered to the heater core through the primary heater hose. The blower motor and fan, which are located inside the heater core housing, remove the heat from the core and push it into the passenger compartment in the same fashion that the engine fan removes heat from the radiator. The passenger control system is operated by a series of cables and levers that control the activation of the blower motor and fan, as well as open and close the air passages and ducts leading into the dash vents. Most cars came equipped with this manual cable and lever-style system, although in later production years, vacuum operated controls and hoses replaced the cables.

Over time, the small and very narrow passages of the heater core become clogged with debris and contaminants from the cooling system. Under pressure of the cooling system, a clogged heater core will begin to expand due to the restriction of flow, and will eventually leak and fail. The first sign of this instant death is a sudden waterfall of coolant into the passenger side floorboard. From here, the heater core must be replaced.

Many people choose to bypass the core by either splicing the two heater hoses together or removing them completely and capping off the open ports. This works temporarily, but every car restoration should include a functioning heater control system.

The worst part about replacing the heater core is clearance, especially with the right-hand inner fenderwell in the engine compartment. Although some have successfully managed to replace the core without removing the inner fenderwell, it really makes the job a lot easier after it's out of the way. Be sure to fully drain the cooling system before removing any hoses or clamps. The heater hoses can be disconnected from the ports on the firewall and set aside. Next, remove the fastener nuts of the heater core cover and fan housing. Disconnect the small wiring harness from the blower motor assembly and remove the cover from the firewall. You may need to exert a little muscle between the cover and the firewall to break the bond of the factory adhesive.

With the outer case assembly removed, you can pull the heater core box from the inside of the firewall. It may take a little time to disconnect the appropriate brackets, cables, and retaining hardware from the heater box. As I said before, clearance is the killer. Be sure to keep track of all the hardware and its location on the box. Next, lift the heater core from the housing and discard it.

With the whole assembly in pieces, clean and inspect the condition of the remaining parts. Lubricate the control levers and cables for smoother operation. Surface rust on the case or the box should be treated and repainted. Also, check the blower motor and fan assembly for positive engagement. This can be done by grounding its case to the negative terminal of a spare battery and running a wire from the spade connection

Access to the heater box can be tight underneath the dash. Be sure to disconnect all cables and brackets from the box before attempting to remove it from the firewall.

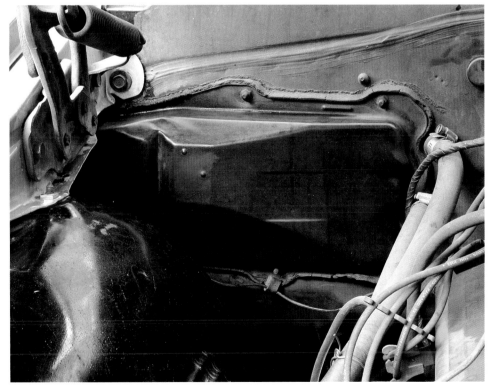

Remove the passenger-side fenderwell, allowing access to all of the cover bolts.

on the motor to the positive terminal of the battery. This will indicate whether or not the motor is working properly. The shaft of the motor should be lubricated at this time as well.

To reinstall, place the new heater core back inside the box and attach the necessary cables and brackets. Locate the box into its original position on the inside firewall and reinstall the fasteners. The sealing surfaces should be scraped clean with a putty knife and treated to new gaskets. Using the same mounting hardware, install the blower motor and fan assembly into the case and attach to the outer side of the firewall. Reconnect the wiring harness and the heater hoses, and refill the cooling system.

Installing an Electric Fan

Time: 2 hours

Tools: Standard socket set, standard wrenches, wire cutters/crimpers

Talent:

Applicable years: All

Cost: $75–$350

Parts: Electric fan, fan relays, wire, and various connectors

Tip: Always double-check your electrical connections before firing the engine. If hot leads are hooked up incorrectly, you can easily destroy and fry your electrical system.

PERFORMANCE GAIN: Improved cooling, less drag on the motor at high rpm

COMPLEMENTARY PROJECTS:

Project 43: Installing a New Fan and Fan Belt; Project 56: Installing a New Radiator and Hoses; Project 89: Removing and Replacing the Battery and Battery Cables

Electric fans have long been popular in the aftermarket scene for their high efficiency and improved cooling. In fact, new cars come equipped with electric fans largely due to their size. As hood clearances and engine compartments become tighter and smaller, there is less and less room for big engine-driven fans. Although there may be ample space for engine-driven fans on older vehicles, electric fans make a great addition to the cooling system, especially in high-horsepower applications. They eliminate high-rpm airflow restriction, because they shut off when the speed of the vehicle creates

enough airflow to cool the engine. This also keeps the fan from robbing engine power at high rpm.

Electric fans are lightweight, durable, and usually come equipped with their own fan shroud. The blade angle or pitch of the fan varies, depending on the size and output of the electric motor used to drive the fan. Larger fans with more drastic blade angles naturally flow more air, due to their size and design. However, they also place a heavier load on the battery and charging system by drawing high amperage. Fans with large pitch angles, both engine driven and electric, are quite a bit noisier on the road as well. A silencing solution is to install a dual-fan setup, which is capable of flowing between 1,250 and 2,500 cubic feet per minute (cfm). These fans are available in both "pusher" and "puller" configurations. A fan that pulls air from behind the radiator on the engine side is known as a "puller." If the fan is mounted in front of the radiator, it pushes the air through the core and cools the fluid. By and large, the puller fan tends to operate more efficiently than a pusher fan because the air flows along the blades toward the engine, creating a low-pressure area behind the radiator and sucking the air through.

When it comes to installing an electric fan, the most difficult part is typically the wiring. There are many different ways to wire the fan, but as with any high-amperage accessory, the use of an external relay is a must. The idea behind fan relays is to run as large an amount of current as possible to the load. This requires the shortest possible amount of heavy-gauge wire between the battery and the load. The relay itself then acts as a conductor between the fan and the battery. Therefore, the switch mounted inside the car operates the relay instead of the fan and only requires a small amount of current to activate it. Depending on how the fan assembly is wired, the interior switch can supply either power or a ground to activate the relay.

Select a fan based on the specific needs of your car. The first consideration should be clearance in the engine compartment. If you will be running an engine-driven fan in unison with the electric fan, measure the distance between the stock fan and the radiator. You should also take measurements between the top of the lower radiator hose and the underside of the upper radiator hose. Once the size of the new fan has been determined, look for a unit that will handle the cooling needs of your engine. Keep in mind that electric fans can be thermostatically controlled to run with the operating temperatures of your engine. If this is not a concern, you can easily install a manual on/off switch inside the car. The switch can be run with 18-gauge wire leads to both the relay in the engine compartment and a "key-on" power source at the fuse block.

The relays should be mounted as close to the battery as possible, such as on the engine side of the core support. This

This large 18-inch electric fan makes a great addition to the aluminum radiator for maximum cooling.

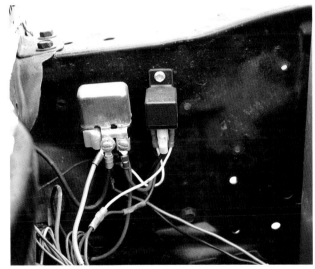

The fan is wired directly to the relay and a dash-mounted switch inside the car activates it.

provides the shortest distance between the battery and the fan and allows for the maximum current to reach the fans. If you are running a dual-fan setup, dedicate one relay to each fan for a little extra insurance. This will prevent the relay from getting too hot and burning out. The same applies with a single high-current fan.

Most fan kits come complete with mounting hardware and detailed instructions. Follow the manufacturer's recommendations on how to specifically install the fan and components.

It always helps to have a reliable monitor on the cooling temperature of the engine.

155

TRANSMISSION

The transmission is a vital part of any performance vehicle. The projects in this chapter focus on modifying and increasing the performance of factory transmissions, and cover both automatic and manual versions. Like the engine, the transmission should be blueprinted specifically for your car.

PROJECT 61
Removing and Replacing the Transmission

 Time: 4 hours

 Tools: Standard socket set, standard wrenches, torque wrench, torque converter holding tool (optional), floor jack, transmission jack (optional)

 Talent: ♦ ♦ ♦ ♦

 Applicable years: All

 Cost: $10–$25 for materials/fluids

 Parts: Transmission fluid, transmission tail-shaft plug

 Tip: After removing the driveshaft from the rear of the transmission housing, install a stop plug over the tailshaft to avoid fluid spilling out.

 PERFORMANCE GAIN: Transmission trouble is never fun. Whether it's for repair, rebuilding, or all-out racing, a finely tuned transmission is a cornerstone of performance.

COMPLEMENTARY PROJECTS: Replacing the transmission mount; Project 62: Removing and Installing the Flywheel/Flexplate; Project 63: Understanding and Installing a Torque Converter

Release the transmission shifter linkage from the steering column.

Removing the transmission assembly from any vehicle is a delicate procedure. It requires time, open space, and plenty of patience. Located smack dab between the engine and the rear drivetrain, the transmission and its various counterparts literally serve as the middle man in the forever-valuable transfer of power. Whether you prefer manual domination or the creature comforts of an auto-pilot, the basic principles and operation of the transmission remain constant. The same goes for removing and installing as well. Although there are many modifications to be made on individual components, this project narrows the focus to getting the beast safely in and out of the car.

As we covered earlier in the engine removal process, you can make the swap as one complete assembly (engine included) or opt for the transmission alone, and it's really just a matter of preference. Regardless, start by disconnecting the negative

Depending on the application, most of the transmission-to-engine mounting bolts can be accessed from the top of the vehicle.

Loosen and remove the two support bolts that connect the transmission mount to the crossmember.

TRANSMISSION

battery cable from its terminal post. Drain any fluids (i.e., coolant, engine oil, power steering fluid, etc.) from the engine that may result in a spill during the process. Disconnect any and all electrical connectors from the engine/transmission assembly. This may include the engine harness, the neutral-safety and back-up light switches (if applicable), and the throttle valve detent switch. The order and approach may vary slightly from one tranny to another, as GM produced and offered more than a handful of different designs over the years. Continue the disassembly by removing the air cleaner and the throttle linkage cable or rods; you want to create as much room as possible for easier access to other areas. Unbolt the shifter linkage at the steering column and remove any retaining clips (see photo 1). Floor-shift cars will require the removal of the shifter boot and housing, the center console (if so equipped), and the shifter mechanism. On a four-speed, disconnect the Z-bar rods and springs. Be careful—these pieces may still be loaded under high spring pressures.

Before going any further, raise and support the car using a floor jack and a sturdy pair of jack stands. You will need to loosen and remove the lower shifter and/or clutch linkage from the side of the transmission case. Anything that may obstruct a clean removal must go. Keep track of and label all of your hardware, clips, and retainers to make the reassembly a much smoother operation. The speedometer cable and oil cooler lines (if applicable) should be next on the list. The speedometer cable will simply unthread from the case and slide right out. Label the cooler lines for pressure or return and tie them back out of the way. Be prepared for a little oil spill when disconnecting the lines. On some models, it may be necessary to unbolt the exhaust pipe(s) from the collector for additional clearance. Sometimes, it's easier just to remove the whole system from the collector rearward, including the mufflers. This is especially true when cross-over bars or X pipes are implemented midway in the exhaust system. At the rear of the car, unbolt the U-joints and disengage the driveshaft from the transmission tailshaft. Refer to Project 65 (Replacing the Universal Joint and Driveshaft/Installing the Driveshaft Safety Loop) for instructions on the disassembly.

Pulling the transmission out and away from the back of the engine requires the torque converter to be loosened from the crankshaft flexplate. Start by removing the flywheel/torque converter cover at the front of the transmission. You should then have sufficient clearance to access the converter mounting bolts. Remove the converter from the plate and secure it to the body of the transmission. Be sure to mark the orientation of the torque converter in relation to the flexplate for reassembly.

Support the transmission housing with a floor jack and remove the transmission-mount-to-crossmember support bolts. Loosen the bolts securing the crossmember to the frame and slide it toward the rear of the vehicle. With the engine properly supported, the transmission-to-engine/bell housing mounting bolts may now be removed. Manual transmissions may be pulled with or without the bell housing. The case is typically mounted to the housing by four bolts. With the transmission isolated, slowly slide the assembly rearward and lower to the ground.

To install, realign the proper match marks and lubricate all bearings and shafts with clean engine oil. Raise the transmission with the floor jack and secure it to the engine block. Reattach the remaining components, linkage, and hardware, and set them to the proper torque values. Refill the transmission case with fresh fluid if necessary.

PROJECT 62
Removing and Installing the Flywheel/Flexplate

Time: 1 hour

Tools: Standard socket set, flat-blade screwdriver, breaker bar, torque wrench, Loctite

Talent:

Applicable years: All

Cost: New flywheels $50–$200 (new GM); flexplates $75–$100

Parts: New ring gear plate, flywheel/flexplate bolts (optional)

Tip: Be sure to research the right replacement part for your application. An improperly balanced rotating assembly will wreak havoc on the rest of your engine.

PERFORMANCE GAIN: A stronger, properly balanced rotating assembly

COMPLEMENTARY PROJECTS:
Project 63: Understanding and Installing a Torque Converter; Project 64: Installing a Clutch; Project 90: Installing a High-Torque Mini Starter

TRANSMISSION

No engine would be complete or useful without the ever-important flywheel or flexplate. These large, ring-gear plates are mounted to the rear flange of the crankshaft at the back of the engine block. In conjunction with the starter assembly, the plates are responsible for "kicking over" the engine when the ignition is fired. Along the outer rim of the plate is a series of geared teeth designed to mesh with the pinion gear of the starter motor. When power is applied to the starter (via the ignition switch), the pinion gear engages the teeth of the

flywheel/flexplate and turns the plate in the direction of rotation. Since the plate is bolted directly to the crankshaft, this quickly gives the engine its initial breath of life and gets things moving.

Although flywheels and flexplates are almost identical in function, they vary slightly in design. The face of a flywheel has a smooth, machined surface similar to a brake rotor. This is strictly for the application of a manual clutch. The pressure plate of the clutch assembly is bolted to the outside ring of the flywheel. The pressure plate applies force to the clutch disc (located between the pressure plate and flywheel) when the clutch pedal is released. This connects the drive of the engine to the transmission and beyond.

A flexplate is intended for automatic-controlled vehicles. Since the torque converter aptly handles the transfer of power between the engine and the transmission, there is no need for the manual clutch and flywheel assembly. Instead, the flex-plate mounts to the rear of the crankshaft (same as flywheel) and simply serves as the mounting point for the torque converter. For this reason, flexplates are typically lighter than their flywheel counterparts.

Whether automatic or manual, the removal of the plate is pretty much the same. The transmission must be disengaged and pulled from the engine in order to access the rear of the crankshaft. Remove the bell housing and clutch assembly (if so equipped). On automatic cars, the transmission case is a one-piece design. Removal of the torque converter from the flexplate is all that's required. For details on these procedures, refer to the appropriate projects in this book.

Using a long breaker bar for additional leverage, loosen and remove the six retaining bolts and washers from the fly-wheel or flexplate. If the plate turns while attempting to remove the bolts, try wedging a screwdriver between the teeth of the plate and the starter gear to lock it into place. Clean the threads of the bolts before reassembly. If any threads are damaged or marred, replace the bolts. A set of new ARP bolts will cost about $10. Closely inspect the surface of the flywheel and the condition of the teeth. If the surface indicates excessive wear in one particular area of the plate, you could have a mis-aligned clutch assembly. If the gear teeth are chewed up or broken, you may need to correct the engagement of the pinion gear to the flexplate, which can be done using starter shims.

When it comes to replacing the flywheel/flexplate, it can be a little tricky. Different displacement engines often come equipped with different plates. This is most evident in the number of teeth on the outside ring of the plate. The diameter can vary as well. Measure the diameter of the existing plate and count the number of teeth present on the ring (usually 153 or 168) to ensure you make the correct replacement.

Flexplates are visibly different than flywheels. There is no machined surface required for a clutch. The torque converter bolts right up to the center of the plate and transfers the power to the transmission.

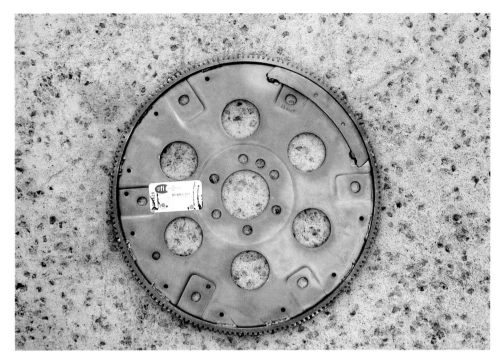

You can still purchase new GM flywheels from the dealership parts counter. It's a good idea to save your old plate so you can match it up to the new one.

TRANSMISSION

In addition to the size and teeth issues, consider the way in which the motor is balanced—internally or externally? An internally balanced crankshaft should be balanced without the flywheel/flexplate or the vibration damper attached. These external components have a neutral balance in the equation and allow for greater interchangeability, meaning an aftermarket flywheel or damper can be installed without throwing the engine's balance out of whack.

An externally balanced crankshaft requires the added components for proper balancing. These cranks are manufactured with lighter counterweights, relying on the external weight of the flywheel and damper to make up the difference.

Once the pieces have been balanced as a package, any part change will require rebalancing of the entire assembly.

Some machine shops actually convert externally balanced cranks into the more-desired internally balanced pieces by adding material to the crank to achieve the "correct" weight. The conversion is not cheap, but it may be worth the extra effort for hassle relief alone.

After the right plate has been selected, the installation is self-explanatory. Reverse the steps listed above and torque all bolts to the recommended settings. Apply a liberal amount of Loctite to the threads before assembly.

160

Understanding and Installing a Torque Converter

 Time: 1–2 hours

 Tools: Standard socket set, standard wrenches, torque wrench

 Talent:

 Applicable years: All

 Cost: $200–$600

 Parts: Torque converter, transmission fluid

 Tip: Consult with torque converter manufacturers before selecting a new converter.

 PERFORMANCE GAIN: Well-balanced driveline, smoother shifts, maximum engine power band

COMPLEMENTARY PROJECTS:

Project 62: Removing and Installing the Flywheel/Flexplate; Project 66: Installing an Automatic Transmission Aftermarket Floor Shifter

The torque converter case mounts as shown to the flexplate with the front snout of the unit mated to the transmission input shaft.

Torque converters are to the automatic transmission what a clutch is to a manually driven transmission. Torque converters allow the engine to idle with the transmission in gear by internally disconnecting the engine rpm from the transmission. Torque converters also allow the transmission to be smoothly shifted through the range without requiring the throttle to be closed during the shift.

Torque converters are spherical metal cases that house three sets of blades. They are bolted to the rear of the crankshaft at the transmission flexplate and generally rotate with the engine at rpm (similar to a flywheel). The first set of blades attaches directly to the converter's case and forms what is called the impeller, or the pump. The second set connects to the transmission output shaft and is referred to as the turbine. The third set of internal blades, known as the stator, mounts onto a hub and a stationary shaft through a one-way clutch.

The torque converter operates in a fashion similar to two fans. If you place two fans close together and supply power to only one of them, the blades of the nonpowered fan will slowly begin to turn. A torque converter uses the same principle; however the medium is fluid, not air.

The primary reason to change the torque converter in your car is to evenly pair up the performance of the engine with the driveline. If you make any significant changes in your engine, the balance between the engine and driveline components will most likely be altered or thrown off (automatic-equipped vehicles only). Selecting the right torque converter can eliminate these problems and maximize the power generated from the engine.

To choose the correct converter, you need to truly be aware of your car's capabilities and its limitations. The engine's power band, the rear gear ratio, the weight of the vehicle, and the vehicle's overall purpose are all very important and relative pieces in the torque converter equation. The most crucial component to consider when

A series of directional blades that carry and transfer fluid make up the internals of the converter.

shopping for a new converter is your camshaft. The profile of the cam dictates the opening and closing of the engine's valves, thus creating its power band. If you run a stock or near-stock hydraulic camshaft, there is no additional load or burden on the torque converter. A stock converter will perform suitably. If the profile of the camshaft is more aggressive and yields long-duration opening and closing of the valves, a higher stall speed torque converter is necessary to allow the engine to enter its higher-than-stock power band.

Aftermarket torque converter companies usually identify and rate their units by stall speed. Stall speed can be defined as the attainable engine rpm at full throttle, while the brakes are locked and the transmission is in gear, before the driven wheels begin to turn. However, the stall speed is only attainable if the brakes can hold the car in place.

Many manufacturers choose to classify converters by the diameter size of the case. Each case size typically represents a small range of stall speeds. The smaller the diameter of the case, the higher the stall speed of the converter. For example, a 12-inch stock converter will produce a stall speed of around 2,000 rpm at its highest point. A smaller, 10-inch unit will produce a stall speed roughly between 2,600 and 3,800 rpm. This is why knowing the power band of your engine is a key element in picking the right converter. Place the stall speed approximately 300 rpm before the engine's torque peak. Most stock V-8-powered, automatic, rear-drive cars have stall speeds in the neighborhood of 1,500 to 1,800 rpm. As the engine is modified and more power is produced, the stall speed of the converter should increase along with it.

To replace the torque converter, the transmission must be removed from the vehicle. The torque converter is mounted to the rear of the crankshaft between the engine block and the transmission case. For tips and procedures on safely removing and reinstalling the transmission assembly, check out Project 61. Remove the flywheel/torque converter

The individual pieces of the torque converter case are welded together at the seams to provide strength and rigidity.

cover and loosen the converter mounting bolts at the flexplate. Remove the transmission from the back of the block, along with the torque converter.

When reinstalling, position the converter back onto the flexplate and torque the bolts to the required spec. Assemble the rest of the transmission and linkage, and fill with clean transmission fluid.

PROJECT 64
Installing a Clutch

Time: 3–4 hours

Tools: Standard socket set, standard wrenches, torque wrench, clutch alignment tool

Talent:

Applicable years: All

Cost: $150–$400

Parts: New clutch assembly

Tip: Always replace any other suspect components when performing a big job like this. Your powertrain and driveline are only as strong as their weakest link.

PERFORMANCE GAIN: Tighter, smoother shifts; increased holding power at high rpm

COMPLEMENTARY PROJECTS:
Project 62: Removing and Installing the Flywheel/Flexplate; Project 65: Replacing the Universal Joint and Driveshaft/Installing the Driveshaft Safety Loop; Project 70: Understanding Rear Gear Ratios

The clutch of the manual transmission is designed to smoothly connect and disconnect power from the engine to the transmission. In order to initiate forward motion, the engine must be allowed to operate without any load until enough engine torque is created to move the car. The clutch assembly physically disconnects the transmission from the engine until the necessary amount of torque has been established. By gradually releasing the clutch pedal, the power and torque from the engine are transferred to the transmission and the rest of the driveline. The clutch disc and pressure plate serve as the connecting links in the system. When the clutch pedal releases, the two components contact each other and tie the engine and transmission together. When the pedal is actuated, the disc and pressure plate separate from each other and allow both the engine to spin freely and the transmission to shift.

The entire clutch assembly consists of the engine flywheel, clutch disc, pressure plate, throwout bearing and fork, and the pedal linkage. The flywheel and pressure plate are attached to the rear of the engine at the crankshaft, and they rotate along with it. The clutch disc is sandwiched between the flywheel and the pressure plate and is splined to the transmission input shaft. The flywheel and clutch pressure plate are the driving members of the assembly. As they rotate with the engine, the "floating" disc is driven and rotated on contact, thus turning the shaft of the transmission.

On the transmission side of the clutch pressure plate, a circular series of springs, in conjunction with the throwout bearing and fork, enables the engine and the transmission to temporarily disengage. When the clutch pedal is fully released, the springs are dished outward, facing the front of the transmission. As the pedal is depressed, the clutch fork is activated, and it forces the throwout bearing forward to contact the diaphragm spring of the pressure plate. The outer edges of the spring are connected to the pressure plate, and they pull it away from the clutch disc when the clutch pedal is depressed. This separation of the plate and disc disengages the clutch and allows the transmission to be shifted into another gear. When the pedal is released, a small coil spring attached to the clutch pedal pulls the throwout bearing and clutch fork away from the diaphragm spring. This causes the pressure plate and clutch disc to reunite and once again transfer the power from the engine to the transmission. The engine, clutch disc, and input shaft are now all rotating at the same speed.

To remove the old clutch assembly, the transmission and the engine must be separated. If the clutch is all that needs work, leave the engine in the car and pull the transmission only. For detailed instructions on removing the transmission, refer to Project 61. This will walk you through step by step how to properly obtain access to the rear of the engine and the flywheel. Once the transmission is out of the way, the clutch assembly is easily accessible and ready for removal.

Before unbolting the pressure plate from the flywheel, mark the orientation of the plate in relation to the flywheel for reinstallation purposes. It's important that the two pieces reattach in the same position. Slowly loosen and remove the clutch cover bolts from the flywheel. Work in an even pattern to remove the bolts to avoid excess loading or warping until all spring pressure is released. Remove the pressure plate and the clutch disc from the flywheel and set them aside.

Now is a good time to inspect the condition of the flywheel. Although the factory often recommends replacing the

The clutch assembly consists of the pressure plate (right), the clutch disc (lower), and the throwout bearing (center). The flywheel is not included.

The clutch disc sits between the flywheel and the pressure plate and is installed using the supplied clutch alignment tool.

Centrifugal clutches are becoming more and more popular with the high-performance crowd, due to their increased holding power, structural strength, and light pedal pressures. When you go to pick out a new clutch, consider your options and all that the aftermarket has to offer. The theory behind these clutches is pure physics. When an object rotates about any axis other than one at its center of mass, it creates an outward-pushing pressure called centrifugal force. The more this object weighs or the faster it turns, the greater the force will be. The centrifugal force is increased by the square of the speed at which the object is rotating. Therefore, by increasing the rpm five times the original amount, the centrifugal force of the clutch increases to 25 times the original amount. These clutches incorporate small weights on the pressure plate, and use the centrifugal force of these weights to increase the holding pressure of the clutch disc to the flywheel as the engine rpm ramps up. In turn, the increased holding power eliminates the need for heavy-duty pressure plate springs and requires less pedal pressure to engage and disengage the clutch.

To reinstall the new assembly, clean the pressure plate and the surface of the flywheel with brake cleaner. You will need a clutch alignment tool (included with most clutch kits) to hold the clutch disc rigidly in position while you properly place and bolt the pressure plate back onto the flywheel. Torque the plate to spec and remove the alignment tool. Be sure to line up the previously made marks with each other to ensure the right balance. Lubricate the ball socket, fork fingers, throwout bearing, and throwout fork groove before final reassembly. Continue the reinstallation of the transmission and the driveshaft.

flywheel, many shops agree that the old one can safely be resurfaced and used again. However, if the flywheel needs more than 0.025 inch of material removed from the surface, replace it with a new unit. Removing too much material may require the use of shims between the flywheel and the rear of the crankshaft to compensate for the difference. While you're at it, check out the rear main oil seal and the clutch's pilot bearing for any signs of faulty operation or damage. These are cheap to replace and could save you the headache of having to tear the whole thing apart again later to fix them. If you replace the pilot bearing, go with the higher-quality needle bearing bushing instead of the solid brass bearing.

Replacing the Universal Joint and Driveshaft/Installing the Driveshaft Safety Loop

 Time: 2 hours

 Tools: Standard socket set, standard wrenches

 Talent:

 Applicable years: All

 Cost: $50 for new U-joints, $50 for driveshaft loop

 Parts: A set of heavy-duty performance U-joints, driveshaft loop (optional)

 Tip: When replacing your driveshaft and/or universal joints, think about adding a driveshaft loop to your driveline for increased safety.

 PERFORMANCE GAIN: A stout, rigid drivetrain capable of handling the high-torque loads of performance motors

COMPLEMENTARY PROJECTS:

Project 61: Removing and Replacing the Transmission; Project 69: Inspecting the Differential Housing and Gear Set

Driveshafts and their ever-important joints are solely responsible for transferring the power and torque of your engine and transmission to the rear-end unit. Most GM muscle cars have conventional, open-type driveshafts. This means there is a universal joint (U-joint) at each end of the driveshaft assembly. The U-joints allow the driveshaft to move freely up and down to match the travel of the rear end. The forward U-joint connects the shaft to a slip-jointed yoke that slides into the back of the transmission. The inside of this yoke is splined and designed to mate with the splines of the transmission output shaft, creating a smooth, gearlike connection. The rear U-joint is located at the rear drive axle assembly and is held in place by two long, U-shaped bolts. At each end of the joint is a bearing cup or cap that houses the needle bearing internals and grease. The caps are secured by conventional snap rings in the recessed groove of the yoke.

Many novice car crafters fall under the assumption that because U-joints and the driveshaft are integral parts of the driveline, they are difficult to replace and should only be handled by a professional. In reality, universal joint and/or driveshaft replacement is one of the easiest projects you can tackle underneath your car. All you need are some good jack stands, a 1/2-inch socket wrench, and a 1/2-inch boxed wrench.

First and foremost, raise the rear of the car to a suitable working level and support it with a pair of jack stands. Try to pick out the flattest open area in which to do so. Before disassembly, mark the location of the driveshaft in relation to the rear-end yoke to ensure the same positioning during reassembly. Loosen and remove the two nuts from each "U" bolt. You may need to lightly tap the U-bolts back out of their respective through-holes, as they make for a pretty tight fit. With the bolts out of the way, the rear universal joint can be removed from the car. If you plan on reusing the same U-joints for whatever reason, tape the bearing caps shut to avoid spilling and losing the needle bearings inside.

At this point, you can slide the driveshaft out the back of the transmission. Place a small container at the front of the yoke to catch any spilled or leaking oil. You can also wrap a plastic bag with a rubber band around the end of the transmission to keep the oil off the floor. Once the driveshaft is disconnected and out of the car, you can easily remove the front U-joint from the yoke.

Although it is possible to overhaul universal joints, I recommend replacing them. For the relatively low cost of new joints and the ease of removal, it's really a no-brainer. If it's necessary to clamp the assembly down in order to remove or install the joints, secure the ends of the yokes for stabilization. Never clamp the shaft with a vise or any other object that could dent or damage it.

The joints and the shaft will return in reversed order. For high-end street use or racing applications, consider a driveshaft loop as long as the driveline components are already

Using both a socket and a boxed wrench, loosen and remove the U-shaped bolts from the joints.

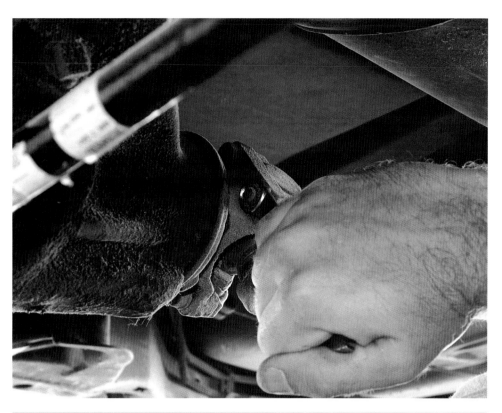

The crossmember mount will serve as the locating point for the new driveshaft loop.

removed from the vehicle. A driveshaft loop is engineered to retain and support the rapidly rotating shaft in the ill event of front U-joint failure. If the rear joint breaks, the shaft will most likely slide out of the transmission and exit the back of the car. However, if the forward U-joint gives way, the front of the shaft will drop, and can very easily stick or plant itself into the pavement. With the rear of the shaft still fixed and mounted to the differential assembly, the likely results can be catastrophic, if not fatal.

Installing a safety loop is relatively simple and only requires two bolts. In fact, you end up using the same two bolt holes in the transmission at the crossmember mount. First, remove the bolts securing the transmission to the crossmember. Using a floor jack, support and slowly raise the transmission just enough to allow ample clearance to slide the mounting plate of the loop between the crossmember and the top of the mount. After the plate is in position and the bolt holes are realigned, insert the new mounting bolts into the mount. The bolts will tie the crossmember, driveshaft loop, and mount to the transmission as one rigid assembly. Contact any aftermarket performance company for the correct driveshaft loop for your vehicle.

Installing an Automatic Transmission Aftermarket Floor Shifter

 Time: 3–4 hours

 Tools: Standard socket set, standard wrenches, power drill and attachments, round file, utility knife

 Talent:

 Applicable years: All

 Cost: $150–$300

 Parts: Shifter kit and hardware (included), transmission shifter cable (if needed)

 Tip: Aftermarket shifters often vary in design. Follow the manufacturer's instructions on the best way to mount and operate the product.

PERFORMANCE GAIN: Tighter, shorter-throw shifts for positive gear engagement

COMPLEMENTARY PROJECTS: Project 61: Removing and Replacing the Transmission

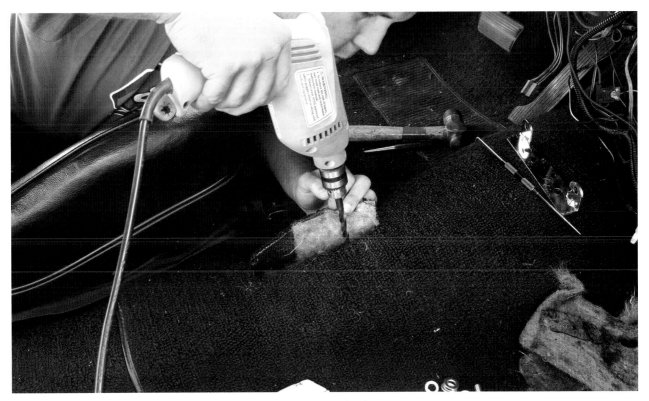

After the carpet is cut, drill four holes in the floorpan for the shifter mounting bracket.

TRANSMISSION

To execute the perfect shift, you need a solid and responsive shifter. Unfortunately, so many automatic-equipped cars rolled off the assembly line with nothing but a sloppy, column-mounted stick. Column-shift cars are forever cool as nostalgic sleepers, but any serious, performance-based vehicle is in need of much more.

Installing an aftermarket shifter has been a popular modification since the majority of these cars were factory fresh. Aftermarket companies, such as B&M and Hurst, design and manufacture shifter kits for every application imaginable and have long proven their advantages in the world of racing.

Dealing with a typical GM small block/TH350 combination, the first thing on the agenda is to get rid of the cumbersome column unit. Disconnect any and all attaching brackets and hardware from the steering column and shaft. As you might have guessed, the floorpan will need to be accessed in order to secure the bottom mounting plate of the new shifter and housing assembly. If your car has a bench seat, it will need to be removed before proceeding any further. Unbolt the seat from the floorpans (front and back) and separate the seat from the seatbelts. The belts should not need to come out. Once the seat is free and clear, remove it from the passenger compartment. This is always a little easier with an extra set of hands. With bucket seats, the conversion can be made without disturbing any other components.

The next step is to locate the new position of the shifter on the floorpans. Place the new unit and housing on the floor while sitting in a normal driving position to determine the best spot to anchor the bracket. Mark the location on the carpet where you will begin cutting. Using a sharp utility knife, carefully make the incision in the rug and underlying sound deadener to accommodate the mounting plate.

Now that you have a clear shot at the pans, the holes for the bracket can be drilled out. Grab a power drill and the appropriate bit, and let the sparks fly. Most kits include the necessary mounting bolts and nuts, so follow the product's recommendation on the size of holes to be drilled. Keep in mind the transmission is closely nestled to the underside of the floorpan. Try to stay shallow with the drill bit once the hole has been punched through. The transmission may need to be slightly lowered to access the bolts and apply the locknuts from the underside.

The transmission shifter cable extends from the body of the shifter, down through the floorpan and attaches to the detent on the transmission case. Drill an oblong hole in the floorpan where the cable can exit the passenger compartment and attach to the transmission. File the jagged edges of the hole smooth to avoid snagging or damaging the cable assembly. Insert a correctly sized rubber grommet into the hole for ease of operation.

The shifter itself is now ready to be installed into the floor bracket. Tighten the bolts down and feed the shifter

Drill several 1/4-inch holes into the pan, creating an oval or oblong shape for the shifter cable to slide down into.

The body of the shifter is finally bolted and secured to the mounting plate with the supplied hardware.

cable through the floor. Attach the opposite end of the cable to the transmission and check for any kinks or resistance in the movement of the cable. Operate the shifter by hand (engine not running) to ensure positive engagement in each gear. Reinstall the front seat, seatbelts, and any other items that have been removed during the installation.

PROJECT 67
Installing a Four-Speed Shifter

 Time: 3 hours

 Tools: Standard socket set, standard wrenches, needle-nose pliers

 Talent:

 Applicable years: All

 Cost: $250–$300

 Parts: Shifter kit, linkage rods and hardware (optional), brake cleaner

 Tip: On new assemblies, smooth out the shift arm holes with a small file to avoid any snagging or binding of the linkage rods.

PERFORMANCE GAIN: Quick, positive engaging shifts

COMPLEMENTARY PROJECTS: Project 2: Installing New Carpet and Sound Deadener; Project 64: Installing a Clutch

The shifter mechanism contains the body of the shifter and the fingered levers for each gear.

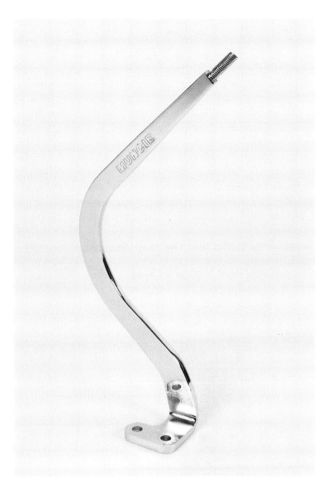

The shifter handle is an entirely separate piece and attaches to the body of the shifter housing with two bolts.

Every four-speed car needs a commanding shifter. The feeling of banging through the gears and executing every shift with violent authority is comparable to none. As gearheads, this all-so-familiar rush and excitement is what we live for. The cars, on the other hand, end up taking quite a flogging over the years and, as a result, produce sloppy shifts, gear crunches, and broken linkage. All of these performance-hindering conditions can easily be solved by stepping up and installing a rugged aftermarket stick, such as one manufactured by the legendary Hurst Shifters.

If you plan on purchasing a new shifter, consider replacing all of the transmission shifter linkage rods and hardware to further complete the package. From years and years of use, the rod ends often get hogged out into oblong holes and create sloppy gear engagements. Rebuild kits are available from Hurst and Mr. Gasket that include a set of nylon or steel rod bushings (depending on preference) and all

of the necessary retaining clips. These kits make a huge difference in the positive feel of your shifts. Typically, nylon bushings are recommended for street use due to their quiet operation and low-wear qualities.

The new shifter may be installed with the transmission still mounted to the chassis of the vehicle. Keep in mind that clearance may be extra tight in some applications. Start by safely hoisting the frame of the car and supporting both sides with a pair of sturdy jack stands. Carefully remove the retaining clips of the linkage rods from the transmission case and disconnect the arms. Take note of the position and location of the rod ends on the case. If the opposite ends of the rods are accessible from underneath the car, remove them in the same manner from the fingers of the shifter. Keep track of all original hardware during the disassembly.

Clear a direct path to access the shifter assembly from inside the vehicle. Remove the seats, console, carpet, and any applicable items to make the job easier. Reaching through the factory-cut shifter hole in the floorpan, release the linkage rods from the shifter body (if not already done) and unbolt the shifter assembly from the top of the transmission case.

To install the new unit, assemble the threaded rod adjustments for each linkage arm. As noted in the disassembly, each rod has its own designation on the shifter. The longest rod is third and fourth, the midsized rod is first and second, and the shortest rod is reverse. Now, place the shifter body into position on the transmission and tighten the bolts. The transmission should be placed in neutral and the supplied alignment pin inserted through all three shifter arms.

To finish the assembly and properly adjust the rods, it's best to start at the transmission case and work your way back to the shifter body. With the arms installed onto the transmission, adjust the opposite end of the rod at the shifter until each arm slides perfectly into place. Start with the reverse rod and move outward to the others, making sure the bushings easily install into the holes. Once all of the rods are attached, remove the alignment pin and check for smooth operation. This is a very important step in determining how your new shifter will perform. If you feel any snagging or abnormal resistance in the shifter, more adjustment is necessary.

The final step of adjustment is at the shifter stops. Every shifter comes equipped with a set of stops to prevent the slider arms from traveling too far and damaging the shifter. The stop for first and third is located at the rear of the shifter, while the second and fourth stop is at the front of the body. Place the transmission in the appropriate gear and turn the stop counterclockwise until only a few threads of the stop are showing. Slowly turn the stop inward until it touches the shifter, and then back it out one turn. Tighten the locknut and repeat the process for the opposite stop.

PROJECT 68
Installing a Transmission Brake

TRANSMISSION

 Time: 6–8 hours

 Tools: Standard socket set, standard wrenches, power drill and bits, pair of calipers, torque wrench

 Talent: 👤👤👤👤

 Applicable years: All automatic transmissions

 Cost: $300–$3,000 (complete transmission)

 Parts: Transmission brake kit or transmission assembly, transmission fluid

 Tip: Wiring the trans brake activation switch to a button on the transmission makes the engagement simple and convenient.

PERFORMANCE GAIN: Consistent staging and improved starting line launches

COMPLEMENTARY PROJECTS:

Project 61: Removing and Replacing the Transmission; Project 63: Understanding and Installing a Torque Converter; Project 66: Installing an Automatic Transmission Aftermarket Floor Shifter

Drag racing is all about knowing your equipment and being able to run consistently with the combination of your selected components. Every time you stage at the lights, a flurry of thoughts and concerns quickly blows through your mind. You may have the perfect winning formula down to a raw science in your head, but when that tree turns green, it's a whole different story. Launching a car from the starting line without red-lighting the tree takes every bit of concentration and focus to pull off correctly.

A transmission brake is designed for these exact situations. It enables the driver to load, or stall, the torque converter with engine rpm without having to simultaneously apply foot pressure to the brakes to hold the car in place. When the trans brake is activated, first and third gears are locked by hydraulic pressure and prevent the output shaft of the transmission from rotating. With the transmission and the car unable to move, you can apply the maximum load of engine rpm to the torque converter. At this point, the car is ready to launch. Disengaging the brake will release the pressure lock on the transmission gears and allow the car to quickly jump forward at the peak of its power band.

The engagement and disengagement of the trans brake all takes place in less than a second. While the brake is inactive, the transmission operates in its normal fashion. When the switch is activated, an electronic solenoid, which replaces the stock vacuum modulator, opens and regulates the flow of transmission fluid between two passages in the valve body assembly. When the fluid enters and pressurizes the passages, first and third gears are engaged at the same time, thus creating the lockup.

By releasing the activation button, the solenoid is disengaged and the fluid modulator valve returns to its original position. This cuts off all flow of fluid to third gear and eliminates the pressurized fluid in the passage through a small hole drilled into the direct drum of the automatic transmission. Once third gear disengages, the transmission instantly shifts into first gear and resumes normal operation.

Transmission brakes are simple in function, yet complex in design. Brake kits usually include a custom-modified valve body, separator plate and gasket, high-rate regulator spring, custom-rate direct drum piston-return springs, and a modulator valve spring. Installing the trans brake yourself requires disassembling the transmission and digging deep into the guts of the assembly to make the necessary modifications.

Transmission brakes can be purchased as a kit or as part of an entire transmission assembly from a number of different companies. Follow the manufacturer's instructions to the letter to ensure proper engagement and operation. You may elect to have a competent performance shop install the kit or transmission for you. Be sure to change the automatic transmission fluid and filter before reinstalling the transmission into the chassis. With the addition of a properly installed trans brake assembly, you will have one less concern on your mind when the time comes to let 'er rip!

172

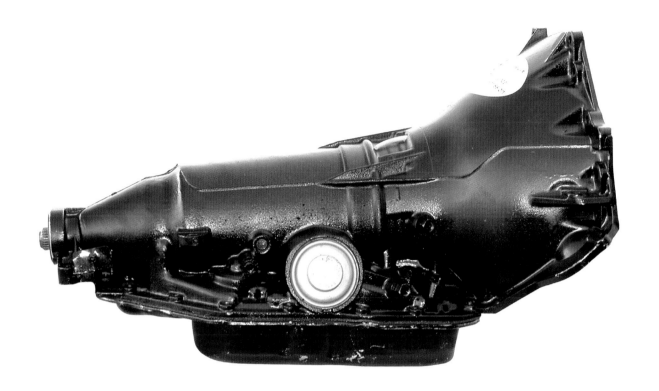

The transmission brake assembly is buried deep in the belly of the automatic transmission. Complete trannies are often sold with the trick valve body already installed.

REAR END

The rear differential assembly handles the transfer of power from the engine and transmission to the rear wheels. Consisting of the ring gear, pinion gear, and the drive axles, the rear end unit is simple in design, but extremely rugged and capable of handling heavy torque loads without failure or slippage. A stout rear axle assembly is always a major priority in any high-performance application.

Inspecting the Differential Housing and Gear Set

Time: 2 hours

Tools: Standard socket set, flat-blade screwdriver, hammer or mallet, gear oil, lubricant additive, clean rags, oil "catch" container

 Talent:

 Applicable years: All

 Cost: $50 for gear oil and new gasket

 Parts: New differential cover gasket

 Tip: Before opening up the rear differential housing, it's best to have a plan of action. Think about the future goals of your car and, more specifically, the rear end assembly and gear sets. Be prepared for the possibility of having to rebuild or replace the gear sets and pinions.

PERFORMANCE GAIN: A clean, well-oiled rear axle assembly will guarantee positive performance in your street or strip vehicle.

COMPLEMENTARY PROJECTS: Replacing the rear axle; Project 70: Understanding Rear Gear Ratios; Project 71: Installing a Powertrax No-Slip Traction System

Many of us often neglect the routine maintenance needs of the rear axle assembly. We figure as long as the rear tires still move when we hit the gas, everything back there must be OK. And unless there is some God-awful grinding noise overpowering the roar of the engine, the differential fluid level is probably good and clean. Ha! The rear end components are some of the toughest around, but everything needs a little TLC now and then. When you think about the strenuous loads and demands that are constantly placed on the differential and the rear axles, you can only assume that breakdown is inevitable. We hope this information reaches your hands before it's too late. Like everything else on your

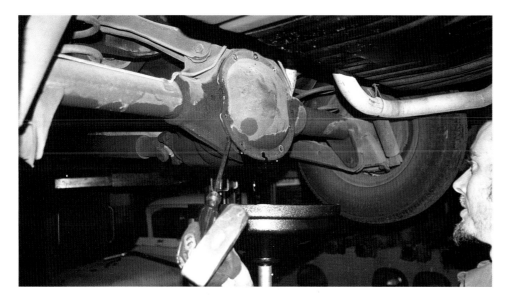

Use a flat-blade screwdriver to break the gasket bond between the cover and the housing surface.

175

Allow the old oil to fully drain from the case into a catch container.

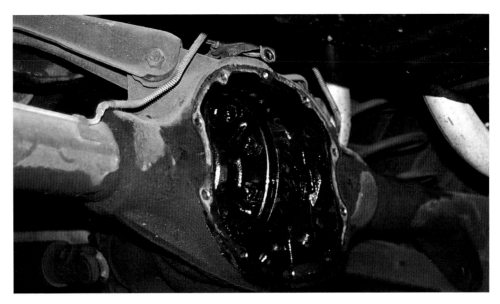

With a clean rag, wipe and remove any sludge or metal shavings from the differential housing.

car, preventative and periodic maintenance can, and usually will, go a long way.

Besides the monetary effect, a poorly kept rear end assembly also costs power and kills performance. All the power in the world does you absolutely no good if the rear end is unable to harness and deliver that power to the driving wheels.

And in order to do so, everything must be in perfect working order. If you suspect problems, or maybe it's just been a while since the gear oil has been changed, the best place to start is with a routine inspection and cleanup.

To initiate the inspection, remove the rear differential cover. With either a shop hoist or a floor jack and jack stands, raise and secure the rear of the vehicle to enable easy access to the cover bolts. One at a time, loosen and remove the retaining bolts from the diff cover. Be sure to have some type of container in position to catch the gear oil from the bottom of the housing. After all of the bolts are removed, you may need to gently pry the cover away from the housing along the edges. The thick rear end gasket can create a pretty tight

bond between the two surfaces. Be careful not to bend or kink the sealing area of the cover plate.

Once the cover has been removed and the fluid drained, inspect the inside of the housing for any built-up gunk or debris. Grab a shop light or a powerful flashlight and remove the sludge (typically found at the bottom of the housing) with some clean rags. Spray cleaners also work well for dissolving old residue and oils.

Closely examine the teeth of the gears for chipped edges or cracking. One side of the ring gear may show excessive wear, which usually indicates sloppy gear engagement and operation. If the teeth appear to be chewed up, replace the gear set while you're at it. Most performance gear sets run around $200–$250 and can make an astonishing difference in the quickness of your car. Differential rebuild kits are also a great idea, and usually cost about $150.

After thoroughly cleaning and inspecting the rear end assembly, install the new diff cover gasket and cover plate. Torque the bolts down evenly to the manufacturer's specs. Refill the case with quality gear oil and check for leaks.

Understanding Rear Gear Ratios

 Time: n/a

 Tools: n/a

 Talent: 🔧🔧

 Applicable years: All

 Cost: $200–$250

 Parts: Ring and pinion set, differential fluid

 Tip: It's best to seek out the help of an experienced professional when changing the rear end gears.

 PERFORMANCE GAIN: Quicker, faster, off-the-line acceleration

COMPLEMENTARY PROJECTS:
Replacing the rear axle; Project 71: Installing a Powertrax No-Slip Traction System

The ring and pinion gears are the key components that comprise the rear gear ratio.

REAR END

Most of us are familiar with the notion that rear axle gears largely affect your car's performance. The "more" gear you have, the faster you go, right? In fact, there are tons of variables that ultimately determine the right gear choice for your machine. The first thing to grasp and really understand is the actual gear ratio and what it represents.

The rear end gear ratio refers to the relationship between the driven gear (ring) and the drive gear (pinion) and is easily calculated by dividing the ring gear tooth count by the drive gear tooth count. For example, if the ring gear has 41 teeth and the drive gear has 10 teeth, the correct gear ratio would be 4.10:1. This also means that for every one revolution of the ring gear, the drive gear will turn 4.10 times. The driveshaft and the rear axles have the same comparable relationship.

The easiest way to understand the operation of the rear gears is to think of them as mechanical levers. They provide a mechanical leverage that multiplies torque to help the power

of the engine move the car. As the gear ratio becomes numerically higher, the gears offer more leverage to assist in acceleration. These types of ratios are commonly referred to as "lower" or "deeper" gears. If the ratio drops numerically (from 4.56:1 to 3.55:1), the gear set becomes "taller" and offers less mechanical leverage. The relationship between the two types of gears is like changing a tire with a socket wrench versus a long breaker bar. It requires much more force to move the small wrench (tall gears) than it does the longer leverage bar (deep gears). Rear end gears work in the same fashion. If the engine and transmission deliver 100 ft-lb of torque to the pinion gear and the gear ratio is 4.56:1, the output torque to the rear wheels would be 456 ft-lb (100 x 4.56). With a taller gear ratio of 3.08:1 in the same car with identical power, the output torque would drop considerably to 308 ft-lb (100 x 3.08). This is why deep gears are always so popular on the drag strip—it's free torque.

However, there is compromise that comes with running a lower gear set. At the top of that list is engine cruise rpm. Lower gears require more input speed or revolutions of the engine in order to produce the same output speed at the tire. A taller gear will not make as much torque, but it requires less engine rpm to make the same tire rpm. Using the aforementioned ratios, the engine would turn 4.56 times for every one revolution of the tire with the lower ratio, 3.08 times with taller ratio. This has a big effect on your highway

The pinion gear is precisely machined for positive engagement and smooth operation.

cruising speeds. By swapping out a 3.08:1 gear with a lower 4.56:1 gear with a 26-inch-tall tire, your cruise rpm at 65 miles per hour would jump from 2,600 to 3,800! The rpm is calculated by multiplying your miles per hour by the gear ratio by 336. Then divide this total by the rear tire diameter (65 x 4.56 x 336 = 99,590 / 26 = 3,830).

When it comes to performance gearing, there are plenty of options. Most drag strip–bound cars usually prefer a gear in the 4.10:1 neighborhood. If the car is particularly heavy or the powerband of the engine is at the upper end of the rpm scale, lower gears (numerically higher) may be necessary. If the car is a little on the light side yet still makes good power, you can get away with running a taller rear gear ratio. Naturally, less torque is required to move a lighter object than a heavy one. For top speed purposes, tall or shallow gears are used to reduce the engine rpm versus the actual road speed. These types of cars may not have quick, low-speed acceleration, but selecting the right transmission can easily compensate for the lack of bottom-end grunt.

The engine's powerband also dictates which gears will work best in your application. For instance, big-cube big-blocks such as BOP (Buick, Olds, and Pontiac) 455s make plenty of low-end torque but fall off a little early in the upper rpm scale. Running a taller gear (numerically lower) will allow the engine's natural torque to accelerate the car off the line. In turn, the tall ratio helps accelerate the car down the track and maintain its miles per hour.

Many other factors affect the gear ratio and vice versa, including transmission type and individual transmission gear ratios, tire diameter, and torque converter stall speeds (automatic). These should all be heavily considered before changing the existing rear gear ratio.

Installing a Powertrax No-Slip Traction System

 Time: 5–6 hours

 Tools: Socket wrenches, center punch, hammer, slide hammer, flat-blade screwdriver, boxed wrenches, white lithium grease, black silicone grease, gear oil, carburetor cleaner

 Talent:

 Applicable years: All

 Cost: $400–$425

 Parts: Powertrax no-slip traction system

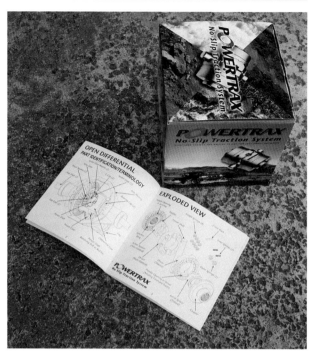 **Tip:** Remove your differential beforehand and work on a flat surface.

 PERFORMANCE GAIN: All the advantages of a Detroit Locker (and more) without grinding your gears

COMPLEMENTARY PROJECTS:
Replacing the rear axle; Project 65: Replacing the Universal Joint and Driveshaft/Installing the Driveshaft Safety Loop

The instruction booklet that comes with the Powertrax kit is second to none.

Space prohibits us from going through the actual installation of the Powertrax unit—we'd need five more pages and about 40 more photographs! Don't let this discourage you. The instructions that come with the product are among the best we've ever seen. The step-by-step guide is technically perfect, with large illustrations and clear directions. We chose this project to make you aware of Powertrax, and to explain how it works and its key benefits.

If you haven't heard of Powertrax yet, don't feel bad. Only a few years new to the marketplace, Powertrax is a highly refined no-slip traction system and it fits right into any open- or closed-end differential carrier. Powertrax is a big step up from a standard factory limited-slip differential in that it incorporates the latest in technology, extrahardened Zytanium components, and simplicity of design. Without getting into all of the technical specifications here (which are covered in great depth in the Powertrax installation manual), we'll at least cover the basics of Powertrax and what makes it work so well.

With limited-slip/posi differentials and locker differentials, there is a big advantage over an open rear end: the added traction allows for better performance. The problem with a limited-slip is exactly that—it's limited. Through various forms of internal friction devices, a limited-slip differential transfers a relatively small amount of power to the nonslipping wheel. The clutch system hurts your fuel economy and easily overheats when slipping. The clutches are also prone to wear and tear and require friction/silencer additives.

Locker differentials, by contrast, "lock" the two drive wheels together. When powering in a straight line, engine torque is delivered equally between both drive wheels. If one

179

wheel loses traction, a locker will deliver power to the wheel with the highest amount of traction—a pretty good system, but there is one major drawback. Although a locker will deliver excellent performance and allow full-wheel differentiation when turning, it is typically harsh and noisy. Disengagement is sudden and abrupt, and it tends to "ratchet" loudly when cornering. Also, reengagement is delayed.

A Powertrax unit is a totally different animal. A relatively simple combination of rings and gears made of high-strength Zytanium, Powertrax greatly improves on all of the effectiveness of a locker differential, while offering incredibly smooth and quiet operational characteristics. Through computer-aided design techniques, Powertrax provides optimal intermeshing of gears, rings, and couplers with precision synchronization.

Before getting started: Since you're going to be working on the differential and removing the axles, you'll need to get the car up off the ground. Use a hoist if you have access to one. If not, get the back half of the car up on a quality pair of jack stands. Set the parking brake, block the front tires, and remove both rear wheels.

The Powertrax system can be installed in all makes of rear-wheel-drive or four-wheel-drive vehicles. It can also be installed in an open or closed differential. Powertrax is not intended for use with front-wheel-drive vehicles.

What makes Powertrax so cool?

•It works. It's the only differential that offers the maximum traction of a locker with the smooth characteristics of a limited-slip/posi differential. It delivers power to both wheels through intermeshing teeth in such a way that one wheel cannot be powered ahead of the other. A specially contoured saddle ensures direct engagement of the teeth. Powertrax is also designed with a precision synchronization mechanism that holds the driver and the coupler disengaged throughout a turn, so the unit remains quiet and operates smoothly, unlike a locker differential.

•It's easy to install. It fits into your existing differential case, so there's no need to realign the ring and pinion gears.

•It's strong. There are no friction clutches to wear out. The sliding motions of the primary torque-carrying components have been engineered to occur under negligible forces for long product life and trouble-free operation.

Don't let the little springs scare you! It's all covered in the book.

SUSPENSION

The suspension on any older vehicle always needs serious attention. The factory rubber bushings slowly deteriorate and collapse under the constant loads of handling and braking. Rebuilding the suspension not only increases performance, but also creates a safer vehicle on the road.

Installing New Front Lowering Springs and Shocks

SUSPENSION

 Time: 5–6 hours

 Tools: Standard socket set, rubber mallet, pry bar, pickle fork (ball joint removal tool), drill with bit for drilling steel, grease gun, grease

 Talent:

 Applicable years: All

 Cost: $125

 Parts: Front 2-inch lowering springs, KYB gas shock absorbers, tie rod ends and polyurethane bushings, upper and lower ball joints, shock mount retainers (if not included with shock kit)

 Tip: Always support the lower control arm when removing the coil springs. If you have access to a hoist (or lift), take advantage. An impact wrench can save you time as well.

 PERFORMANCE GAIN: Our 2-inch lowering springs will drop the car's center of gravity, offering vastly improved handling, not to mention the cool lowered stance.

COMPLEMENTARY PROJECTS:

Project 77: Installing a Rear Sway Bar; Project 86: Bleeding the Brakes

Ever notice how the topic of road handling never seems to crop up when people start talking about their muscle cars? Most older street machines do well as long as they're going in a straight line. Get into the corners, however, and a lot of these cars simply give up; some of them even become downright dangerous. Very few cars from the late 1960s and early 1970s exhibit any kind of ability to tackle corners without excessive body roll, mostly due to the lack of attention paid to the car's underpinnings. After all, the name of the game was quarter-mile domination. Well, in this project we'll cover the basics of installing a new set of lowering springs and shocks.

The purpose of installing lowering springs is to slightly lower the car, giving it a better center of gravity. The springs used in this project will lower your vehicle by approximately 2 inches. When you're done, you'll have one mean-lookin' road machine with greatly improved road manners.

It's important that you start with solid suspension parts. Make sure the upper and lower ball joints and tie rod ends are in decent shape. Ours were in pretty rough condition, so we decided to replace both. You can work with your vehicle raised on a hoist or a quality set of jack stands. Take the necessary precautions while working under your vehicle.

Since you're going to remove the original coil springs, you need to support the lower control arm with a heavy block of wood and whatever further support is available (jackscrew, etc.). Remember, the spring is under great pressure and once the spindle assembly is removed, it can literally launch into the air. Use extreme caution. To avoid damaging the brake flexible lines, we disconnect them at this stage.

Unless your upper and lower control arms are severely bent or damaged, you will use your existing parts. As shown in our first photo, we've removed all the front end cotter pins. Next, we remove the sway bar and end links using standard socket wrenches. An impact wrench saves time and effort. The old rubber bushings on the tie rod ends can be cut, drilled, or punched out. Then, we remove the old shock absorbers.

With the lower control arms (and coil spring) fully supported, we remove the castle nuts that secure the ball joints and pull the spindle/brake assembly. At this point, it's a good idea to check the upper and lower ball joints. Take the threaded pin that fits through the spindle and try to move it with your fingers. If it's loose and moves from side to side, it's time to replace them. The originals are riveted into place, so you'll have to drill them out and install new ones. New ball joints are affixed with nuts, and cannot be riveted back in as the originals were.

We then gently release pressure on the support under the lower control arm. Go slowly—the object is to gradually release the spring. Stand clear of the spring in case it pops from the pockets in the control arms. You may need to use a large screwdriver or pry bar to coax the spring out. As stated before, use extreme caution.

The next step is to insert the new spring. The original springs on your car are variable rate, as opposed to today's

With our car up on a lift, we've removed the front wheels. This shot shows us removing the cotter pins. You'll need to remove them from the upper and lower ball joints as well as the tie rod ends.

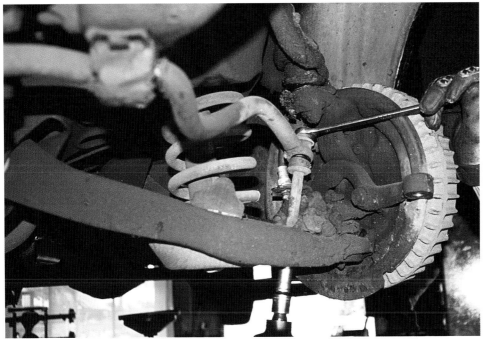

In this shot, we're removing the sway bar from the top of the end links. An impact wrench speeds up the process.

much stiffer progressive-rate springs. We use 2-inch lowering springs (Part Number C990098, Original Parts Group). These are specially developed variable-rate springs, which actually do a couple of things. The new springs are designed to offer a much more comfortable ride, at the same time providing excellent road feel and control.

Important: Make sure the end of the spring sets into the lower-most portion of the spring pocket. The holes in the pocket are for water drainage. If you have trouble getting the springs to set properly into the upper and lower control arm spring pockets, hold the lower arm up in place with one hand and rotate the spring until you feel it move into position.

Here's where the "pickle fork" comes in handy. You can use it to bust out old bushings (as we're doing in this shot) and ball joints. You can also cut or saw out bushings.

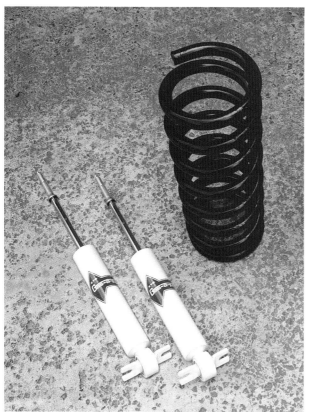

Our new 2-inch lowering coil springs and KYB Gas-A-Just shocks.

Tighten your support under the lower control arm until you can fit the spindle/brake assembly over the top of the ball joints. Install castle nuts and secure with new cotter pins.

On the lower control arm, you'll need to replace the lower shock mount retainers. The old retainers will be damaged after you remove the original shocks. The KYB gas shocks are inexpensive and help provide excellent control. Push them up through the bottom of the lower control arm and fasten at the top of the shock mount. Attach the lower portion of the shock to the lower control arm. Follow the manufacturer's enclosed instructions.

Remember to lubricate the upper and lower ball joints, using a grease gun.

Next, we attach new tie rod ends and bushings. Before securing them to the steering knuckle, coat them with grease. Don't forget to reattach the brake lines.

The final step is to reattach the end links and sway bar. A typical upgrade would move from a 7/8-inch bar up to a 1 1/8-inch bar. Check the brake fluid and bleed the brakes.

Important: We highly recommend following through with rear suspension modifications, including installing the rear sway bar. A car with a beefed up front end and a factory stock rear can experience severe control problems during moderate-to-hard cornering. The rear of the car is very likely to lose road adhesion and may come around 180 degrees under certain driving conditions.

Installing a Front Sway Bar

 Time: 1 hour

 Tools: Standard socket set, standard wrenches, lubrication grease

 Talent:

 Applicable years: All

 Cost: $125

 Parts: Front sway bar, new sway bar bushings

 Tip: Before removing anything from the car, take note of the sequence of the bushings in relation to the lower control arm and the sway bar.

PERFORMANCE GAIN: A tighter, better-handling front end and longer lasting components

COMPLEMENTARY PROJECTS: Installing new sway bar end links and polyurethane sway bar bushings

Many factors contribute to creating a well-balanced and tuned suspension system. From braking, cornering, and steering to tire traction and various weight transfers, the highly detailed equation of suspensions can be overwhelming and often leave us in the dirt.

Traction is at the top of the list in any application. Whether you rely solely on the bite of the rear meats for quick quarter-mile action or the four-wheel gripping force in heavy side-to-side cornering, the traction yielded from the tires ultimately determines how your car handles. You can invest thousands of hard-earned dollars into expensive handling components, but if the car will not hook on the pavement, what good is it really doing?

Most of these cars were factory-equipped with a fairly marginal suspension system. Although well designed and durable, they were not built with high-performance handling in mind. Even when new, they pale in comparison to the standards of performance and safety that we know today, leaving us plenty of room for improvement.

Enter the front anti-roll bar. The primary function of the front sway bar is to limit and control the side-to-side body roll of the vehicle. Attached to both the frame and the lower

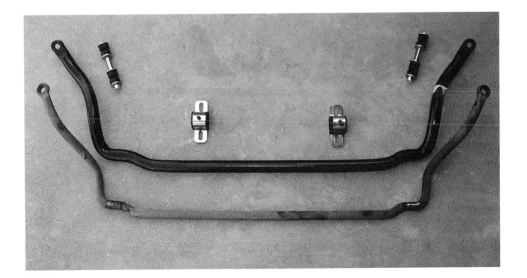

When upgrading or increasing the size of your sway bar, you must also buy a pair of matching bushings (1 1/4-inch versus 7/8-inch stock in this case). We decided to replace the end links with a quality polyurethane set as well.

185

The end links slide up from the bottom side of the lower control arm. The sway bar is sandwiched between a series of bushings and washers on the top side, and is secured with a single nut.

After loosely fitting the sway bar into place at the control arms, tighten the sway bar brackets to secure the bar to the frame. Thoroughly grease the insides of the bushings prior to installation.

control arms, the sway bar rigidly ties both sides of the suspension together, naturally decreasing its flexibility. In addition, it contributes to balancing the rolling front-to-rear weight transfer.

Most GM A-body cars were shipped with a stock 7/8-inch sway bar. Considering the sheer size and weight of these machines, the pencil-thin bars and their rubber bushings (see photo 1) have seen more than their share of stress and abuse over the years. Constant flexure, road grime and debris, and extreme temperatures all play a part in the deterioration of these pieces.

With so many aftermarket suspension companies now offering complete upgrade kits for almost every GM product, the process of beefing up your existing front end is relatively painless. We decided to swap out the stock sway bar with a monster 1 1/4-inch bar and matching polyurethane bushings. For an extra $20, we also replaced the sway bar end links.

Starting off with the front end in the air, loosen and remove the end link bolts and bushings. Note the proper

sequence of bushings and washers to help during the reassembly. With the end links gone, unbolt the brackets from the frame. At this point, the sway bar should literally drop down into your hands.

The install is just as easy. Be sure to apply plenty of grease to the bushings before installing them on the bar. Slide the new end links through the bottom of the lower control arms, followed by the nut on top. Attach the sway bar brackets to the frame and loosely snug them down, allowing for slight adjustments before final tightening.

You'll notice results from upgrading the front sway bar and bushings immediately. A positive, more responsive front end will increase the overall handling and performance of your vehicle without question. Furthermore, polyurethane bushings will far outlast their rubber counterparts and will help reduce suspension deflection. Changing the diameter of your front sway bar is one of the most dramatic changes you can make in your front-end suspension.

PROJECT 74

Installing a Quick-Ratio Power Steering Box

 Time: 3 hours

 Tools: Standard socket set, standard wrenches, Pitman arm puller, power drill and bits

 Talent: 🔧🔧🔧

 Applicable years: All

 Cost: $0–$300

 Parts: Rebuilt or remanufactured power steering box, power steering lines and hoses (optional), hose/line fittings, power steering fluid

 Tip: Always research your projects before tearing apart a section of your car. You may find problems or obstacles that steer you in more practical and effective direction.

PERFORMANCE GAIN: Upgrading your steering control from the cumbersome 20:1 factory ratio to the late-model 12.7:1 ratio will make a night and day difference in the response and precision of your steering and front suspension.

COMPLEMENTARY PROJECTS:
Project 72: Installing New Front Lowering Springs and Shocks

In high-performance applications, the original slow-turn steering boxes always leave a little to be desired. The vague feeling of barreling down the road with inches of free slop in the steering wheel is unnerving and unsafe. However, in the early days of manufacturing, this was all that was available. In fact, it was not until the late 1970s that things started to turn around, literally. Often referred to as the dawn of the late-model era, the 1978 production year underwent major changes in model size, style, and engineering. Of these mechanical changes, the quick-ratio steering box vastly improved the handling and performance of these cars and restored confidence in the hands of drivers as well.

Swapping out the steering box on any old GM A-body vehicle is easy. The factory box is located tightly against the left-hand frame rail and is a clear shot from the top or bottom of the car. First, disconnect the front sway bar from the frame and allow the bar to hang suspended from the control arms. On early vehicles (1964–1967), it may also be necessary to unbolt the left front bumper bracket and brace from the frame after marking their locations. Disconnect the steering shaft coupling and mark the Pitman arm in relation to the shaft. Using the appropriate Pitman arm puller, remove the arm from the assembly and set it aside.

To successfully remove and replace the steering box, the steering shaft will also need to be removed from the old unit. For proper instructions on removing the shaft from the steering gear, check out Project 3. Once the gearbox is free and clear of the shaft, loosen and remove the box-to-frame mounting bolts and carefully lift the box from the engine compartment.

Late-model steering boxes typically use a 3/4-inch, 30-spline steering shaft, as opposed to the early style 13/16-inch, 36-spline shaft. You will need to change the coupler, or rag joint, at the entry point of the steering gear. Depending on the year of your vehicle, slight drilling and modification may be necessary to properly adapt the new rag joint to the original steering shaft and column. The actual box will mount in the same manner and location as the old unit, utilizing the same holes in the frame rail for attachment.

For the power steering aspect of the project, the hookup is rather simple. The factory high-pressure lines are capable of withstanding load amounts in excess of 1,800 psi at full lock and are interchangeable with the new quick-turning gearbox. You may need to install an 18-millimeter double-flare nut on the pressure side to adapt to the fitting on the box. The return line should be a quality Weatherhead-type hose with the required fittings.

After the plumbing is complete, place the new steering gear back in the engine compartment and snug the mounting bolts. Leave the rag joint coupler loose to find its new home. Make sure the box is fitted squarely to the frame rail, and return to properly torque the bolts. Reattach the steering shaft to the box and align the match marks for the Pitman arm. Tighten the Pitman arm nut and the steering coupler nuts to their recommended spec.

SUSPENSION

187

The steering box and power steering pump are easily accessible from the front of the vehicle.

The steering coupler, or rag joint, adapts the steering shaft to the gearbox.

Remanufactured quick-ratio steering boxes are available from many aftermarket parts suppliers.

Installing Subframe Connectors

 Time: 2 hours

 Tools: Standard socket set, standard wrenches, power drill and drill bits (if applicable)

 Talent:

 Applicable years: All F-body models

 Cost: $100–$150

 Parts: Subframe connector kit and hardware

 Tip: Buy quality products. There are tons of companies making subframe connectors, but not all of them implement heavy-duty materials and quality construction.

 PERFORMANCE GAIN: Subframe connectors are a must for any high-performance small car without a full frame. They offer strength and improved handling under heavy loads.

COMPLEMENTARY PROJECTS:

Project 72: Installing New Front Lowering Springs and Shocks; Project 73: Installing a Front Sway Bar; Project 76: Installing Rear Shocks and Lowering Springs

Although the majority of projects featured in this book are universal in application (A-body, F-body, X-body, etc.), the installation of subframe connectors is specific to the F-body design. Most commonly installed on Novas, Camaros, and Firebirds, aftermarket subframe connectors offer additional strength and rigidity to a less-than-stout factory platform.

These compact cars of yesteryear were engineered and crafted with a front partial frame only. They lack the brawn and sheer ruggedness of the larger, full-frame vehicles such as the Pontiac GTO and the Chevy Chevelle and Impala.

Having only a shortened frame at the front of the vehicle dramatically affects the chassis' ability to handle any kind of serious horsepower. Other than the car's sheetmetal body, there is no connection between the front and rear suspensions. Under heavy loads (such as a drag launch), the body can distort and twist from the high energy created by the powerplant. Needless to say, this is not a good thing. In addition to warping and possibly even cracking major stress points on the body, this intense "torque flexing" can also hinder your beloved ETs.

When energy intended for the rear wheels is lost and absorbed into the body and suspension, the results can be very disappointing. Subframe connectors will dampen and eliminate these kinds of problems. Constructed of boxed steel tubing (similar to a frame rail), the reinforcement connectors literally tie the two ends of the chassis together. When installed, they run parallel to each other down the length of the floorpans. The shorter subframe car now takes on the burly persona of a full-frame vehicle. There will always be a certain amount of chassis flex under acceleration. However, the harmful effects are greatly minimized when all of the pieces are firmly secured together.

Depending on the year of the vehicle, the installation procedure may vary slightly from one car to another. By far, the most popular subjects are the '68–'72 Novas and the first- and second-generation Camaros and Firebirds. They all share the same subframe and suspension design. The connectors simply attach between the rear of the front frame horns and the forward spring perch on the rear suspension. The body bushings at the frame rails must be removed to allow the connectors to slide into place. In fact, the connectors attach to the frame using the same body bushing bolts and hardware. The rear mounting point is at the forward leaf spring perch, again utilizing the existing hardware. The design is extremely simple yet effective. The aftermarket manufacturers have made the process fairly easy.

On the early Chevy II Novas ('62–'67), the design is similar, but not exactly the same. These cars are well known in the performance world for their poor handling and weak suspension designs. Nonetheless, they have a very popular body style and definitely one worth fixing. The aftermarket offers plenty of quality upgrades for the less-than-impressive factory setup. There are even complete front end replacement kits available for these micro-Novas.

Although it may not be necessary in all applications, our subframe connectors required a fair amount of drilling. At the front of the car, we drill mounting through-holes in both the connectors and the frame rails. The bolts slide through the holes and secure the connectors to the flange of the frame. At the rear spring perches, we also create one hole on each side for the same purpose.

SUSPENSION

The front of the connector arm "boxes" the frame rail and is secured by two bolts.

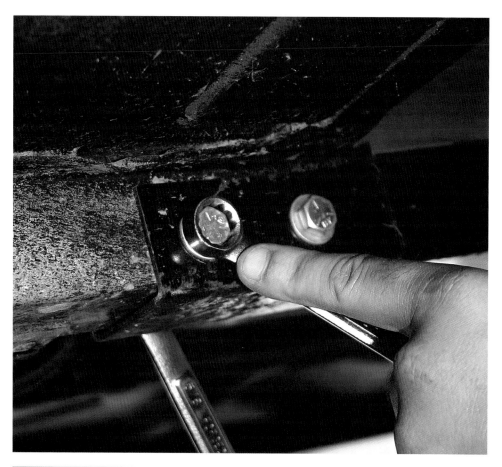

For added strength, we drill the connector arm and the rear flange of the spring perch and bolt them together.

Left: Once the connector is in position, tighten the spring perch bolt and nut.

Below: This angle gives you an overall look at the clean, finished product.

With the car safely supported by jack stands, we start at the front frame rails. The connectors attach to the frame through the newly drilled holes and the bolts are securely tightened. At the rear of the car, we remove the through-bolt at each spring perch and install the connector arm. We retighten the bolts and slowly lower the vehicle. Be sure to check for any binding or twisting in the connectors at the front and rear mounting points.

Installing Rear Shocks and Lowering Springs

 Time: 2 hours

 Tools: Standard socket set, standard wrenches, floor jack and jack stands

 Talent:

 Applicable years: All

 Cost: $200–$250

 Parts: One pair of rear lowering springs, one pair of matching shock absorbers

 Tip: Always work on a flat, level surface when underneath a car supported by jack stands. Chock the wheels on the ground for added safety.

PERFORMANCE GAIN: A more positive, responsive rear suspension with improved handling and a smoother ride

COMPLEMENTARY PROJECTS: Project 77: Installing a Rear Sway Bar; Project 78: Installing Boxed Rear Control Arms

SUSPENSION

With the car securely supported on jack stands, remove the lower shock absorber nut and mounting stud.

The rear suspension design on any older car with coil springs is about as basic as it can get. It consists of two upper and two lower control arms, a pair of coil springs, and a couple of shock absorbers. The rear springs are located between brackets on the axle tube and the spring seats in the frame. Sitting in a saucer-type seat, the springs are held in place merely by the weight of the car. The rear shocks, which also aid in spring retention, are mounted at a slight angle between the spring seat (top) and the axle housing (bottom). Depending on the year of the vehicle, the shock absorbers are either both mounted behind the axle housing (pre-1968) or in a staggered configuration (1968 and newer). The staggered configuration cuts down on excess wheel hop and further improves the car's rear-end traction.

If you own and actually drive one of these cars on a regular basis, you know full well what a 35-year-old stock suspension feels and handles like. Although the longevity and sheer toughness of this cave-man design is impressive, it leaves a little to be desired. Years and years of speed bumps, potholes, and not-so-delicate cargo have taken a hammering toll on your rear springs and shocks absorbers.

In any high-performance car, whether for the street or the strip, the suspension plays a prominent role in determining its physical capabilities. For example, a rear drag-car suspension is set up to take the initial and sudden weight transfer from the front, plant the rear end and the tires, and steer the car down the track in a rigid, straight line. A canyon-carving street car is designed to do the exact opposite. It relies heavily on tuned suspension systems for extreme side-to-side cornering, braking, and acceleration. No matter what your drive, it's important to lay down a solid foundation.

We'll start by swapping out the old, dilapidated springs and now-useless shocks and replacing them with a new set of lowering springs and gas shocks. Get the rear of the car up in the air and secured on a pair of jack stands. Place the floor jack underneath the axle for support and disconnect the shock absorber (lower first, then upper). With the shock removed, slowly lower the jack and allow the axle to drop. By releasing the load, the rear springs should be free of all tension. Carefully pry the lower end of the spring over the retainer and remove. If the springs are still loaded after lowering the axle, a spring compressor should be used to safely remove them from their seats.

When installing new springs—either stock or lowered—don't be fooled by the height of the new springs compared to your old ones. The true difference lies in the spring rate. It's impossible to tell how the car will sit with any pair of coil springs simply by looking at them. If they truly appear suspect, call the manufacturer and double-check the part number before scuffing them up and installing them.

Most cars came equipped from the factory with rear spring insulation pads. These small rubber pads are installed between the top of the spring and its upper retainer to avoid rubbing or excess noise. The new springs may take a little extra muscle to place, but they should basically go in the same way the old ones came out. Make sure the entire diameter of the bottom coil is fully seated in its groove.

The new shocks are now ready to be installed. Starting at the top mounting location, secure (hand tight) the upper end of the absorber to the spring seat (two bolts). Again utilizing the floor jack, support and raise the axle to meet the lower mounting stud of the shock absorber and loosely install the nut. Return to the top and tighten; then tighten the lower.

With the car back on the ground, forcefully bounce the rear end and check for any signs of leakage or geometry problems. New springs need time to settle in place and find their home in the seats. So hit the road, and enjoy the ride.

As you can see, the old springs and shocks were long overdue for replacement. The Gabriel Hi-Jackers (the rear shock of choice throughout the 1970s) were completely collapsed and offered zero support in dampening the rear end travel. We decided on a pair of KYB GR-2 gas shocks to fix the problem.

By removing the shock absorber and allowing the axle tube to drop, you should have plenty of room to place the new spring into position by hand. (Note the rubber insulator at the top of the spring.)

When reinstalling the shocks, start at the top and loosely secure the nuts to allow for any angle adjustment on the bottom.

Installing a Rear Sway Bar

 Time: 30 minutes

 Tools: Standard socket set, standard wrenches, power drill and drill bits

  Talent:

 Applicable years: All

 Cost: $100

 Parts: Rear sway bar, sway bar mounting kit (includes bolts, washers, and necessary spacers)

 Tip: Always be patient and take your time when measuring pieces for drilling.

PERFORMANCE GAIN: A solid, well-planted rear suspension that works in unison with your front-end components

COMPLEMENTARY PROJECTS: Project 76: Installing Rear Shocks and Lowering Springs; Project 78: Installing Boxed Rear Control Arms

The rear sway bar is an often-overlooked piece of the rear suspension. Most of these cars were built and sold sans rear anti-roll bar. Back in those days, only the special high-performance vehicles were granted rear reinforcements. Even a large number of Chevrolet's factory Super Sports did not have a rear sway bar. The reason? The factory was mainly interested in production and keeping all costs as low as possible. Since many General Motors manufacturers shared the same or similar platforms (and parts), it made more sense to utilize the parts available from each other than to make each rear-end assembly different. And as we all know, the vast majority of assembly line cars at the time were not performance vehicles. Truth be told, most car buyers were not interested in the performance arena or plainly could not afford it.

SUSPENSION

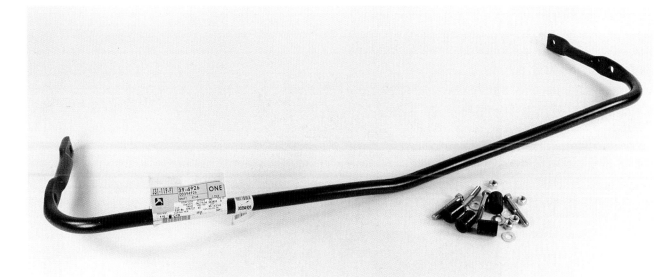

Most aftermarket rear sway bars, complete with mounting hardware, sell for around $100. This is one of the best nominal investments you can make for your car's suspension and handling capabilities.

In this photo, we show the sway bar bolting right up to a fully boxed control arm. If you use a stock (unboxed) control arm, the supplied spacers will fit right inside the arm, adding strength and rigidity.

And what am I getting at? When used in any high-performance application, the poor geometry and flexibility of the stock rear suspension needs work. In addition to control arms and bushings (covered in Project 78), the rear sway bar is one of the first improvements that comes to mind, and one of the easiest.

If your car was not originally equipped with a rear sway bar, chances are you will need to drill two holes in the sides of your existing lower control arms to mount the bar. Making sure you have marked the arms to be drilled evenly and symmetrically is key. If your measurements are even slightly out of whack, it can hurt your car's performance. Don't take any chances—double-check your work.

The easiest way to obtain the correct placement of the sway bar mounting holes is to measure a pair of predrilled factory lower control arms. If you are unable to use a factory template, carefully measure the distance from the forward end of the control arm to the location of the sway bar. Have a friend or two help you out with the mockup. Once its position is determined, remove the arms from the vehicle and place them on the workbench. Scribe a mark in the same location on each arm, representing the sway bar. Transfer the hole pattern of the sway bar to each control arm. Now, you are ready to drill.

The sway bar mounting kit comes complete with hardware and spacers for nonboxed control arms. The bolts supplied are 3/8 inch–16 (thread count), so make your holes accordingly. If at all possible, use a drill press to punch out the control arms. Your holes will come out clean and straight every time. If not, use a hefty power drill and be careful. When drilling larger-diameter holes, always use a center punch and a smaller pilot drill bit before reaming the final size. This will keep the larger drill bit from "walking" out of position on the surface and throwing off your placement.

Now, we are ready for the install. With the lower control arms bolted back in place, lift the sway bar to meet its newfound mounting holes. Just to be safe, install the bolts and washers through the sway bar first. If anything crazy ever happened and the bolt fell out, this would keep it from getting caught in the rear wheel. The spacers that come in the mounting kit actually belong inside the lower control arm (see photo 2) to prevent excess load or stress on the sidewall of the arm while tightening the nuts and bolts.

While holding the nut in place on the back side with a wrench, crank the socket down on the bolt head to securely tighten.

Installing Boxed Rear Control Arms

 Time: 1–2 hours

 Tools: Standard socket set, standard wrenches

  Talent: 👤👤

 Applicable years: All

 Cost: $200 (new), $30 (conversion)

 Parts: Factory-style or aftermarket boxed rear control arms (new bushings included), or weld-in boxing plates (new bushings optional)

 Tip: When replacing older rear control arms, use polyurethane bushings to help stiffen the rear end and reduce deflection.

PERFORMANCE GAIN: Positive gripping force to help eliminate wheel hop

COMPLEMENTARY PROJECTS:
Project 77: Installing a Rear Sway Bar; Project 76: Installing Rear Shocks and Lowering Springs

Rear coil-spring suspensions are extremely simple in design and easy to understand. Along with the shock absorbers and springs, the rear upper and lower control arms receive the torque and weight coming from the front of the vehicle and transfer it downward, planting the rear tires on the ground. Inside each end of the arms is a rubber bushing. The lower arms are mounted between the rear axle assembly and the frame. Their job is to maintain the fore-and-aft

relationship of the axle to the chassis of the car. The upper control arms are centered and mounted at the top of the axle. They help control the torque loads placed on the axle assembly during driving, braking, and cornering. Together, these components are responsible for the handling of your vehicle under load.

Everyone who enjoys a slightly overpowered rear-wheel-drive car is more than familiar with the ever-present condition of wheel hop. Just one heavy mashing of the pedal and your rear end is wildly dancing up and down like a hippo on a pogo stick—not exactly what I would call high performance. The constant tweaking and flexing of an ill-handling, sloppy rear suspension can not only lead to broken parts and failure, but also to substantially slower timeslips at the track.

Most factory lower control arms are of the nonboxed sort, meaning that one side of the square arm is open (see photo 3). Consequently, it leaves plenty of room for twisting and distorting while under torque loads from the axle assembly. The end result is poor, unreliable performance, plain and simple.

By replacing your existing open-style arms with a pair of beefed-up boxed units, you can drastically increase the strength and longevity of your rear suspension. The cool thing about this swap is that you have a couple of options. If you need a factory-correct part for restoration accuracy, you should be able to pick up a pair of original arms at any good swap meet.

SUSPENSION

With the rear end of the car securely supported on jack stands, loosen and remove the control arm from its rear mounting point at the axle bracket.

197

Use a socket wrench and a long extension through the frame to access the front mounting bolt of the control arm.

It goes without saying, but performance aftermarket companies also have plenty to offer. Most of their control arms are already installed with upgraded polyurethane bushings. You can also retrofit your stock arms by welding in the extra support bracing. A pair of properly fitted "boxing" plates sells for around $30.

Assuming the rear of the car is securely hoisted, start by removing the shock absorbers from each side. It may be helpful to also remove the rear wheels to gain a little more working room under the car. With the shocks out of the way, use a box wrench and a ratchet to disconnect the arm from its rear mounting location. Depending on the car, you may need a ratchet with a long extension to access the front bolt of the control arm (see photo 2). On our '69 Skylark, the bolt head is positioned deep inside the frame rail. After unbolting the front of the arm, remove and repeat the process for the opposite side. If you decide to retrofit your stock control arms with weld-in plates, now is a good time to think about drilling them for the addition of a rear sway bar (if needed). Most factory and aftermarket boxed arms come predrilled to accommodate anti-sway bars.

When reinstalling the arms, there is a right and a wrong way. Install the added boxed side of the arm, where the sidewall is flared into a lip, so that it faces the pavement. Additionally, the drilled sway bar holes should be toward the rear of the vehicle. If the arms are stubborn in finding their proper position, don't be afraid to smack 'em around a little bit using a rubber mallet. Once everything is back in place, tighten the nuts and bolts and reinstall the shocks.

Whether you opt for boxed replacement arms or perform the boxing yourself with weld-in plates, the improvement is dramatic. The new-and-improved arms will hold up far better than the stock pieces.

198

Installing Rear Antihop Bars

 Time: 3 hours

 Tools: Standard socket set (large), standard wrenches (large), power drill and bits, torque wrench (optional), threadlocker

 Talent:

 Applicable years: All

 Cost: $150

 Parts: Antihop bars (hardware included)

 Tip: When reinstalling the upper control arms, use a small amount of threadlocker to prevent the nuts and bolts from vibrating loose.

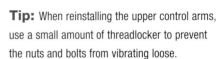 **PERFORMANCE GAIN:** Wheel hop is annoying and squanders the power made by the engine. Antihop bars fight to prevent the loss of traction and rear end control under heavy horsepower loads.

COMPLEMENTARY PROJECTS: Project 77: Installing a Rear Sway Bar; Project 78: Installing Boxed Rear Control Arms

As we covered in earlier projects, the rear end suspension plays a huge role in your car's traction and straight-line performance. In addition to the springs, shocks, and control arms, rear traction (antihop) bars can greatly increase and improve your power-harnessing capabilities. Stock components tend to fall a little short when it comes to handling high-horsepower loads.

Rear traction bars have been around the aftermarket scene for a long time, as they are tried-and-true performers. The relative design of the bars is simple. They install onto the center of the rear axle carrier at the differential. The lower end of each bar is mounted into the webbing of the diff housing for added strength. The upper, bushed ends of the bars serve as the new mounting location for the upper control arm assemblies. By unbolting the control arms from their stock mounting points at the diff and moving them upward, you decrease the amount of rear end deflection and improve the overall geometry of the rear suspension. Just below the new mounting location, the antihop bars lock into the diff housing, where the control arms were before. This design ultimately plants the rear tires of the vehicle downward with much greater force.

As always, break out the floor jack and throw the rear end of the car on some sturdy jack stands. A flat, level driveway or garage is optimum. Be sure to chock the front wheels before hoisting the car into the air. You will need as much room as possible to access the control arms and install the traction bars. Removing the wheels at this point may be a good idea. This will also allow more natural light into the confined work area.

With the car firmly supported, locate the floor jack underneath the pinion area of the rear end housing. It's highly important to maintain the pinion angle and support the assembly during the removal and reinstallation of the control arms. Start by removing the left (driver's side) upper control arm from the rear end bushing. Slightly loosen the front mounting bolt to allow the arm to pivot. Carefully remove the bushing from the differential housing and set it aside. Using the supplied steel bushings, install the left antihop bar with the grease fitting facing the rear of the vehicle. The new bar will mount into the old control arm bushing location on the housing. Most traction bars come equipped with new control arm bushings already pressed in and installed. Simply attach the control arm to the upper end of the traction bar bushing.

To secure the lower end of the bar to the housing, you must first drill a 1/4-inch hole through the front webbing. You will notice that the antihop bars have already been drilled out for this purpose. Be sure to leave enough material between the hole and the edge of the housing for rigidity. Use the traction bar as a guide to mark and drill your holes. When completed, install the 1/4-inch bolts, washers, and locknuts according to the manufacturer's specs. Return to the upper bolts and nuts and tighten to the specified torque value. Repeat the same procedure for the right (passenger) side of the vehicle.

Keep in mind a couple of things about installing aftermarket traction bars (Edelbrock or not). They are aftermarket pieces, not original. This means they often fit a wide variety of cars and require slight modifications, such as grinding and additional drilling, for them to work properly. Most of the time, the modifications are fairly minor, not enough to discourage and scrap the whole project.

SUSPENSION

Edelbrock produces a top-of-the-line traction bar kit complete with urethane bushings, grade 8 hardware, and a clean powder-coated finish.

Loosen and remove the upper control mounting bolt from the rear end housing and bushing.

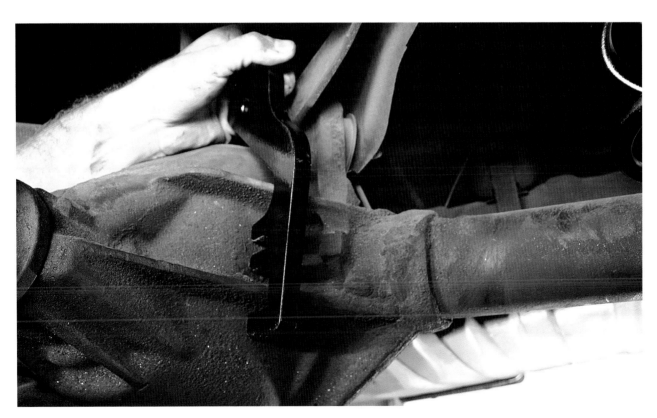

The lower end of the antihop bars is designed to mate and secure to the webbing of the housing.

Shimming the Rear End Ride Height

SUSPENSION

 Time: 1 hour

 Tools: Standard socket set, standard wrenches

 Talent:

 Applicable years: All

 Cost: Fabrication costs will vary, but expect to pay $20–$30 to have them made. If you purchase your own material ahead of time, factor in about another $10.

 Parts: A small plate of aluminum stock; 6061 aircraft alloy is the most common and least expensive.

 Tip: You can save some money by making the shims yourself if you have a wide assortment of hole saws or a knockout punch. They may not produce the cleanest results, but they will work nonetheless.

 PERFORMANCE GAIN: None, just the peace of mind knowing your car is sitting level and straight

COMPLEMENTARY PROJECTS:
Project 76: Installing Rear Shocks and Lowering Springs

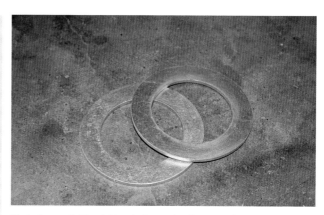

Made from a lightweight, yet strong aluminum stock, these rings/spacers are the perfect trick to level out an uneven stance.

How many times have we all seen a car, either in our driveway or going down the road, that is constantly listing or favoring one side?

A while back, I was helping a friend install a new pair of rear coil springs and shocks into his GM muscle car. After thoroughly wallowing in the road grime underneath the car, we finally got everything back in place and slowly lowered the car onto the ground. Everything appeared to be fine and dandy at first glance. However, when we took about 10 paces back, we could not help but notice a slight rake in the car's stance. I'm not talking about the classic 1970s-era stinkbug kind of rake. I mean the car appeared to be sitting as if one of the rear tires was slightly deflated compared to the other. After retracing our steps and double-checking the work to make sure no bonehead maneuvers were made, we were still scratching our heads. Everything seemed to check out as it should. At that point, we busted out the tape measure in an effort to obtain an accurate reading from the ground to the lip of the rear wheelwells. Lo and behold, we had a problem—taking our measurements from several different locations on a flat, true surface, we determined that the rear right side of the car sat lower by a solid 1/2 inch.

We decided to test our fabrication skills by making a couple of shims, or spacers, to quick-fix this nagging problem. The best way we found was to actually make a template out of cardboard first, measuring the overall diameter of the spring seat and the diameter of the inside retainer.

With the help of a local machine shop, we were able to duplicate the cardboard template using the aluminum we had previously purchased. On a machine lathe and mill, the job will be a walk in the park for any veteran machinist. Approximately 15 minutes and $20 later, we had our magic shims in hand and were ready to put them to the test.

Made from lightweight, durable aircraft aluminum, the spacers simply drop down inside the spring seat underneath the bottom coil. Depending on your car and how jacked up it might be, you may need to use multiple shims or a thicker stock alloy to correct the offset. With the shim(s) in place, reinstall the spring and shock absorber. Lower the car back onto the ground and repeat your measurements. Remember, driving the car will naturally help things to settle a bit, so give it some time and check it again.

Above: To access the lower spring seat, disconnect the shock absorber and allow the axle to slowly drop, releasing all tension on the coil spring.
Below: With the spring removed, installing the spacer requires nothing more than dropping it into position at the bottom of the spring seat.

Lowering Your Car

SUSPENSION

Time: 3–5 hours

Tools: Standard socket set, standard wrenches, spring compressor, ball joint separator, air compressor and cutoff wheel, grinder (optional)

Talent: ▮▮▮

Applicable years: All

Cost: $0–$300

Parts: Lowering springs (optional), rear lowering shackles

Tip: Do not be deceived by the free height of uninstalled coil springs. Just because one set of springs is taller or shorter than another, it does not mean the coils will maintain the same relationship to each other once under load.

PERFORMANCE GAIN: Improved handling and response

COMPLEMENTARY PROJECTS:
Project 72: Installing New Front Lowering Springs and Shocks; Project 76: Installing Rear Shocks and Lowering Springs

The act of lowering a vehicle has become a fine science. There are many approaches to achieving the desired look, but not all are safe and sound practices. It's easy enough to grab a torch and watch your springs collapse under the extreme heat of the flame, but it takes good planning and a little geometry refresher course to pull it off correctly. Lowering a car is not just about cosmetics either. By lowering the center of gravity, you increase the responsiveness and agility of the suspension and allow the car to outperform its factory standard.

Ride heights are determined by a number of factors, such as the spring rate, spring load, and the sag. The spring rate of the active suspension, whether coil or leaf spring equipped, is defined by the amount of weight required to deflect the spring 1 inch at a time. Measured in pounds, it represents the rate at which the spring compresses and returns to its original state. The width and diameter of the coils, as well as the pitch between the coils, greatly affect the traveling rate of the spring. Typically, the stouter the spring is built, the higher its spring rate.

The amount of weight that a spring can handle at any given compressed height is known as the spring load. For example, if a 12-inch-tall spring at free height with a 150-lb/in rate were compressed to a height of 8 inches, it would be supporting 600 pounds at that height. The sag of a spring slowly increases over time due to general overuse and will eventually lower the car as the springs weaken.

Dropping the front end of any vehicle can be done a number of ways. Ideally, the most straightforward method is to replace your existing springs with aftermarket lowering springs. They are rated by the measurement in inches the car will drop from factory ride height (1-inch drop, 2-inch drop, etc.). Manufacturers spend countless hours researching and engineering their springs to work and perform in a wide variety of applications. The springs are designed to lower the ride height and improve handling with a stiffer spring rate. The high-rate springs may increase vibrations or create a slight harshness in the ride compared to a factory spring, but with the right choice of shock absorbers, the change in ride quality will be minimal.

With lowering springs, keep in mind the drop is determined with factory ride height as the baseline. The stock suspensions on these cars were rather lofty, and by today's standards, they would be considered off-road vehicles. Therefore, a 2-inch drop spring may actually raise the ride height of your car from where it currently sits, especially if the worn-out factory springs are still in place. Check with the manufacturer before purchasing or installing the springs to determine the right choice for your car.

An alternate method to drop the front end is to cut coils from the factory spring assemblies. This is by far the least expensive route to lowering your stance and, if done properly, the subtraction of coils can lead to an increased spring rate and improved handling. In fact, cutting a stock spring will increase the spring rate by 10 to 15 percent for every one coil that is removed. Cutting half a coil generally equals approximately 1 inch in spring drop. Your overall drop should not equal more than 2 inches total. Cutting deeper into the spring body will significantly affect the car's ride qualities and pose the threat of bottoming out the suspension.

The easiest way to remove coils from a spring is to use an air-powered cutoff wheel or grinder. A bench-mounted chop saw also works well for this purpose. Always wear protective

Left: Coil springs can be safely cut and altered with an electric grinder or air-powered cutoff wheel.

Below: The shock absorbers must be fully compatible with the modified springs. In some cases (3-inch drops and more), special lowering shocks will be required.

eye gear when cutting or grinding. After the springs have been cut, carefully reinstall them into the control arms and lower the vehicle to the ground. Allow the springs to settle and find their resting point within the suspension before deciding to remove any more coils. Follow the same steps for any rear coil spring vehicle.

For leaf spring applications, purchasing and installing de-arched springs is the way to go. The springs are press-bent to the desired height, as the overall arches in the leaf spring assemblies are altered. De-arched springs lower the center of gravity, increase the spring rate of the leaves, and improve the handling of the rear suspension. You may also use lowering blocks to drop the rear end. Lowering blocks are mounted between the rear axle assembly and the lower spring pad, causing the axle to be raised from the arc of the leaf and placing the rear housing closer to the frame. Lowering blocks work fine in mild applications (up to 2 inches of drop), but begin to pose problems in the pinion angle and geometry of the rear suspension when taken to extremes.

SECTION NINE
BRAKES AND WHEELS

The brakes are the most important components on your classic car. They provide all of the necessary stopping power to keep things under control during normal driving conditions on the street and racing on the track. There are many different designs and styles of braking performance, and all should be considered in meeting your braking needs.

PROJECT 82
Installing a Master Cylinder/Power Booster

 Time: 2 hours

 Tools: Standard socket set, standard wrenches, brake bleeder (optional)

 Talent:

 Applicable years: All

 Cost: $200–$250

 Parts: Master cylinder/power booster

 Tip: Always bleed the brakes repeatedly anytime changes are made in the brake system.

 PERFORMANCE GAIN: A new dual-circuit master cylinder and power booster will enhance the ease and safe operation of your brake system.

COMPLEMENTARY PROJECTS:
Project 83: Rebuilding Drum Brakes; Project 84: Installing Front Disc Brakes

After the fluid has been drained, remove the old cylinder from the firewall.

Most vehicles on the road today, both old and new, use hydraulic systems to actuate the brakes. Hydraulic systems allow pressure to be delivered through small-diameter hoses and lines from the pedal to the braking surfaces at each wheel without taking up a large amount of room. They also decrease the amount of foot pressure required by making the surface area of the master cylinder pistons smaller than that of the wheel cylinder or caliper pistons.

The master cylinder consists of a fluid reservoir mated to a cylinder and piston assembly. Late models (typically post-1967) came equipped with a dual-reservoir master cylinder. The dual reservoir was designed to separate the front and rear braking systems hydraulically in case of a leak. These dual-circuit master cylinders utilize two pistons, a primary and a secondary, to keep the braking system safely in order. The primary piston is actuated mechanically by the linkage of the brake pedal. The secondary piston, located directly behind the primary, is set in motion by trapped fluid between the two pistons. If a leak occurs forward of the secondary piston, it will move forward to the front of the master cylinder and the trapped fluid between the two pistons will operate the rear brakes. If the rear brakes develop a leak, the primary piston advances until it reaches the secondary, forcing it to apply pressure to the front brakes.

In the unfortunate circumstance of a system failure or leak, most dual-circuit systems use a switch to warn the driver that only half of the braking system is working properly. This switch is either mounted on the firewall or on the frame of the vehicle below the master cylinder. A hydraulic piston receives equal pressure on both sides from the two circuits. If the pressures remain even and stable, the piston is stationary. If there is a leak in either circuit and the piston is pushed to one side, the switch is closed and the warning light is activated.

On disc-brake cars, this switch mechanism also contains a metering valve and often a proportioning valve. Metering valves restrict pressure to the front brakes until the rear shoes have been engaged to the drums. Proportioning valves, on the other hand, control fluid pressures to the rear brakes to avoid rear wheel lockup during extreme braking.

To check for leaks in the system, slowly apply pressure to the brake pedal. If the pedal sinks to the floor, a leak is guaranteed. If no external leaks are detected along the brake lines or at the wheel cylinders, the problem is inside the master cylinder.

207

Many aftermarket companies sell master cylinders and power boosters complete as one assembly.

When the hydraulic system is at rest, it is full of fluid. Applying pressure to the brake pedal forces the trapped fluid in front of the master cylinder pistons through the lines and to the wheels. On drum brake systems, the wheel cylinder pistons are pushed outward by the fluid toward the brakes shoes and retrieved by return springs. The pistons are directed inward toward the rotors on disc brake applications and returned by spring seals. When the pedal is released, a spring located inside the master cylinder returns the pistons to their normal position. The pistons will retract faster than the return flow of fluid; therefore the fluid from the reservoir is used to prevent a vacuum in the system.

The addition of a power booster in conjunction with a dual-circuit master cylinder translates to lighter foot pressures and shorter distances of travel in the brake pedal. In other words, power boosters make life easy. They are actuated by vacuum pressure from the intake manifold through a small diaphragm located at the front of the master cylinder. A check valve is placed at the port of the diaphragm to ensure that brake-assisted vacuum will not be lost during periods of low manifold vacuum. When the brake pedal is depressed, the vacuum source is shut off and atmospheric pressure is allowed to enter one side of the diaphragm. This causes the pistons of the master cylinder to move and apply pressure to the brakes. By releasing the pedal, vacuum is applied to both sides of the diaphragm, and springs return the master cylinder pistons to their original position.

The clevis and lock pin at the rear of the booster attach directly to the linkage of the brake pedal.

To remove the old master cylinder from the firewall, first suck the brake fluid out of the reservoir with a siphon. Loosen the fittings and disconnect the brake lines from the side of the master cylinder. It's important to cover or cap the lines to prevent contaminants from entering the system. Remove the nuts and washers securing the master cylinder to the firewall. Remove the clevis lock pin and disengage the master cylinder pushrod at the brake pedal.

To install the new master cylinder with the power booster, attach the pushrod to the pedal and line up the booster's mounting holes on the firewall. Loosely tighten the booster to the studs and reattach the hard lines to the master cylinder. Once everything is in place, tighten as necessary. Refill the reservoir with clean brake fluid and check for any leaks. The new assembly may require alteration or replacement of some hard lines. If you are unable to make the old lines adapt to the placement of the new master cylinder, check out Project 99 on hand bending and fabricating new lines. Be sure to thoroughly bleed the entire system before attempting to move the car (Project 86).

PROJECT 83

Rebuilding Drum Brakes

Time: 3 hours (per pair)

Tools: Lug wrench, flat-blade screwdriver, rubber mallet, needle-nose pliers, specialty brake tools (recommended)

Talent:

Applicable years: All

Cost: $100

Parts: Brake shoes, drum brake hardware kit

Tip: When doing your brakes, only disassemble one side at a time. The other side will serve as an accurate point of reference when putting all of the pieces back together.

PERFORMANCE GAIN: Better brakes! Periodically replacing your shoes and rebuilding the brake assemblies will increase your chances of ever seeing old age.

COMPLEMENTARY PROJECTS:

Project 82: Installing a Master Cylinder/Power Booster;

Project 86: Bleeding the Brakes

Let's face it—the brake system is the single most important set of components on your vehicle. Street enthusiasts and racers alike often regard drum brakes as safety hazards and marginal performers. The stopping power and control of a drum fails to match the ever-increasing standard of its favored sibling, the disc. However, with the right selection of quality parts and a little massaging, you can cheaply transform your factory binders into rock-solid performers.

The mechanical principles of drum brakes are fairly basic. The design consists of two brakes shoes mounted on a stationary backing plate. The spring-mounted shoes are positioned inside the drum, which rotates with the wheel assembly. The shoes move toward the drums while braking and maintain proper alignment of the linings and the drums. At the top of the backing plate is the wheel cylinder. When the brakes are deployed, hydraulic pressure forces the actuating links of the wheel cylinder outward and against the top surface of the brake shoes. The tops of the shoes are then forced against the inner linings of the drums, causing the revolution of the wheels to be slowed. When the pressure is released from the brake pedal, the return springs pull the shoes back away from the drums.

To access the drum and brake assemblies, you must first remove the wheel from the hub. Safely raise and support your vehicle with a floor jack and jack stands. Loosen the lug nuts before lifting the tire off the ground. Once the wheel is removed, the drum is fully exposed and can be eliminated. Remove the cotter pin and spindle nut from the front of the hub assembly. It may be necessary to retract the adjuster on the back side of the drum. Remove the plug from the back side of the drum and turn the adjuster with a small flat-blade screwdriver to release any excess tension between the shoes and the inner linings of the drums. Using a rubber mallet, tap the rear edge of the drum forward over the wheel studs. Inspect each drum closely for any cracks, scores, or grooves in the surface. If the unit is cracked, replace it. Deep scores and grooves can be handled by any automotive machine shop on a lathe. If the damage is minimal, try using some fine emery cloth to smooth out the roughness or burrs.

Before digging into the mess, spray the shoes, springs, and hardware down with brake cleaner. Do NOT use compressed air—brake shoes contain cancer-causing asbestos. One at a time, remove the springs, screws, pins, and levers from the inner brake assembly. Specialty tools are readily available at any parts counter to make this chore a little easier. When approaching the shoes, notice the difference in size of the primary and secondary linings. The primary (leading) shoe has a shorter lining than the secondary (trailing) shoe and is mounted to the front of the wheel.

To remove the shoes, pull back on the secondary lining and disengage the parking brake strut and strut spring (rear drum brakes). Remove the shoe and disconnect the parking brake cable. By releasing the primary hold-down pin and spring, you can extract the leading shoe. Check the condition of the seals on the wheel cylinders for any leaks or cracks and replace if necessary. Inspect the wheel bearings, wheel seals, and hydraulic brake hoses, too.

The reinstallation requires only a few special details. Lightly lubricate the backing plate contact points before positioning the new shoes. Be sure the right and left adjusting screws are not mixed up during the process. Focus on one side

BRAKES AND WHEELS

209

Once the tension has been released and the cotter pin and spindle nut removed, simply pull the drum from the hub assembly.

Although a spring puller is highly recommended, the job can be done with a set of needle-nose pliers.

at a time, using the opposite side as a visual reference. When installed correctly, the star wheel adjuster should be closest to the secondary shoe. When complete, properly adjust the drum brakes and bleed them if necessary.

To adjust the drums, remove the rubber plug from the adjusting slot on the backing plate. Insert a brake adjusting spoon into the slot and engage the lowest possible tooth on the star wheel. Lower the spoon to move the star wheel upward and to extend the adjusting screw. Continue this movement until the brakes lock, preventing the wheels from turning. Using a small screwdriver, push and hold the

adjuster lever away from the star wheel. Now engage the topmost tooth on the star wheel with the spoon and begin backing off the tension until the tire and wheel spin freely with a minimum of drag. Keep track of the number of turns the star wheel is backed off to create an even balance between both sides. Perform this method of adjusting the brakes while the car is supported on jack stands and the wheel is installed.

In addition to the drums and brake shoes, rebuild kits are often sold and installed to enhance the performance of tired drum brakes. The kits typically include all of the springs, screws, pins, and miscellaneous hardware needed for the job.

PROJECT 84
Installing Front Disc Brakes

 Time: 3–5 hours

 Tools: Standard socket set, standard wrenches, floor jack and jack stands, rubber mallet, ball joint separator or pickle fork, mini sledgehammer, wheel bearing grease, brake fluid, brake cleaner, small rubber hose, "catch" container

  Talent: ▮▮▮

 Applicable years: All

 Cost: $500–$1,500

 Parts: Disc brake kit

 Tip: A much-overlooked detail in the disc brake conversion is the placement of the wheel by the hub assembly. Often, the mounting plane of the new hub will cause the wheel to sit further outward in the wheelwell. Depending on the wheel and tire size, the slight variance can create all sorts of clearance problems. Check it out before installing or assembling the parts.

PERFORMANCE GAIN: Disc brakes are far superior to the age-old design of drums. They stop faster, last longer, and improve the agility of your vehicle.

COMPLEMENTARY PROJECTS: Project 82: Installing a Master Cylinder/Power Booster; Project 86: Bleeding the Brakes

Many disc brake kits come complete with everything you need to improve your car's braking performance.

BRAKES AND WHEELS

Today, disc brakes are a staple in the performance game. Although factory drum brake systems can be modified to increase performance, the stopping power is simply not there. At high speeds, drum brakes require a much longer skid pad (similar to that of an airplane landing strip) to finally bring the car to a halt. They are also highly vulnerable to brake fade from excessive heat and water. Truth is, we often get so caught up in horsepower and going faster that we forget that at some point, we have to slow down.

The only safe and effective way to harness big power is to add disc brakes. Although discs require greater pressure, they offer superior stopping resistance and handling under heavy braking. With discs, you also have the option of upgrading to larger-diameter rotors and calipers to further improve control. (You may need to switch to a larger wheel to accommodate the new-and-improved rotors. Be sure to check your clearances beforehand.) If you're working off a budget and simply can't afford the high-dollar items, vented or slotted rotors and carbon-metallic pads offer better-than-stock braking performance at an affordable price. In addition, they keep the rotor and pad surface cleaner, lower operating temperatures, and improve wet braking.

Since most of the stopping force derives from the front wheels (approximately 60 to 70 percent on rear-wheel-drive cars), it goes without saying that the forward units should be addressed first. Front disc brake kits are everywhere. They are packaged and sold in various stages of completion and range anywhere from $500 to $1,500. Some kits include rotor assemblies, calipers and pads, master cylinder/power booster, and all of the necessary hard lines to adapt to your application. Others, however, take a more bare-bones approach. Either way, the aftermarket supplies front discs for just about any older car.

Getting down to business, remove the front wheels from the car. If you are not familiar with proper jacking and support techniques, see Project 54. With the wheels removed from the hub assemblies, gently pry the grease cap from the front of the hub. Next, remove the cotter pin, the castle nut and washer, and the outer wheel bearing from the spindle. Be sure to keep track of your hardware and the order in which it was removed. The old hub and drum are now free and clear for dismissal. It may be necessary to retract the shoes from the drum linings using the adjuster slot in the drum's backing plate. Insert a small flat-blade screwdriver into the slot and back off the adjusting screw. If the drum continues to put up a fight, it may take a little "coaxing" from a rubber mallet to get things moving.

At this point, I recommend draining the brake fluid from the system. Start by using a siphon to draw out as much fluid as possible from the master cylinder reservoir. Attach a small hose to the bleeder screws and allow the remainder of the brake fluid to be drained from the master cylinder and the brake lines into an empty container. Remove the soft brake hoses from the wheel cylinders. Be careful not get brake fluid on any painted surface. The stuff is nasty and will eat the paint right off.

There are numerous brake kits for all different cars. Although it's not uncommon for some manufacturers to include replacement spindles as a part of the package, some kits are designed and intended to reuse the existing drum spindles. The step-by-step sequence may vary greatly,

Grease the bearings heavily before installation.

depending on your selection of parts and the kit that best suits your needs. Follow the manufacturer's instructions first and foremost during the procedure.

On our project car, we are able to reuse the factory drum spindles. However, we opt to remove them anyway for cleaning and repainting. Using a pickle fork and a mini sledgehammer, we separate the tie rod and the ball joints from the spindle assembly. For specific instruction on the removal of these items, refer to the front-end rebuild project (Project 72) in this book. If you prefer, you can remove the drum and hub assemblies as one complete unit without disengaging the steering knuckle. Simply unbolt the backing plate from the spindle assembly and remove the unit as a whole.

If you purchased a fully assembled kit, the rest is pretty straightforward. Attach the knuckle assembly to the control arms and tie rods, and refasten the lines and hoses. Although our kit came unassembled, it was pretty straightforward in its own right. After the fresh paint on the knuckles has dried, we install the supplied spindle brackets and the new backing plates. Thoroughly grease and install the new inner wheel bearings in the hub/rotor assembly. It is highly important to keep the bearings clean and free of all dirt and debris. Lightly tap the bearings into place with a clean, rubber mallet or large socket. Be careful not to damage the lip or the seal of the bearing.

The freshly packed rotor may now be installed onto the shaft of the spindle. Install the outer bearings and grease heavily. Fit the spindle nut and washer loosely over the bearing, but do not tighten. Assemble the calipers and install them onto their designated rotor. Once the unit is complete, mount the spindle assembly back into the car and torque the bolts to the proper spec. To seat the outer wheel bearings, torque the spindle nut to approximately 15 ft-lb while spinning the rotor. Back off the nut 1/2 turn, retighten, and install a new cotter

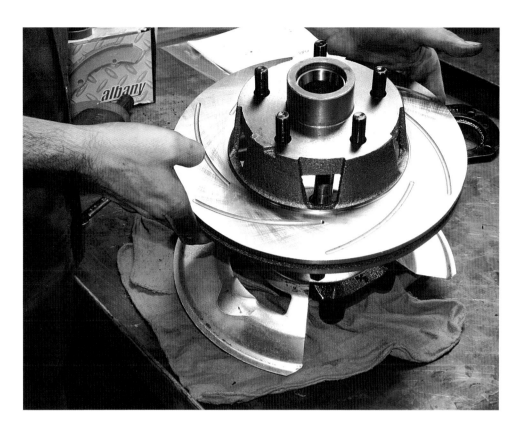

Install the rotor assembly onto the shaft of the spindle as shown.

Secure the caliper to the caliper mounting bracket with grade 8 bolts and lockwashers.

pin and grease cap. Refill the system with the recommended brake fluid and bleed thoroughly.

As with any aftermarket kit, be prepared for the unexpected. Fabricating new hard lines is not uncommon with a disc brake swap. Neither is relocating or replumbing a propor- tioning valve. There are many factors to consider before laying down the plastic and ordering a new kit. It's always a good idea to call the tech support lines prior to purchasing and pick their brains on any gray areas. Each kit will be different in one way or another. Always follow the instructions keenly.

213

PROJECT 85
Installing Rear Disc Brakes

 Time: 3–4 hours

 Tools: Standard socket set, standard wrenches, flat-blade screwdriver, bearing puller

 Talent: 👤👤👤

 Applicable years: All

 Cost: $700–$900 for kit

 Parts: Rear disc brake kit, brake fluid, gear oil (if applicable)

 Tip: Most rear disc brake kits require the use of at least 15-inch-diameter wheels to clear the rotor assemblies. Check with the manufacturer before purchasing.

 PERFORMANCE GAIN: Rear disc brakes add extra stopping force and consistent braking and handling performance.

COMPLEMENTARY PROJECTS:

Project 82: Installing a Master Cylinder/Power Booster; Project 84: Installing Front Disc Brakes

Making the switch from rear drum brakes to rear disc is not practical in every situation. Most of the time, a front disc conversion and factory rear drums will do the mundane job of slowing and stopping just fine. But for high-end, big-horsepower cars, sometimes you need absolutely all that you can get. Installing an additional pair of rotors and pads out back will improve your stopping power and increase the responsive handling of your car.

The procedure for installing a rear disc brake kit is much like the front. The stock drums are removed and replaced with new rotor assemblies and brake pads. Modifications to the brake lines and plumbing are minimal, and provisions for such are included in most kits.

After the car has been lifted and supported on a sturdy pair of jack stands, remove the rear wheels from the vehicle.

It's easier to crack the lug nuts loose while the tires are still on the ground. Once all of the nuts can freely spin, release the parking brake, raise the car, and remove the wheels. Now the drums may be removed. Release the tension of the rear brake shoes from the inner drum linings by backing off the adjusting screw. This screw may be accessed through the small slot in the backing plate of the drum assembly and rotated with a flat-blade screwdriver. By turning the adjuster counterclockwise, you will gradually pull the shoes away from the drums and allow the drum assembly to be removed from the rear axles. If the adjuster is all the way backed off and the drum still seems to be stuck in place, use a hammer to tap the drum loose.

Drain the brake system before moving any further. Using a siphon, remove the excess brake fluid from the master cylinder reservoir. Open the bleeder screws at the wheels and allow the remaining fluid in the system to drain into a small container.

In order to remove the drum backing plate assemblies, the rear axles must first be pulled from the rear end housing. There are typically two types of axles used on these cars, the C-clip type and the non-C-type. C-type axles are retained by C-shaped clips that fit into grooves at the inner end of the shaft. Non-C-type axles are retained by the brake backing plate and are bolted to the axle housing. To figure out which type of axles you have, unbolt and remove the differential cover and visually check inside the carrier. With a non-C-type axle, remove the nuts holding the retainer plate to the backing plate. Disconnect the brake line and plug the opening to prevent contaminants from entering the system. Using a slide hammer/axle puller, remove the axle shaft and bearing assembly. Once the shaft is out of the carrier, collapse the edges of the bearing to dislodge it from the axle shaft. The brake backing plate may now be removed from the axle housing.

If you are working on a C-type axle, place a large container beneath the axle housing, loosen and remove the cover bolts, and drain the gear oil. The next step is to remove the differential pinion lock screw and the pinion shaft, both of which are located inside the differential housing. Slide the flanged end (wheel) of the axle toward the center of the carrier and remove the C-clip retainer from the groove in the axle shaft. The axle shaft is now free and may carefully be removed. Use a bearing puller or a slide hammer to remove the bearing from the axle shaft. Follow the installation instructions of the new disc brake kit. As always, this will vary, depending on the manufacturer and the kit you select. Assemble the new rotors and calipers and install them onto the axle shafts. Reroute any necessary plumbing and reattach the brake lines at the wheels. Many kits come complete with new lines, hardware, and a separate rear brake proportioning valve.

Once the kit is fully assembled and installed, refill the master cylinder reservoir and the lines with clean brake fluid and bleed the entire system.

BRAKES AND WHEELS

214

Above: Rear disc brake kits can be purchased with large slotted and vented rotors.
Below: Most kits come complete with the necessary brackets and hardware to adapt to the existing setup.

PROJECT 86
Bleeding the Brakes

 Time: 2 hours

 Tools: Standard wrenches, vacuum bleeder or pressure bleeder (optional, but recommended), brake fluid, clean rags, rubber hose

 Talent:

 Applicable years: All

 Cost: $20 for fluid and supplies

 Parts: None

 Tip: When working with brake fluid, always be extra careful. Brake fluid can quickly and permanently ruin paint jobs. Even a slight film on your hands can leave its mark on the car. It's a good idea to wear rubber gloves and cover all painted surfaces around the master cylinder reservoir.

 PERFORMANCE GAIN: Proper bleeding will ensure safer and more responsive braking.

COMPLEMENTARY PROJECTS: Project 82: Installing a Master Cylinder/Power Booster; Project 83: Rebuilding Drum Brakes; Project 84: Installing Front Disc Brakes

Bleeding the brakes is never a fun thing to do. It's a tedious, patience-testing process that often takes numerous attempts before getting it right. The act of bleeding involves filling the lines with fluid and removing any trapped air pockets or bubbles from the brake system. Although there are different approaches to bleeding, they all share the same common goal and result. Thorough bleeding of the brakes is an absolute must when it comes to performance and safety. When air pockets form in the brake lines, the pedal becomes soft and spongy because air compresses more easily than fluid. When the pedal is mashed, the trapped air compresses and expands much like a spring. In turn, the air absorbs the energy from the pedal and prevents the delivery of fluid to the brake caliper.

The most straightforward and effective method is manual bleeding. Before the introduction of vacuum and pressure bleeders, there was just one way to properly bleed the brakes—the hard way. The only drawback of manual bleeding is the need for a second set of hands (or feet, I should say). With an assistant at the pedals, the bleeding is performed by hand at each wheel, one at a time. By depressing and pumping the brake pedal, fluid rushes through the system at a high velocity. Air bubbles and trapped particles are quickly flushed from the system by the flow of fluid.

To bleed manually, attach a small rubber hose to the brake caliper nipple. Route the opposite end of the hose into a container to catch the fluid. With your auxiliary pair of feet,

firmly pump the brake pedal a few times, holding the last stroke of the pedal down to the floor. With the pedal depressed, slightly loosen the nipple to allow the pressurized fluid to exit the system. The fluid should come rushing out, so be careful. It's not a bad idea to wear some safety glasses while near the wheel. However, if the fluid slowly dribbles out the end of the hose, the lines are probably clogged with contaminants. Check the condition of all brake lines and hoses before moving forward. At this point, it's critical to maintain pressure on the pedal. Premature release will only permit air back into the lines. Simply tighten the nipple and release the pedal.

An alternative method to bleeding the brakes is to use a handheld bleeding tool. The pressure-style bleeder works similar to manual bleeding. The kit usually attaches to the top of the master cylinder and pressurizes the fluid out of the reservoir and through the system. Take the same approach at the wheels to release the fluid from the nipples. Pressure bleeders are effective in eliminating air pockets from the lines and are relatively inexpensive (approximately $50). You can easily bleed the whole system single-handedly, without the help of an assistant.

Another option in the bleeding game is to reverse the strategy and use a vacuum bleeder. It attaches to the caliper nipple and draws the fluid through the lines from the master cylinder. These bleeders are extremely easy to use and perform fairly well. It's best to perform a "final bleed"

Top: Slowly open the bleeder valve on the backing plate to drain the fluid. Above: The vacuum bleeder attaches to the valve and draws the brake fluid through the system from the master cylinder.

manually after vacuum bleeding (and pressure bleeding). Air can still be trapped in the system, even after numerous bleeds.

Regardless of the method used, always start the bleeding process at the wheel farthest from the master cylinder, working your way back to the left front wheel. This will help minimize the air in the system. It's also beneficial to bleed each caliper more than once. Working your way around the vehicle several times can be quite time consuming, but the more you bleed, the better you brake, plain and simple. Be sure to keep an eye on the reservoir and fluid level as you bleed. If the reservoir begins to run dry, you'll suck air back into the lines. You don't want to start over!

PROJECT 87
Installing a Line Lock

Time: 2–3 hours

Tools: Standard socket set, standard wrenches, tubing bender (if needed), brake bleeding tool

Talent: 👤👤👤

Applicable years: All

Cost: $125

Parts: Line lock system and installation kit, brake fluid

Tip: Always bleed the brakes thoroughly after repairing or modifying your brake system.

! PERFORMANCE GAIN: Controlled, effortless burnouts for ultimate rear tire traction

COMPLEMENTARY PROJECTS:
Project 82: Installing a Master Cylinder/Power Booster;
Project 86: Bleeding the Brakes

The line lock switch and solenoid easily plumb into your existing brake system with minor modifications.

In order to produce consistent quick times at the track, rear wheel traction is of the utmost concern. It starts with building a stout and responsive rear suspension capable of handling and directing the power loads from the engine and transmission to the rear wheels. From there, it's all up to the tires and their ability to bite into the pavement and propel the vehicle forward.

Anytime an object is severely heated, it becomes softer and more pliable. This is why you see every driver lay down a massive, four-alarm smoky burnout before each pass at the track. The heat generated by the extreme friction causes the tires to gum up and stick to the asphalt when the car is launched. Although you never need a good reason to ruthlessly smoke the tires, it actually plays an important part in the science of going fast.

This is where line locks enter the picture. A line lock is a control device that applies line pressure to the front (or rear) brakes after your foot has been removed from the brake pedal. When the lock is activated, fluid surges to the front brakes and locks them in place, while the rear brakes are still disengaged. This altered condition allows the driver to then step on the gas pedal and roast the rear treads. The back tires are free to spin without fighting any brake pressure. Once the cloud of tire smoke engulfs your car, simply release the lock button and proceed to stage at the lights. Your tires are now fully heated and ready to bite.

Regardless of style or brand, line locks are generally installed in the same manner. The first thing to examine is the type of brake system used on your car. The master cylinder, either single or dual reservoir, and the distribution block are key pieces in the way the line lock will mount and plumb into your existing brake system. Most line locks require rerouting the rear brake line to the kit-supplied T-fitting and installing the lock switch between the fitting and the original distribution block. The line lock solenoid installs between the master cylinder and

The line lock activation switch is a designated part of the shifter assembly.

the switch block and should be as far away from the exhaust as possible. The lines exiting the switch block lead to both the right and left side brake and wheel assemblies.

Depending on the line lock and installation kit (often separate) purchased, you may need to fabricate and hand-bend new hard lines to hook up to the rest of the system. This gives you the chance to route everything neatly and out of the way of other intruding components. Be sure to pay close attention to the factory brake light switch, as it may require slight modification to work with the new line lock system.

Mount the interior line lock switch in a convenient, easy-to-reach location. Although most switches are installed as a part of the transmission shifter, there are other alternatives. One trick approach is to temporarily mount the switch using a generic plug and socket that mates into the cigarette lighter (if you have one). The indicator light may also be used in this location when it comes time to fry those meats!

PROJECT 88
Changing the Wheels and Tires

 Time: 1 hour

 Tools: Straightedge or ruler

 Talent:

 Applicable years: All

 Cost: n/a

 Parts: Wheels, tires, lug nuts, wheel studs (if needed)

 Tip: Be sure the tires can handle the load of the vehicle they are installed on. Every tire has a maximum load rating (per one tire) at maximum inflation pressure.

PERFORMANCE GAIN: Safer handling and braking, increased acceleration

COMPLEMENTARY PROJECTS: Project 84: Installing Front Disc Brakes; Project 85: Installing Rear Disc Brakes

Changing the wheels and/or tires on your car makes a huge difference in a number of different areas. First, the outward appearance and attitude of a wheel change are night and day. It's amazing what a properly fitted wheel and tire combination can do for the aesthetics of a classic vehicle. On the other hand, there's a lot more to it than just looks. The wheels and tires play a special role in the performance and handling of your machine.

The factory standard in wheels was typically a small-diameter steel wheel (13 or 14 inches) encased in a tall, bias-ply tread. The width often varied, but most fell in the range of 5.5 to 7 inches. These nostalgic wheels and tires are eternally cool and work great for that classic, factory-correct look. Nevertheless, the aftermarket is absolutely flooded with alternatives. Aluminum mags have long been a popular choice for just about every car imaginable. They are manufactured in all sizes, both factory original and larger, and are available with custom backspacing and offsets if needed. They also shave a fair amount of unsprung weight from the vehicle versus the original steelies. Chromed wheels are yet another favorite.

Before choosing a set of wheels, it is important to understand the basic physical aspects of your vehicle's rollers. The wheels are responsible for supporting the tires as your car rolls down the road. They must be capable of withstanding the loads generated from acceleration, braking, and cornering. Every application will have different criteria for the required strength of the wheels. For example, every wheel has a maximum load rating. To determine if a certain wheel will work in your application, divide your car's gross vehicle weight (GVW) by four (the number of wheels) and compare the number to the manufacturer's rating.

A wheel typically has two basic parts, the spider and the rim. The center section of the wheel that bolts to the brake drum or rotor is known as the spider. The rim forms the outer lips of the wheel that contact and retain the tire. On most wheels, these two separate pieces are welded, riveted, or bolted together to form the final product.

Taking proper measurements is highly important in selecting the right wheel for your car. The most common measurement is the wheel's diameter. The diameter is determined by measuring across the face or back of the wheel between the opposite points where the tire rests. This measurement will come into play in tire selection as well. The diameter of the wheels and the openings of the tires must be the same to fit. The width of the wheel is measured between the two lips of the rim where the tire is mounted.

The rear spacing, or backspacing, is the distance between the wheel's inboard edge and its mounting surface. The backspacing can easily be calculated by placing a straightedge across the back edges of the wheel (face down) and measuring down to the rear mounting pad. Deep backspacing allows larger wheels to fit inside the fenderwells without altering the placement of the tires.

The wheel's offset is the distance from the wheel center to its mounting pad. A positive offset indicates the mounting pad of the wheel is in front of the rim centerline. With a negative offset, the mounting surface would be behind the rim centerline.

Factory wheels are constructed of solid steel and look great on original cars.

Rally wheels are very popular for their sleek looks and classic styling.

Bolt patterns vary between different makes and models. The bolt circle diameter is the imaginary circle drawn through the centers of the bolt holes. Depending on the wheel, the bolt pattern is the distance between two opposite mounting holes. Even-numbered wheels (four, six, or eight lugs) require a measurement from the center of one hole across the wheel to the center of its direct opposite hole. Five-lug bolt patterns are determined by measuring from the center of one hole to the center of the farthest hole in the pattern. The number will be slightly smaller than the actual bolt circle measurement.

Tire selection is just as crucial in the equation to performance. Tires must work in unison with the wheels and provide the necessary traction, control, and stability for the car. Deciphering the codes on a tire's sidewall is basic, yet informative. On a 275/60R15 tire, the "275" represents the

221

The bolt pattern is measured from the center of one stud hole across the wheel to the farthest stud hole (five-lug wheel).

A wheel's backspacing is the distance from the center mounting pad of the wheel to its outer edges.

The width of the wheel is taken by measuring the distance between the two points where the tire rests.

tire's section width in millimeters when the tire is mounted on the recommended wheel size. This value will increase or decrease approximately 1/4 inch for every 1/2-inch increase or decrease in the wheel width. The "60" designates the tire's aspect ratio, which is expressed as a percentage. The aspect ratio, or profile, is the ratio of the tire's section height to its section width (275). The section height of this tire is 60 percent of the section width. The section height is the measurement of the inflated tire from the bottom of the tire bead to the top of its tread.

Installation of wheels and tires should be left to a competent shop. The shop has the specialized tools and equipment that make the job easy and safe, and can balance each wheel and tire prior to mounting.

ELECTRICAL

E lectrical systems can prove to be a true nightmare. Troubleshooting and repairing these components requires much patience and often the use of specialty tools or equipment. The projects listed in this chapter serve as a general introduction to electrical systems and the items commonly replaced.

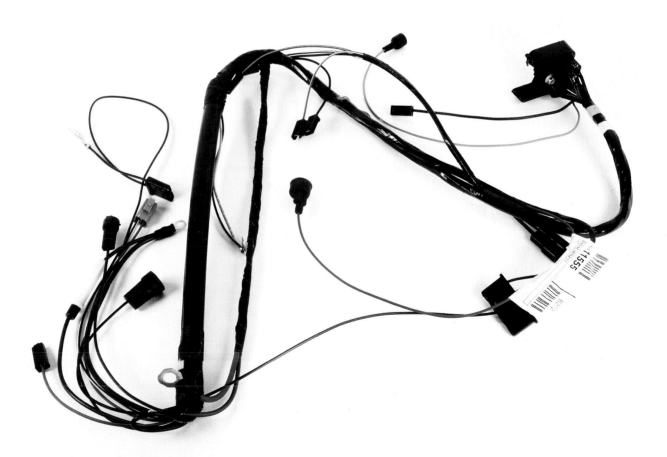

Removing and Replacing the Battery and Battery Cables

 Time: 1 hour

 Tools: Standard socket set (with extensions), standard wrenches, wire cutters/crimpers, wire brush

 Talent:

 Applicable years: All

 Cost: $50–$150

 Parts: Battery and cables, terminal ends (optional)

 Tip: Always remove the negative battery cable from the terminal post before the positive. Any sparks from or around the terminals could ignite battery gases and cause personal injury.

 PERFORMANCE GAIN: More reliable starting power and performance of your 12-volt accessories

COMPLEMENTARY PROJECTS: Replacing the battery hold-down clamp and battery tray

Loosen the nut from the battery terminal and remove the cable from the post.

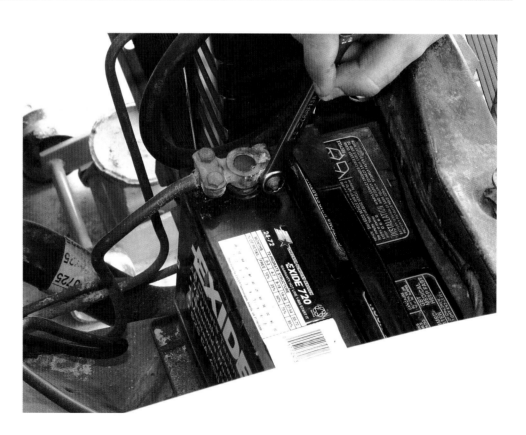

ELECTRICAL

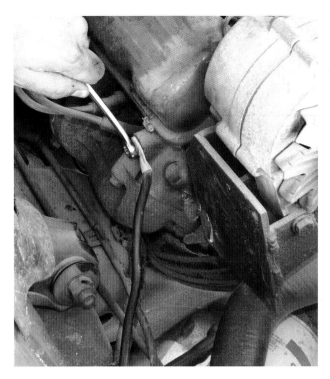

The negative battery cable is typically easy to access and remove.

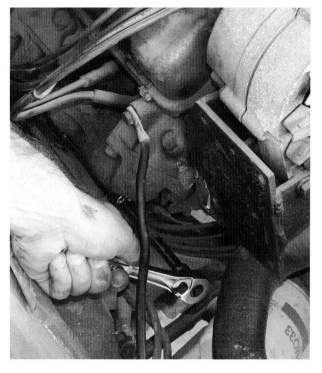

Using a socket wrench and multiple extensions, unbolt the positive cable from the solenoid on the starter motor.

Your vehicle's electrical system can be broken down into three major groups: the starting system, the charging system, and the ignition system. The starting system mainly consists of the battery and the starter. Together, they provide the means and the muscle with which to kick the engine over and begin the beautiful act of combustion.

The battery is typically first on the scene to get things moving. By cranking the engine with the key in the ignition switch, electrical energy is temporarily removed from the cells of the battery and delivered to the starter motor via the positive battery cable. The sudden surge of juice enables the starter pinion gear to engage and turn the flywheel at the crankshaft. For a more in-depth, detailed explanation of starter function, check out Project 90 on starter assemblies.

During this critical transfer of energy, the battery relies solely on the operation of the charging system to recoup its precious resources. If the charging circuit is working properly, the electrons will be replaced and returned to the battery core by the alternator (or generator). However, if the system fails to perform its primary duty of rejuvenation, the battery will simply die. The charging system must produce and maintain a greater voltage than the storage battery in order to reverse the flow of energy back into the cells and recharge the core. In addition, the charging system simultaneously supports and is responsible for all ignition and accessory components.

The voltage regulators are designed to limit the flow of voltage and protect the battery from being overcharged and damaged during the transfer of electrical power. The accessory items are also protected from the dangers of excessive voltage. Some early vehicles were equipped with externally mounted voltage regulators. They are typically bolted to the inside of the core support and linked to the generator or alternator through the engine harness. In later years (mid 1970s and later), the use of internally regulated alternators became widely popular and replaced the earlier design.

To remove the battery from the engine compartment, first release the battery hold-down clamp or retainer. The negative battery cable should ALWAYS be removed from the battery post prior to the positive cable to eliminate any possibility of arcing at the terminals or damaging the electrical system. After the ground cable has been disconnected, remove the positive cable from its post and lift the battery from the mounting tray.

The other ends of the battery cables are attached to the starter (positive, +) and the block or frame (negative, -). The negative cable is usually easy to access and remove. Simply trace the cord back to its mounting location and loosen the retaining bolt. The positive cable connects directly to the solenoid of the starter motor. To remove from the top of the vehicle, attach a long extension and socket to your wrench and slide the tool behind the exhaust manifold or header. Once you have located the socket on the locknut, loosen the nut and remove the cable end from the mounting stud. In some applications, it may be easier to access the positive cable from underneath the vehicle.

When replacing the battery, always refer to the manufacturer's recommendations for the proper size and amount of cranking power necessary for your vehicle. Determine whether you need top-post or side-post terminals. If you plan to reuse your battery cables, inspect the shielding for any cracks or frayed ends before installing the new battery. Battery cables and terminals should be periodically cleaned and maintained with a wire terminal brush and baking soda.

ELECTRICAL

PROJECT 90

Installing a High-Torque Mini Starter

 Time: 1 hour

 Tools: Standard socket set with extensions

 Talent: ▮▮▮

 Applicable years: All

 Cost: $150–$200

 Parts: Mini starter, starter bolts and shims (included)

 Tip: After the new starter is in position, have a friend "bump" the starter over with the ignition key. Underneath the car, check for proper spacing, clearance, and meshing of the pinion gear to the flywheel ring gear. Make sure the car is in park with the emergency brake on.

 PERFORMANCE GAIN: A more powerful, lighter starter that is easier to install and access

COMPLEMENTARY PROJECTS: Project 89: Removing and Replacing the Battery and Battery Cables; Project 92: Installing a New Alternator

The starter motor is a specially designed, direct current (DC) electric motor capable of producing a large amount of power. The rapid rotating speed of the starter's pinion gear enables the unit to drive the larger flywheel gear at the rear of the motor and thus start the engine.

Mounted on the side of the starter assembly is a small magnetic device known as the starter solenoid. It receives current from the starting switch circuit of the ignition switch. This circuit consists of the starting switch contained in the ignition switch, a transmission neutral safety or clutch pedal switch, and the appropriate wiring to connect these to the solenoid. When the ignition key is rotated to the start position, a plunger inside the solenoid becomes magnetically

activated. It slides the starter's pinion gear to the flywheel ring gear by a collar and spring. This small pinion gear is mounted to a one-way drive clutch that is splined onto the starter's armature shaft. If the two gears mesh properly, the flywheel is engaged and the engine is cranked. However, if the teeth of the gears are misaligned, the spring will compress and force the two gears together when the starter pinion gear rotates into position.

After the engine is started, the clutch mechanism allows the pinion gear to spin free of the armature shaft, protecting the starter motor from operating at excessive speeds. When the key is released from the start position, the solenoid is no longer energized. The solenoid assembly retracts the pinion gear and breaks the flow of current to the starter.

Electrical systems such as the starter motor and its harnessing are especially vulnerable to the elements over time. The starter is located at the bottom of the engine, wedged tightly between the exhaust header and pipe and the engine block. Although the starter only operates intermittently, it is constantly subjected to the extreme heat generated from neighboring components. Cracked and frayed wires, contact corrosion, and heat fatigue and failure are not uncommon. The starter consistently plays an integral part in the daily operation of your vehicle. Eventually, starter replacement is in high order.

When the time comes to rejuvenate your starting system with a new starter motor, consider a high-torque mini starter. As the name implies, this micro unit is equipped with a 3.73:1 gear reduction pinion to increase your starting torque by 40 to 50 percent. It weighs roughly 11 pounds and is 33 percent smaller in overall size compared to a factory replacement starter. This allows for plenty of clearance and protection from the heat, especially with the use of headers.

When working with any electrical system, the first priority is to disconnect the negative battery cable. Depending on your car, it may be easier to access the starter motor connections from below the vehicle. Raise and support the vehicle safely using jack stands. Disconnect the starter leads at the terminals of the solenoid. Make sure to label the mounting location of each wire prior to removal. If you are unable to reach the posts of the solenoid, you can unbolt and lower the starter to access the wires. Be careful not to let the starter motor fall and snap or sever the solenoid leads. Remove the starter motor mounting bolts and slowly pull the unit out. If shims or flat washers are used to space the starter to the flywheel, keep track of them and their designation. With the mini starter, the gap or clearance may be slightly different. The new starter should come complete with shims and mounting bolts.

Follow the instructions in the reverse order and be sure to reconnect the leads to their proper terminals. After the new starter is in place, reattach the negative battery cable and secure it to the terminal.

ELECTRICAL

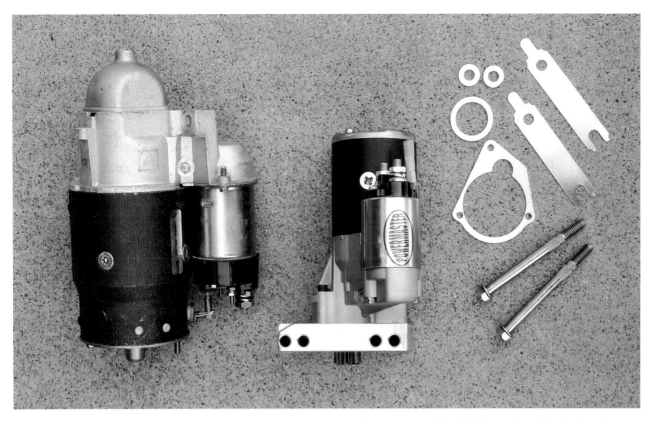

Above: The high-torque mini starters come complete with shims and new bolts. They are compatible with both small- and big-block engines.
Below: Often, shims must be used to obtain the proper pinion-gear-to-flywheel-gear clearance.

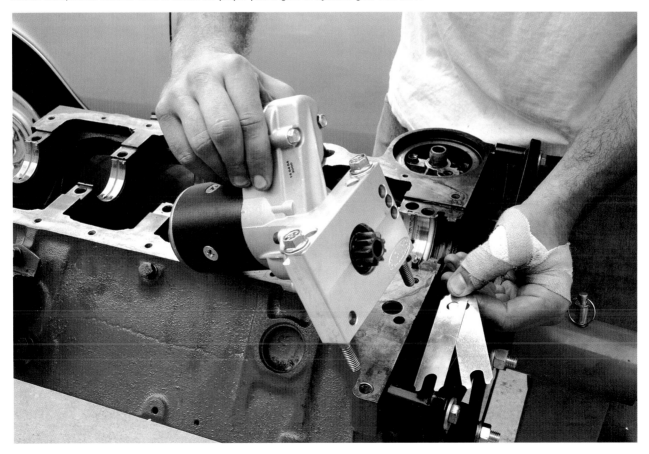

Installing a Wiring Harness

 Time: 30–60 minutes

 Tools: Flat-blade screwdriver

 Talent: 👤👤

 Applicable years: All

 Cost: $25–$500, depending on application

 Parts: Rear lamp wiring harness (for '67 Chevelle) approximately $125

 Tip: Keep everything orderly. Get the correct harness for your car's wiring. (Custom made is even better.)

PERFORMANCE GAIN: No more "voodoo wiring." This project will ensure bright lights and proper performance.

COMPLEMENTARY PROJECTS: Project 92: Installing a New Alternator

We ordered a new rear lamp harness, available from any classic car parts supply company, for our 1967 Chevelle.

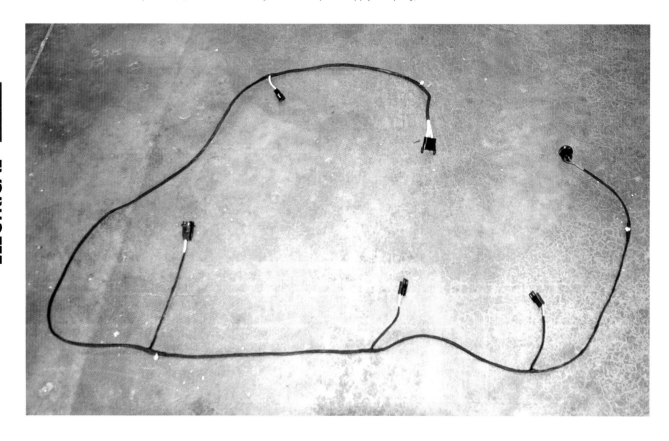

ELECTRICAL

You may be the greatest wrench-spinner in your club, but when it comes to wiring, most backyard mechanics would gladly pay someone else to do the job. Complicated tangles of wire, fuse blocks, and fear of torching your ride can be downright intimidating. Not to worry—there are plenty of companies out there that specialize in wiring harnesses for all years and applications. Companies like Painless Performance Products have changed the way people think about automotive wiring. There are others, but Painless has taken perhaps the scariest wiring problems imaginable and made solving them almost idiot-proof. Let's say you're faced with the prospect of totally rewiring your dash. There's a kit out there that includes all the necessary hardware wrapped up in an easy-to-install package. Each wire is preprinted with the application, so you know exactly what it's supposed to do. Terminals are coded by either color or shape (or both), so you can tell exactly where they're supposed to plug in. It's not child's play, but it's well within the realm of most backyard mechanics.

With the multitude of GM cars that were built from the early 1960s through the mid-1970s, there are countless wiring applications. From forward lamp harnesses, to power window harnesses, all the way up to full 18-circuit muscle car engine harnesses, spread out over many years and car lines . . . well, you get the picture. If you're not interested in a one-size-fits-all harness, there are companies that specialize in totally custom applications. Lectric Limited (www.lectriclimited.com) will take your old existing harness (no matter the application) and create a brand new one for you, tailored to fit your car perfectly. Wire type, color, gauge, striping, connectors, lamp sockets, tape type and color, etc., are all exactly as per your car's original specs. Many other classic GM-based restoration parts companies will offer a huge selection of original-style harnesses as well.

Obviously, space does not allow us to cover all wiring applications here. For this project, we've taken our '67 Chevelle and elected to replace the rear lamp harness.

The key to starting out right is organization and cleanliness. As with most wiring harnesses, this one looks a lot less intimidating when it is laid out properly. It's a good idea to unravel your new harness and get acquainted with it. Instead of just climbing in the trunk with the wiring tangled around everything, lay it neatly out in the trunk, matching up what goes where.

As you can see by Photo 2, the original wiring has become brittle and cracked. Someone has taken frayed wires and tried to twist them back together. This can only result in poor connections, leading to lights that look dim, blink when they're not supposed to, or don't even come on at all. Replacing the harness was definitely the right choice. We proceed to unplug the old connectors, and remove all that old, dried-up wiring.

To install the new wiring, we start with the harness end and plug it into the outlet that protrudes into the back of the trunk from the car's interior. To test the power, insert new bulbs into all the sockets: taillamp/turn signal, reverse lamps, and the license plate lamp. Voilà! They all fire up, glowing intensely. We then remove the bulbs and proceeded to route the new wiring. With our custom-made harness, everything fits to a tee. The correctly wrapped wire sits snugly in the Chevelle's trunk wiring tabs. All the bulb sockets line up with their respective holes and twist in perfectly. The whole process takes about 30 minutes, and the end result is well worth it.

You can take this same approach to any wiring harness replacement on any car. Stay organized and, when at all possible, lay out the entire harness the way it would fit into the car. Test-fit first, and make notes on paper if you have to. Rewiring is not scary, and with the products that are on the market today, it's now a whole lot easier.

Wiring that was perfect in 1967 has deteriorated to the point that replacement is a must. This wiring is cracked, brittle, and ready to give up any moment.

The new harness is a perfect reproduction of the original, right down to the correctly spaced light sockets and tape-wrapped wiring.

Installing a New Alternator

  Time: 1/2 hour

 Tools: Socket set or boxed wrenches, heavy flat-blade screwdriver or pry bar

 Talent:

 Applicable years: All

 Cost: $65–$150

 Parts: New alternator

 Tip: When choosing a new alternator, always shoot for more power.

PERFORMANCE GAIN: Better idle stability—great for that monster stereo

COMPLEMENTARY PROJECTS:

Replacing the external regulator; Project 91: Installing a Wiring Harness

ELECTRICAL

Even though some of the earliest cars covered in this book are running on a generator, the vast majority of the '65 through mid-'70s cars came with alternators with external regulators as standard equipment. The information in this project is intended to give you a brief overview of how your alternator works, how to replace or upgrade your alternator, and what to look for in a new one.

Once you turn the key to fire up your muscle car, your battery does 100 percent of the work. It supplies the energy needed to turn over the starter motor. Once the engine comes to life, however, it's the charging system that takes over. The charging system provides voltage for all of your car's electrical components. There are basically two different types of voltage-producing generators. One is the direct current (DC) generator (found on the very early cars), and the other is the alternating current (AC) generator, more commonly referred to as the alternator. The alternator utilizes a spinning magnetic field to produce voltage in windings, putting out the current via solid-state diodes. As automotive design, power, and electronic luxuries increased in the mid-1960s, the alternators quickly took over from the generators. The direct current generators are not capable of maintaining a proper voltage (especially at idle speeds) to support the newer car's electrical needs.

An alternator is composed of two main electricity-generating components: the rotor and the stator. The rotor is nestled in the center of the housing. It is made from field-coil windings mounted on a shaft that is supported by ball bearings. Brushes and slip rings permit the battery's current to be fed into the rotor's windings. All of this creates a magnetic field around the windings. When the drive belt spins a pulley mounted on one end of the rotor shaft, the rotor assembly starts to turn. This produces a rotating magnetic field. Two poles, each of opposite polarity, surround the windings and increase the magnetic field's strength. Internal cooling fans help circulate air through the alternator to keep the temperatures low. Surrounding the rotor is a fixed or stationary set of three output loops wrapped around an iron ring. This is called the stator. As the rotor spins, its magnetic field cuts through each loop, infusing them with voltage. The rotating magnetic field has a north-south polarity, so with each rotor revolution, each loop gets exposed to this polarity. The result is alternating current voltage (AC). The AC current starts to flow, keeping your car's electrical components lit.

All of this is well and good and, compared to the old generators, the new-for-the-1960s alternators were a space-age breakthrough, smaller, lighter, and way more powerful. But that was then, and this is now. Most of these older muscle-car-era alternators output little more than 55 amps. Even the big-block Corvettes of the mid-1960s only offer a top-of-the-line 60-amp unit. But compared to the lowly generators, this was the big time. Today, alternators with ratings of 80, 100, or even 200 amps are available. Depending on your particular needs, you can install as much juice as you want.

With all that basic knowledge under your belt, let's move on to the upgrade. The first step is to neutralize the battery. Do this by disconnecting the negative battery cable. Next, we're going to remove that old alternator.

Choose your new alternator carefully. If you're running a plethora of electricity-hogging accessories (stereos, power goodies, etc.) and some state-of-the-art electronic components under the hood, you may want to step up to at least a 100- or 120-amp unit. A great retrofit unit for classic muscle cars is GM–Delphi's CS-130 alternator. It offers a smaller size, lighter weight, and increased performance at engine idle.

Installing the new alternator is as simple as reversing the steps listed in the photo captions. As pictured in Photo 4, you'll need to provide enough pressure on the alternator to keep the belt tight. Once you've got everything reconnected (don't forget the battery's negative cable), fire it up and enjoy all that newfound energy and dependability.

230

Above: Using a socket or boxed wrench, remove the bolt that secures the alternator to the top alternator bracket.
Below: Disconnect or unplug all wiring from the alternator. If you're unsure how to put it all back together, jot down which wire connects to which terminal.

Above: Using a socket or boxed wrench, remove the nut that secures the alternator to the mounting post.

Below: After securing the alternator to the mounting post, use a heavy screwdriver or pry bar to "push" the alternator into position. The belts must be tight; then you can tighten the nut that secures the alternator to the upper alternator bracket.

Installing a New Turn Signal Switch and Cancel Cam

 Time: 2 hours

 Tools: Steering wheel puller, standard socket set, Phillips screwdriver, flat-blade screwdriver, dielectric grease, length of twine

 Talent:

 Applicable years: All

 Cost: $60–$120

 Parts: Turn signal switch assembly, canceling cam, turn signal lever (optional)

 Tip: When removing the old switch from the column, tie a piece of string or twine to the end of the connector to feed and guide the new harness down through the shaft cover.

PERFORMANCE GAIN: There's just something about external signal lamps that makes the roadways a safer place.

COMPLEMENTARY PROJECTS: Replacing the external turn signal bulb; Project 3: Removing, Inspecting, and Refinishing the Steering Column

Although not a major mechanical crisis, a broken turn signal switch can be rather bothersome and a safety hazard. This highly important switch is responsible for activating the signal lamps at the front and rear of the vehicle. Along with the canceling cam, it is tightly nestled into the steering column housing just behind the center hub of the steering wheel. The turn signal lever attaches directly to the body of the switch through a small slot in the steering shroud. On the back of the switch is a series of wires and an electrical connector that runs down the length of the steering column. The long, flat connector plugs into the underdash wiring harness and bridges the gap between the switch and the power source. Activated by upward or downward movement of the lever, the internal switch and its contacts enable the signal lamps to turn on and off.

Due to the excessive use of the turn signal switch, the plastic body and various actuating springs and levers often wear down and are rendered useless. Corrosion is yet another culprit in the premature failure of the switch. The dielectric grease used to lubricate and protect the contact points is commonly found contaminated, dried up, or even burned off. The turn signal switch is one of many overlooked components that fall into this forgotten category. Fortunately, the swap is pretty painless and only requires the removal of the steering wheel to accomplish. In fact, while you're there, you may want to look at replacing other suspect pieces such as the turn signal lever, horn buttons and contacts, or even the steering wheel center cap.

When working with anything remotely electrical, the first priority is to disconnect battery power from the rest of the vehicle. Grab a wrench or socket and remove the negative battery cable from its terminal post. Turning your attention to the steering wheel, carefully remove the center cap and retainer or trim pad (depending on year). Most early vehicles with a spoke-style wheel have a center emblem cap. Using a small, flat-blade screwdriver, gently pry one edge of the cap up and out of the retainer. The later, trim-pad style steering wheels are fastened by retaining screws in the back side of the wheel.

You'll need a steering wheel puller to remove the wheel from the steering shaft. The puller can be found at any parts supply store and is a great tool to have readily available in the box. The horn ring, contacts, and retainer will need to go first in order to fully access the steering wheel nut. A small Phillips screwdriver should handle the order. Before approaching the wheel, mark the positioning in relation to the shaft to ensure that the wheel is reinstalled correctly and straight. Remove the locknut and washer and use the specialty tool to pull the wheel from the steering column shaft.

On later models, the switch assembly is secured to the shaft by a C-clip retainer. Use a compression tool to compress the lock plate and remove the C-clip. The cancel cam can be removed and replaced by hand. It simply slides down and around the shaft in front of the signal switch. Take note of the way it's installed prior to disassembly. The turn signal lever

The turn signal switch assembly is a tight fit. The C-ring holds the cancel cam, spring, and washer in front of the switch.

and the four-way flasher knob (if applicable) can now be unscrewed from the body of the switch. On some automatic-equipped vehicles, the transmission indicator will need to be removed as well. The switch is fastened to the steering column housing by three small retaining screws. Once the switch is loose, unplug the connector from the dash harness at the base of the steering column. It may be necessary to first unbolt the column from the dash carrier. Be sure to properly support the column after removing its bracing. Do not allow the column to "hang" suspended by the lower support only.

To eliminate the switch from the column, the applicable column covers and housings must be removed to allow clearance for the connector to slide through. Different years and models will have similar, yet special circumstances. Carefully guide the harness and its connector body up through the column.

Reverse your steps to install the new components. Make sure the turn signal switch is in the neutral position prior to installing the cancel cam, spring, and washer. The flasher knob should be in the "out" position.

Three small retaining screws fasten the switch to the housing.

The harness for the switch slides down inside the steering column cover.

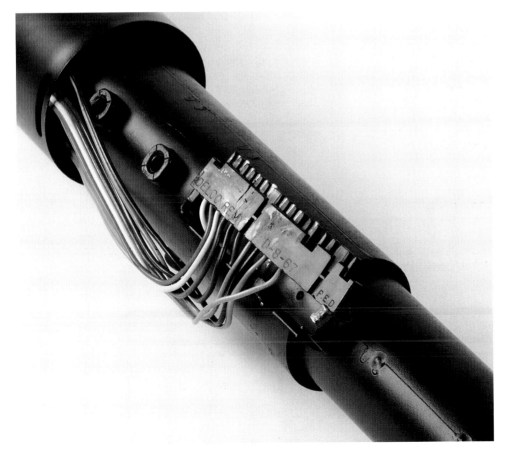

At the other end, the switch connector plugs into the underdash wiring harness.

Restoring the Windshield Wiper System

 Time: 2–3 hours

 Tools: Standard socket set, standard wrenches, wiper arm removal tool

 Talent:

 Applicable years: All

 Cost: $50–$150

 Parts: Wiper switch, wiper motor and washer pump (if needed), bulk hose, washer reservoir (if needed)

 Tip: Be sure to replace your wiper motor with the correct part. In some model years, both two-speed and three-speed wiper motors were offered. Although they may appear the same, the motors had different wiring connectors and are not interchangeable.

 PERFORMANCE GAIN: Safe and reliable windshield wipers

COMPLEMENTARY PROJECTS:
Project 91: Installing a Wiring Harness

ELECTRICAL

Although a finely-tuned windshield wiper system has never netted raw horsepower, it is among the necessities for any street-driven vehicle. The wiper system consists of three major components: the wiper switch, wiper motor and linkage, and washer pump and reservoir.

Due to continuous use, the wiper switch is most commonly the weakest link in the system. It relies on a series of electrical contacts to switch on/off and to vary the operating speed of the wiper arms. Over time, the electrical contacts become corroded and fail to engage or disengage the wipers. Faulty connections inside the switch may also cause intermittent operation of the wipers. It is possible to remove the wiper switch from the dash or the steering column (depending on the year of the vehicle) and repair the contacts and loose connections. However, replacing the wiper switch altogether is a far better alternative. The switches are inexpensive and plug directly into the dash harness, just like the originals.

A dash-mounted wiper switch (pre-1968) is secured to the front panel of the dash by a simple retaining ring. The switch is plugged into the underdash wiring harness and fed through the opening in the back side of the instrument panel. The wiper switch knob then attaches to the front of the shaft. To remove the switch, disconnect the negative battery cable and unplug the wiring harness connector from the wiper switch. Remove the front retaining ring or bezel and carefully slide the switch out of the instrument panel.

The windshield wiper motor is mounted to the firewall panel inside the engine compartment. On the back side of the motor is a small crank arm that attaches to the mechanical linkage under the cowl grill. The linkage rods transfer the movement of the wiper motor crank arm to the windshield wiper arm and blade assemblies. If the wiper blades use a press-type release tab at the center, simply depress the tab to remove the blades. If no tab is present, carefully press the center spring of the blade with a small screwdriver to release the assembly. The wiper arms require the use of a specialty tool to remove them from the serrated shafts of the linkage rods. Insert the tool underneath the wiper arm to leverage the base from the shaft. Remove the cowl grill from the top of the fenders to access the arms and the rear of the wiper motor. Disconnect the linkage rods from the crank on the motor and remove the linkage assemblies. Be sure the wiper motor is in the park position. The wiper motor may now be removed from the firewall.

On some models, the washer pump was integrated into the wiper motor assembly. It can be removed from the motor and serviced separately. The washer pump is responsible for the function of washing the windshield with concentrated fluid. The pump is actuated by the wiper switch inside the dash. When power is applied to the switch, the washer pump draws the fluid from the washer reservoir and sprays the windshield. The arms are briefly activated to help clean the dirty surface.

It's important to check all the seals of the pump and the hose connections for any leaks or deterioration. Replace any cracked or brittle lines with new hose.

Above: The windshield wiper motor and pump is a self-contained unit located on the driver's side firewall.
Below: Wiper switches are easy to install and only require a single connection.

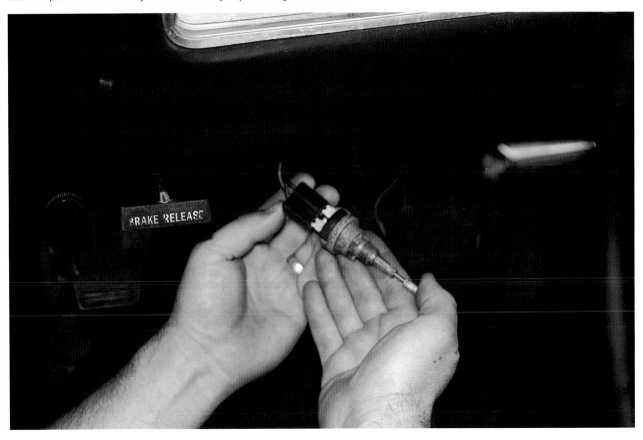

Installing an Aftermarket Tachometer

 Time: 1 hour

 Tools: Wire strippers/crimpers, flat-bade screwdriver, standard wrenches, 12-volt test light (recommended)

 Talent:

 Applicable years: All

 Cost: $50–$300

 Parts: Tachometer, electrical connectors, hose clamp (optional), HEI connector (if applicable)

 Tip: Buy plenty of electrical connectors. They come in a wide variety of designs and sizes. Splicing bare wires together and covering them up with a ball of electrical tape is not smart or good practice.

PERFORMANCE GAIN: Reliable, consistent shifts to help maximize your vehicle's performance

COMPLEMENTARY PROJECTS:
Project 26: Replacing the Distributor Coil, Cap, and Rotor

ELECTRICAL

Adding an aftermarket tachometer is one of the best investments you can make in prolonging the life of your engine. In the excitement of the moment, it's far too easy to recklessly pin the throttle and overrev the engine. Transmissions need to shift. Believe it or not, there is an optimum point at which the shift should be executed. Depending on a multitude of factors (camshaft profile, carburetor/intake arrangement, timing curve, etc.), your engine routinely performs within a certain power band. The optimum shift point for the transmission will naturally be at the top end of your horsepower range. Exceeding this invisible marker can not only prove to be counterproductive by hindering your track ETs, but it can also grenade your engine beyond repair. The simple installation of a tachometer comes in very handy.

Most cars were delivered from the factory without a tachometer. Only the special high-performance models of the day were graced with the RPO (regular production option) item. Although desirable, many conservative-minded consumers deemed the racelike instrument an unnecessary expense.

If you prefer (as I do) the simplistic ruggedness and control of a four-speed, a tachometer is an absolute must—end of story. However, with automatics, there seems to be a little more flexibility. Not every small V-8 paired with a two-speed will benefit from the installation, but manually shifted automatics on both the street and the strip are constantly gaining in popularity. Automatics are simply easier to handle at the track, especially during the launch. They relieve the left-foot responsibility at the clutch pedal and allow the driver to focus on making crisp, consistent shifts. In one single pass, so much is either gained or lost solely in the timing and execution of the shifts, regardless of your transmission. You can easily hear it as a car makes its way down the track. Often, our adrenaline gets the best of us. With so much to think about in only a matter of seconds, it's easy to miss that perfect shift.

Although there are more than enough choices for the "right" tachometer, the approach and hookup are all the same. Most are calibrated for V-8 applications. If for some reason you run with a six, the tach will need adjusting. The connection usually consists of four leads exiting the back housing of the tachometer. They are color coded and should be explained in your instruction diagram regarding their designation. One lead attaches to the ignition switch (red), one to the battery or ground (black), one to the ignition coil (green), and one to a 12-volt light source (white). This may vary, depending on your existing ignition setup (HEI, ignition box, ballast resistor, etc.).

You can tap into the ignition switch underneath the dash. Locate the "hot" ignition wire and trace it back to a point that will allow you to make the splice. Be sure to disconnect the negative battery cable before making any cuts or connections in the harness. Some manufacturers recommend installing an inline fuse from the tachometer to the ignition switch for added safety. This is a good idea and will protect your components if anything ever goes haywire.

While you're under the dash, look for an accessible wire that connects to any 12-volt light source, such as an instrument panel lamp. Splicing into the wire using a "crimp-on" connector or a wire nut will supply the face of the tach with light. To double-check the wire for 12 volts before cutting, use a 12-volt test probe. This handy, electrical tool resembles the shape and size of a common screwdriver. However, the handle is clear and contains a small light bulb. When the sharp probe is pushed through the outer sheathing

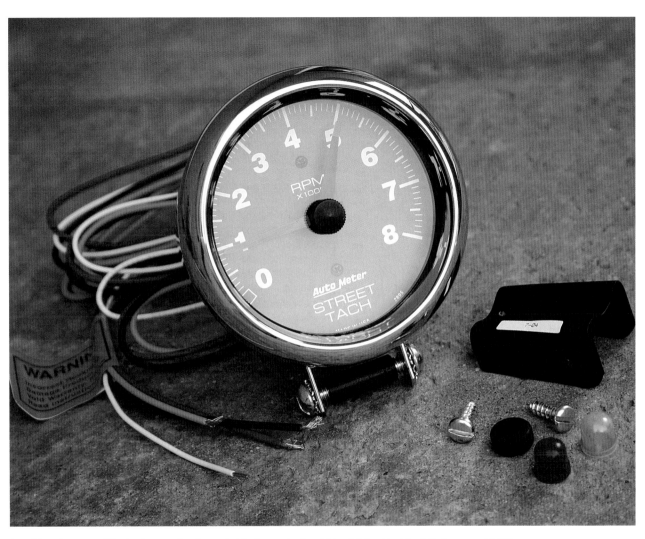

Auto Meter has one of the best names in aftermarket instruments. Its mid-level "street tach" retails for around $100.

and makes contact with the wire, the handle will illuminate if 12-volt current is present.

The remaining two wires will exit through the firewall and into the engine compartment. The black lead should connect to the negative (ground) terminal or cable of the battery. The green (or other) lead will attach to the negative terminal of the ignition coil. On HEI ignitions, you will need to purchase an HEI adapter to connect the lead to the "TACH" terminal on the distributor. Try to find an existing hole in the firewall to feed the wires through. If drilling is required, make it small and neat and use a rubber grommet to protect the wires from the sharp metal.

If you run an aftermarket ignition box, consult the manufacturer before the installation. In fact, consult the manufacturer prior to purchasing the new tachometer. Some tachs are not compatible with these systems.

After the tach is wired in, choosing a practical and functional point for mounting can sometimes be tricky. Depending on the layout of your dash, the tach should be as centrally mounted as possible to keep the diversion from the road to a minimum. An always-popular location is the top of the steering column, directly in front of the instrument panel. Use the mounting bracket and a large hose clamp and place a thin strip of rubber between the clamp and the column to protect the paint or the column cover. I fervently try to avoid drilling holes in these cars, especially when it comes to the interior. If you have no other option, take precise measurements and do the job justice.

239

Installing Aftermarket Gauges

Time: 2 hours

Tools: Standard socket set, standard wrenches, wire cutters/crimpers, 12-volt test light, power drill and bits (if needed)

Talent:

Applicable years: All

Cost: $75–$100

Parts: Gauge cluster (or individual), thread-sealer compound or Teflon tape, 18-gauge wire, and various connectors

Tip: Use a sealing compound or tape on all pipefittings and threads (NPT) to avoid any leaks from surfacing.

PERFORMANCE GAIN: Reliable monitoring of your engine's vital statistics

COMPLEMENTARY PROJECTS:
Project 56: Installing a New Radiator and Hoses; Project 95: Installing an Aftermarket Tachometer

ELECTRICAL

The engine of your car is a very complex animal. It has multiple systems that are constantly performing different tasks, all at the same time. As the operator and commander-in-chief, you need to know the status of these systems in order to give the engine what it needs. The advent of detailed instrument gauges has carried out these orders and given us the necessary information within the comfy confines of the passenger compartment.

In production years past, most vehicles rolled off the assembly lines devoid of elaborate instrumentation. A speedometer and a fuel gauge were the basic package. The remainder of the monitoring systems functioned by a series of what are commonly referred to as "dummy lights." As the

name implies, a simple red or orange light would appear inside the instrument panel if one or more of the systems were triggered by a malfunction. The light would not indicate what exactly went wrong, only that something was not right. Half of the time, these idiot lights were tripped by other gremlins in the vehicle not directly related to the source of the signal lamp. This was and still is a common, frustrating occurrence.

Installing aftermarket gauges is a quick and highly efficient method to keep tabs on all of the engine's systems. This applies for both normally street-driven vehicles and full-on racers. The standard gauge set usually consists of an oil pressure, water temperature, and amps or volts gauge. With the addition of a tachometer, these are the three main components for monitoring the vitals of your engine. They can be purchased individually or in a complete set with a mounting bracket. You also have the option of choosing different styles, faceplates, and mechanical or electrical operation.

For some, installing aftermarket gauges right into their factory dashboards and instrument panels is preferable. However, this often means cutting holes in the dash and destroying the originality of the car. It's usually easy to find a small, unobstructed area in which to mount the gauge cluster. The bottom side of the dash carrier is a popular spot. It provides a clear visual for reading the gauges and looks clean when properly mounted. All of the gauges come equipped with means for their own light source, so night prowling is never a problem. It's important to decide on the location of the bracket before starting the installation.

Getting started on the installation requires locating an accessible water port on the engine block or cylinder heads, an oil pressure port on the engine, and a 12-volt ignition lead. As always, disconnect the negative battery cable from the terminal post when performing any electrical work on your car.

To install the water temperature gauge, a 7/8-inch hole will most likely need to be drilled in the firewall to allow the temperature-sensing bulb to pass through and thread into the water port on the engine. Scout a location on the firewall away from any moving linkage or excess heat. Install a rubber grommet into the hole to avoid chafing of the wire and carefully push the sensor into the engine compartment. The cooling system will need to be fully drained in order to unplug the sensor port on the engine. The coolant can be saved and reused after the installation. Use the supplied bushing (if necessary) and slowly thread the plug of the sensing bulb into the port. Be sure to coat the threads of the plug with a sealer compound or Teflon tape prior to installation. The gauge at the other end may now be mounted into the faceplate, using the U-shaped retaining bracket.

The amps gauge or voltmeter install is purely electrical and only requires three connections. First, strip the ends of one wire (18-gauge recommended) and attach it to the positive side of the gauge backing plate. Loosely place the gauge into the

Aftermarket companies, such as Auto Meter, make gauge clusters for just about every application.

mounting faceplate to determine the length of wire you need to cut. Attach the other end of the wire to a 12-volt "keyed" ignition source such as the fuse box. Keyed means that when the ignition key is switched to the "on" position, power is present at that location. Now strip another wire and attach it to the negative terminal on the backing plate of the gauge. This lead will go directly to either a chassis ground inside the engine compartment or a fixed grounding point located on the underside of the dash carrier.

Last, but not least, is the oil pressure gauge and sensor. The gauge reads the oil pressure found at the engine through a small diameter nylon tube. Remove the oil sending unit from the engine and insert the supplied pipe bushing. Again, coat the threads of the bushings and the connectors with

some type of sealant to ward off any leaks. Install the compression nut and ferrule over the nylon tube and attach the nut to the new fitting. As you slowly turn the compression nut, the seal between the end of the tubing and the inside of the adapter fitting will become tight. The tubing will route back through the firewall (drill hole if necessary) and attach to the back side of the oil pressure gauge using the same method. Install the gauge into the faceplate and secure the plate to the dash.

All gauge lamps should be spliced into a 12-volt light source underneath the dash. Refill the cooling system with coolant/water and tighten any loose fittings. Once all connections are made and secured, fire the engine and inspect both the ports and the gauges for any signs of leakage.

The temperature sensor comes equipped with a pipe-thread bushing that installs into the larger plug in the block.

The oil pressure gauge uses a length of nylon tubing, which connects to the engine. It is secured to both ports using a ferrule and a compression nut.

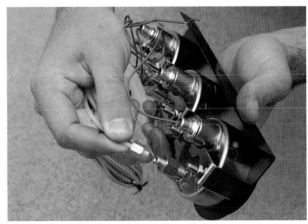

Installing a Safety Cutoff Switch

 Time: 2 hours

 Tools: Standard socket set, standard wrenches, flat-blade screwdriver, Phillips screwdriver, hole saw

 Talent:

 Applicable years: All

 Cost: $50

 Parts: Safety switch kit and hardware, electrical connectors

 Tip: Always follow the required safety regulations, even if track inspectors fail to enforce them.

PERFORMANCE GAIN: Safer racing environments for all

COMPLEMENTARY PROJECTS: Installing a trunk-mounted battery

Whether on the street or the track, safety should always be top on the list. This especially applies to high-horsepower cars dedicated to racing. If you frequent any type of racetrack, you are already familiar with the rules and regulations enforced by the tech inspectors. Sanctioning bodies of racing, such as the NHRA, have their own set of rules for what is and is not allowed on the track. Most of these rules depend on what type of vehicle is being raced and how fast it is. However, tech enforcement tends to vary quite a bit from track to track, which puts you at a greater risk, along with everybody else sharing the track with you.

To help in the front-to-rear transfer of weight when a drag car launches, it has become common practice to install the battery inside the trunk compartment. Therefore, the NHRA mandates that any vehicle with a trunk-mounted battery must have a battery kill switch. "The cutoff switch must be connected to the positive side of the electrical system and must stop all electrical functions." This is strictly for your own safety and the common well-being of the track's safety crews. In the event of an accident, the crews need to be able to shut the car down externally to prevent the possibility of a fire or explosion.

To install a cutoff switch, you first need to figure out where the switch will be mounted at the rear of the car. It needs to be easily accessible and visible for safety crews. The most popular mounting location is in the rear bumper. Although it means drilling a hole in the chrome, it's a better alternative than hacking the body. To do this, you will need a quality hole saw and a power drill. Using a pair of calipers, measure the diameter of the switch to determine what size the hole needs to be. Hole saws can be purchased in a variety of diameters from any hardware store. Next, mark the spot on the surface where the switch will be mounted.

Once the location of the switch has been determined, the wiring is next. The positive battery cable stretches from the battery (trunk) to the "switched" post on the switch. The terminal end may need to be replaced to adapt. If you need to purchase new cables, use a heavy-duty 2-gauge wire. In addition, you need to splice a lead from the "hot" ignition source (key) and run it to the same terminal post as the positive battery cable on the cutoff switch. The opposite post on the switch will be linked to the positive terminal of the ignition coil and the starter motor. Be sure to make solid connections in the wiring and use shrink tubing for extra insurance.

Many companies manufacture cutoff switches for all types of vehicles and applications. The system described here uses a switch with a built-in relay and an accessory terminal to allow other accessories, such as an electric fuel pump, to be shut down also.

Once the switch is securely installed, test the unit by starting the vehicle and allowing the engine to idle. With the engine running, hit the switch to make sure everything is working properly. The car should immediately shut off without hesitation. Try the switch again at an increased rpm to ensure safety in all possible scenarios. Label the switch in bold, black marker as to the position to cut power, such as 'PUSH OFF.'

ELECTRICAL

All safety cutoff switches must be easily accessible and clearly marked.

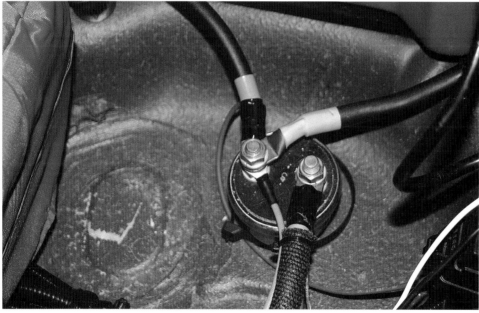

The wiring is very straightforward and only requires a few connections.

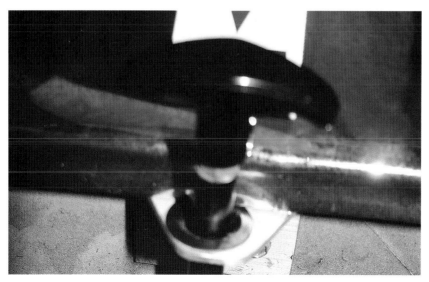

The switch easily mounts to the underside of the trunk pan.

SECTION *ELEVEN*
MISCELLANEOUS

This section contains miscellaneous projects or repairs that are popular in just about every restoration and buildup. They are relatively simple but offer insight into the finishing touches and minor obstacles found in car crafting.

Painting the Engine

 Time: 5–8 hours

 Tools: Wire brushes

 Talent:

 Applicable years: All

 Cost: $50

 Parts: Masking tape and paper, engine degreaser, clean rags, engine paint, latex gloves, lacquer thinner, and valve stem seals (optional)

 Tip: Wearing latex gloves while painting not only prevents paint-stained hands, but also helps keep the engine clean and free of all oils and dirt.

PERFORMANCE GAIN: A freshly painted engine is a must for any classic restoration. The entire engine compartment appears orderly and is a much cleaner place to work as well.

COMPLEMENTARY PROJECTS: Repainting the firewall and inner fenders; Project 32: Installing Valve Cover Gaskets and Studs

The engine compartment is not naturally pretty. It takes the worst of all the elements found on the road and stores them up until the engine resembles that of a giant dirt clod. From built-up road sludge to nasty oil leaks, the engine is constantly subjected to a de-beautification process that is, without question, a killer on the engine paint.

Repainting the engine is not hard; it's just time consuming, especially if the engine is left inside the engine compartment. However, pulling the entire engine out of the car just for the sake of fresh paint is not always the most practical alternative. With some basic guidelines and tips, restoring the luster and shine of your engine can easily be accomplished in an afternoon, while removing only the necessities. The supplies and materials list is inexpensive, and the items can typically be purchased from your local auto parts store.

The absolute first thing you need to do is clean. Using warm water and a mild soap, lightly wash the surface of the engine and its surrounding areas. Remove any pieces that may interfere with the cleaning and/or painting. The air cleaner assembly and the carburetor are easy to remove and should be set aside during the painting. The air cleaner can be painted separately once it's already off of the car.

To break down heavy and stubborn grime, use an industrial engine degreaser. Coat the engine with the degreaser and allow it to soak for a few minutes before rinsing it off. The chemical agents in the degreaser attack the heavy buildup and help remove the unwanted grime.

Once the engine is totally clean and dry, it's time to start masking. Mask off everything on and around the engine that should not be painted. Take your time and make the seams of the tape straight and even. When it comes to painting, 99 percent of the job is in the preparation. To help in the masking, cut a small piece of cardboard and use it as a shield to protect other items in the engine compartment from overspray. Heavy-duty masking paper also works well for this purpose. Items such as vacuum hoses, spark plug wires, and even valve covers can be temporarily removed to ensure full coverage of the paint in tight places.

It's a fact: Paint always adheres and responds better in warmer climates. Spray paint is best suited for temperatures in the 80- to 90-degree (Fahrenheit) range. A popular trick is to prewarm the paint can before spraying in order to allow the paint to slightly thin for better application and finish. Use hot water from the tap to make sure the paint or the can does not get too hot. The engine may also be started prior to painting and allowed to reach its normal operating temperature. When heated, the block, cylinder heads, and the intake will help spread the paint evenly and quickly. A warm engine also reduces the possibility of runs in the paint and makes for quicker drying times.

Test the nozzle of the spray can on a scrap piece of metal or cardboard before starting on the engine. It's always best to apply several lighter coats of paint rather than one or two heavy coats. When each coat is almost dry, yet still tacky, proceed to lightly recoat the area. If the can is running low on

Above: Clean-up is an absolute must before painting an engine.

Right: Carefully mask off the surrounding areas using a thick paper and masking tape.

paint and starts shooting more air than paint, stop. The moisture in the compressed air can create runs in the paint and cause the finish to look spotted. Be sure to purchase more than enough paint to cover these could-be problems.

When all of the coats have finally dried, you can go back and remove any overspray from the engine compartment. Do not be alarmed; this is highly normal. With a little lacquer thinner and few clean rags, the oversprayed paint can easily be cleaned off. Be careful not to spill the lacquer thinner anywhere near the other painted surfaces of the car or engine compartment. It will quickly blemish and ruin the finish of the paint. Additionally, do not use lacquer thinner to clean any paper or vinyl stickers or decals. It is much too strong and will permanently damage them.

PROJECT 99

Fabricating Hard Lines

 Time: 1–3 hours

 Tools: Tubing bender, flaring tool, tubing cutter, hacksaw (optional), small fine-tooth file

 Talent:

 Applicable years: All

 Cost: $100

 Parts: Bulk tubing (aluminum or stainless steel), AN line end fittings (if necessary), wire hanger

 Tip: It's a good idea to flare one end of the tubing before making the bends. If the bends are made and the flare happens to go sideways, you have wasted that whole length of tubing.

 PERFORMANCE GAIN: Clean, professional fit hard lines

COMPLEMENTARY PROJECTS:

Project 40: Installing a Nitrous Oxide System; Project 41: Installing a Mechanical Fuel Pump and Fuel Pressure Regulator; Project 82: Installing a Master Cylinder/Power Booster; Project 87: Installing a Line Lock

In the automotive world, knowing how to hand-bend and flare hard lines is a must for any true do-it-yourselfer. Just about every modified street machine is equipped with some form of custom hard lines. Anything from disc brake conversion kits to nitrous oxide systems require the implementation of newly formed lines. Manufacturers generally do their best to supply what is needed with their products, but the task of producing a single hard line for every application is just impossible. Truth be told, hand-fabricating lines is easy; it just takes a little time, patience, and planning.

When the lines are done and neatly fitted back into position, the car instantly becomes a cleaner, leaner machine.

For some, the idea of making hard lines by hand is intimidating. Where do you start? How do you make them fit right? Having the right tools is Priority 1 on the list. A quality tubing bender is a sound investment for anyone starting to make his or her own fabrications. Benders come in a variety of sizes and styles. Vise-mounted benders are a popular choice for stability and precision. Some even feature stamped markings on the face of the bender that indicate the angle of the bend radius. Tubing size will also determine proper bender selection. The tubing is rated and sized by the measurement of its outside diameter (OD). Look for a bender that works with the diameter of tubing you will most often use. Brake and fuel lines generally range from 3/16 to 3/8 inch.

In addition to a bender, you will need a tubing cutter, a good hacksaw, and a flaring tool. If you plan on cutting and bending stainless steel, buy tools capable of doing the job. Some cutters and flaring tools work fine with softer steel and aluminum tubing but will not hold their own when it comes to manipulating hardened stainless. Although more difficult to bend and flare, stainless steel will far outlast other materials and prevents flaring cracks with its seamless construction. Stainless steel also has a strong reputation for beautiful polishing.

Getting started on the project, make a template of the new line out of a wire coat hanger or some mechanic's wire. Mock up the wire in the correct location and form, including all bends and radiuses, to ensure the new hard line will fit perfectly. After the template is made, simply transform the hard line to duplicate the bends of the wire. Remember to leave extra length of tubing on each end of the new line for flares. Besides, it's always easier to start with a tube that is too long, rather than one that is too short.

To cut the line, use a sharp, 32-tooth hacksaw blade or a tubing cutter. With the saw, clamp the line firmly in the jaws of a vise and cut the needed length. A tubing cutter slices the line by tightening and rotating the cutter's blades in a circle around the outside of the stainless rod. Tighten slowly as you feel the blades cut into the tubing. If you go too fast, the cut end of the tube may be crushed or slightly deformed.

Flaring stainless steel requires a 37-degree single flare to be made in the tubing. Position the tubing inside the flaring tool, depending on the size of the line, with approximately 0.100 inch of tubing protruding from the flush surface of the tool. Place the head of the tool over the tubing and tighten the side lever slowly. After the tube is secured, tighten the top handle of the flaring tool until you feel it release tension. When the flare has been made, rotate the handle in the opposite direction and remove the tube. Always be sure to install the flare nuts and fittings before flaring both ends of the tube.

MISCELLANEOUS

Bending your own hard lines requires the use of specialty tools. This vise-mounted tubing bender is easy to use and indicates the degrees of each bend.

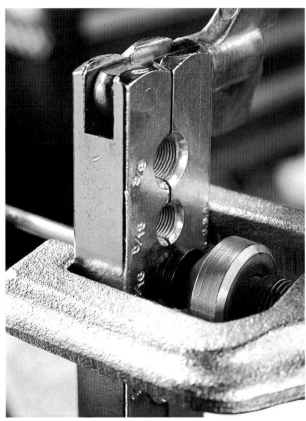

This simple tool will flare the ends of the tubing.

Insert the end of the tube into the correct hole and flare by hand.

Using your wire hanger as a template, insert the tubing into the bender and slowly begin to copy the radiuses of the wire. Although you may be working off a degreed scale, the bends will still be rough estimates. Check each bend on the car as you go to make sure everything is correct.

When routing and installing the lines, safety should be considered first. Pay close attention to all nearby components, such as wheels, driveline pieces, or any other moving parts. Route the lines away from any heat sources and secure with rigid clamps. These safety considerations need to be part of the initial game plan prior to making templates or hand-forming any hard lines.

248

PROJECT *100*
Repairing Threads

 Time: 1 hour

 Tools: Tap handle or socket wrench, power drill

 Talent:

 Applicable years: All

 Cost: $50–$150 for tools and supplies

 Parts: Taps, HeliCoil set, cutting fluid, clean rags

 Tip: Pay close attention to the thread types that are used on your original parts. Taps and inserts are made in both fine and coarse threads (metric and standard).

 PERFORMANCE GAIN: Increased longevity of old and often abused parts

COMPLEMENTARY PROJECTS: Installing stainless-steel high-strength bolts

Snapping the head off a hard-to-reach bolt is one of the most frustrating things that can happen during a project. The threads and shank of the bolt become stuck in the hole and can be a real nightmare to dislodge. Total disassembly is often necessary just to access the broken member with hand tools. Depending on the location and purpose of the bolt, it may not always be worth the extra time and energy to remove and replace it. However, most broken bolts will need proper repair.

After the head has been sheared, determine the best way to gain access to the remaining threads. You may need to use a power drill and wrenches to get the job done, so allow yourself

After drilling the hole, secure the tap into the handle and run the tap through the hole in a clockwise fashion. Be sure the tap enters the hole perfectly straight from all angles.

Taps and handles come in all different sizes, depending on the size and thread count of the bolt being used.

Dyes are used to clean up slightly marred or collapsed threads on a bolt. Using the handle, the dye runs over the bolt threads and cuts the correct thread and taper into the shank of the bolt.

plenty of room. Attempting to repair the blunder at an awkward angle can sometimes just make matters worse. On the bright side, there may be enough shank sticking out of the hole to grasp and loosen with a pair of locking pliers. Try this first; it could save you a lot of time. If the shank is snapped down inside the hole, drill the center of the bolt with the proper removal bit and reverse the direction to break the bolt loose. This is a tricky process and can often damage the threads of the existing hole. If the inside threads appear to be in good shape, run a clean bolt through them by hand to make sure there are no snags before reattaching the parts and tightening the new bolt. If the old threads got chewed up while removing the broken bolt, drill and enlarge the bolt hole and create new threads with a correctly sized tap.

To thread the new hole, you will need a tap, tap handle (or socket wrench), and cutting oil. The idea is to create new threads for the installation of a HeliCoil insert. Constructed of stainless-steel wire, the screw-thread insert is slightly larger in diameter than the threads in the newly tapped hole. Once inserted, the high-tension coil begins to expand against the tapped hole and provides an inner set of threads for the new bolt. This keeps all of the bolt sizes uniform and interchangeable.

Tapping a new hole requires patience and attention to detail. First and foremost, it is highly critical to keep everything straight. Create enough room around the area to position the drill completely perpendicular to the surface. If the bit goes in at a slightly crooked angle, the alignment for the new bolt will be off center. Once the hole has been redrilled, secure the tap into the handle and carefully start the new threads. Oil the tap and the hole periodically while carving the surface. If the tap begins to tighten in the hole, stop and reverse the direction a couple turns. It may be necessary to back the tap all the way out to clean the cut material out of the ridges. Taps are very brittle (hardened steel) and easy to break. It is near impossible to drill broken taps out of new holes, so be careful and go slow.

Inserting the HeliCoil is easy using the supplied installation tool. Rotate the insert into the tapped hole until the top of the insert is approximately 1/4 to 1/2 turn below the new threads. If a deep sink is required, the inserts may be stacked, one atop the other, and trimmed to fit.

PROJECT *101*

Selecting Bolts and Hardware

Time: n/a

Tools: n/a

Talent: n/a

Applicable years: All

Cost: n/a

Parts: n/a

Tip: Choose bolts and hardware that are suitable for the job. For most general automotive applications, commercial grade hardware (SAE Grade 5, SAE Grade 8) is sufficient.

PERFORMANCE GAIN: Confidence in knowing your car is put together well and will stay together

Choosing the right hardware for a project is important, although so much time is spent engrossed in the planning and building of a vehicle, we often forget about the key pieces holding everything together. It's often not until final assembly that we even think about the nuts and bolts, much less their condition or uniformity. Instead, we rely on a half-dozen last-minute trips to the parts store and every mechanic's infamous bucket-o-bolts. This works fine in a pinch, but proper hardware selection should be considered part of the project, not a mere afterthought. You never know—it could save your life.

When it comes to picking out the right bolts or fasteners for a job, the first thing to examine is the present load on that particular bolt. All bolts are rated for their strength in tension and shear forces. A tension load represents two individual pieces being drawn and clamped together. The force of the load is applied along the length of the shaft, as seen in connecting rod and cylinder head bolts. As the name implies, tension loads pull and even have the capability of stretching bolts. Seeing most of the tension force from the load, the threads of the bolt are the greatest risk and are often the first to give or fail.

Bolts subjected to sideways or bending forces are said to have a shear load. These types of loads apply heavy force directly to the shank of the bolt and can ultimately cause the bolt to break in half. In shear load applications, the threads of the bolt are almost irrelevant and are not subjected to any sideways forces. Single shear refers to a bolt that is only supported on one side of the load. In this arrangement, the

Bolts are commonly identified by the markings or patterns found on their heads. The two bolts at left are commercial grade. The smaller two bolts at right are aircraft grade.

MISCELLANEOUS

251

Allen head bolts or cap screws are widely used in the aircraft industry for their high tensile strength and recessed keys.

bolt is much more vulnerable to breaking than with double shear support (support on both sides of the load).

In the world of hardware, you have two basic options: commercial grade and aircraft grade. Commercial-grade bolts are readily available at just about any hardware or auto parts store and are fairly inexpensive. The downside to using commercial-grade hardware is the general application which they are constructed for. The manufacturer has no idea of the amount of load and type of force the bolt will see in service. The threads are typically cut long on commercial bolts to allow them to be used in blind-hole and other applications. The shanks of the bolts are turned with a slight neck for an even compromise between shear and tension loads. In any high-load assembly, such as the bottom end of an engine, use specific bolts and hardware engineered and rated for that purpose.

Aircraft-grade bolts are by far the superior of the two, especially in shear load applications. The threads are shorter than those found on common commercial bolts, leaving just enough bite for an aircraft washer and locknut. Aircraft-grade shanks are slightly thicker as well to create a tight fit in the hole and increase their shear force capability.

The easiest way to determine the rated strength of a bolt is to take note of the markings (or lack thereof) on the head. Most SAE-grade hardware has a pattern of lines stamped into the head to signify the bolt's rated strength. (See photos.) Commercial-grade Allen bolts, or cap screws, are not stamped but offer high-strength reliability. Common airframe bolts have markings of their own, but with less regularity and association. Ask any qualified hardware representative for help identifying and locating specific bolts for your project.

RESOURCES

No project is ever completed without a set of informative reference manuals and technical resources. Below is a list of books and parts suppliers that are extremely helpful in the restoration and performance of your car.

Factory assembly, body, and service manuals are all invaluable resources when it comes to correctly restoring a car. They provide the original spec sheets, drawings, and instructions for the entire vehicle.

Chilton and Haynes service manuals are less-expensive alternatives to factory manuals and serve as handy references for basic automotive maintenance. However, these manuals should be used in conjunction with a more detailed, application-specific book.

Classic Industries is a major aftermarket GM supplier for Camaros, Firebirds, Impalas, and classic trucks. 800-854-1280, ext. 5-210; www.classicindustries.com

Holley Carburetors, by Dave Emanuel, clearly defines and explains everything you need to know about the mysterious world of Holley carburetion. The book starts with the history of Holley carburetors and works its way through just about every Holley model and part number. This book is specific and informative, and a must for any serious tuner. MBI Publishing Company; ISBN 1-8840-8928-3

How to Build the Small-Block Chevrolet, by Larry Atherton and Larry Schreib, is a great reference manual depicting the step-by-step process of building an engine. The book offers helpful tips not commonly found in other how-to engine guides. MBI Publishing Company; ISBN 0-9314-7226-1

Original Parts Group is one of the largest aftermarket manufacturers and retailers of licensed GM A-body parts and accessories. Well-organized catalogs cover the complete GM line and are full of helpful information. 800-243-8355;

INDEX

MOTORBOOKS WORKSHOP

The Best Tools for the Job.

Corvette Performance Projects 1968-1982

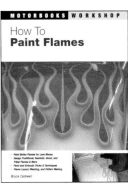
How To Paint Flames

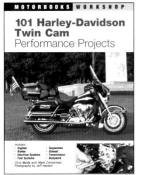
101 Harley-Davidson Twin Cam Performance Projects

Ultimate Garage Handbook

Other Great Books in this Series

Performance Welding Handbook
2nd Edition
0-7603-2172-8 • 139436AP

How To Paint Flames
0-7603-1824-7 • 137414AP

How To Build
Vintage Hot Rod V-8 Engines
0-7603-2084-5 • 138703AP

Honda & Acura
Performance Handbook
2nd Edition
0-7603-1780-1 • 137410AP

Hot Rod
Horsepower Handbook
0-7603-1814-X • 137220AP

How To Build the Cars of
The Fast and the Furious
0-7603-2077-2 • 138696AP

How To Tune and Modify Engine Management Systems
0-7603-1582-5 • 136272AP

Corvette Performance
Projects 1968–1982
0-7603-1754-2 • 137230AP

Custom Pickup Handbook
0-7603-2180-9 • 139348AP

Circle Track Chassis
& Suspension Handbook
0-7603-1859-X • 138626AP

How To Build A West Coast
Chopper Kit Bike
0-7603-1872-7 • 137253

101 Harley-Davidson Twin-Cam
Performance Projects
0-7603-1639-2 • 136265AP

101 Harley-Davidson
Performance Projects
0-7603-0370-3 • 127165AP

How To Custom Paint Your Motorcycle
0-7603-2033-0 • 138639AP

101 Sportbike Performance Projects
0-7603-1331-8 • 135742AP

Motorcycle Fuel Injection Handbook
0-7603-1635-X • 136172AP

ATV Projects: Get the Most Out
of Your All-Terrain Vehicle
0-7603-2058-6 • 138677AP

Four Wheeler
Chassis & Suspension Handbook
0-7603-1815-8 • 137235

Ultimate Boat
Maintenance Projects
0-7603-1696-1 • 137240AP

Motocross & Off-Road
Performance Handbook
3rd Edition
0-7603-1975-8 • 137408AP

How To Restore Your
Wooden Runabout
0-7603-1100-5 • 135107AP

Ultimate Garage Handbook
0-7603-1640-6 • 137389AP

How To Restore John Deere
Two-Cylinder Tractors
0-7603-0979-5 • 134861AP

How To Restore Your Farm Tractor
2nd Edition
0-7603-1782-8 • 137246AP

Mustang 5.0
Performance Projects
0-7603-1545-0 • 137245AP